History of

The American Constitutional

or

Common Law

with

Commentary Concerning

Equity and Merchant Law

By:

Dale Pond
Howard Fisher
Richard Knutson
North American Freedom Council

Edited by: Dale Pond

THE MESSAGE COMPANY

LIBRARY OF CONGRESS CATALOG CARD NUMBER: 94-72953

ISBN: 1-57282-010-1 (Paperback)

PRINTED IN THE UNITED STATES OF AMERICA

Publisher's Cataloging in Publication

History of the American constitutional or common law with commentary
 concerning equity and merchant law / by Dale Pond ... [et al.] ;
 edited by Dale Pond.
   p. cm.
   Includes bibliographical references and index.
   Preassigned LCCN: 94-72953
   ISBN 1-572-82010-1

   1. Common law--United States--Popular works. 2. Equity. 3.
Civil rights. 4. United States--Constitutional law.   I. Pond,
Dale.

KF394.Z9H57 1995   340.57
                              QBI94-21332

Published and distributed by:

The **Message** Company
RR 2 Box 307MM
Santa Fe, NM 87505

505-474-0998

Table of Contents

Court Arguments and Briefs

On the History of the Common Law; Common Law versus Equity/Merchant Law.

by Howard Fisher

The Anglo-American system of jurisprudence is the only one which developed out of what is called the Common Law, that is, the general law of private property known in the British Isles. Common Law was designed through the years to secure the rights of individuals to property; to make it difficult for property to be taken away without due process of law. The Common Law was expounded over the years in case decisions as a result of trials in which the Common Law jury acted as the Judges, and in which they exercised the authority to hear and decide questions of both Law and fact, and Common Law deals with legal relationships, powers and liabilities, and types of actions rather than theoretical definitions of abstract legal concepts.

It is from such controversies involving property that all of our Rights have come. Property is known as Substance at the Common Law, and includes hard money in the form of gold and silver coin.

Controversies involving these matters carry with them a Law jurisdiction, a jurisdiction in which all of our Rights are found. The Judge in a Court of Law is an impartial referee of the dispute, and he is bound to protect the Rights of the parties to the dispute, or he will have lost whatever jurisdiction he may have had, or claimed to have had.

Gold and silver Coin are the only Things recognized at Law to be money. Money is Substance in possession and not a Chose (thing) in action. When a debt is paid, at Law, the debt is extinguished; debt no longer exists; the debt is paid. Debt can only be paid with gold and silver Coin, or certificates redeemable on demand, at par, in gold and silver Coins. This is the legal meaning of the expression "tender in payment of debt", as found in Article I, Section 10 of the Constitution of the United States. (emphasis added)

Thomas Jefferson placed great emphasis on the concept of Rights. He said we did not bring the English Common Law, as such, to this continent; we brought the Rights of Man.

The Common Law of the States of the United States is the Common Law of England adopted by the original Constitution of the United States, so far as not modified by any alterations made by the Constitution of the State at the time of admission to the Union, and so far as not in direct conflict with the Constitution of the United States of America. And the Common Law of the States may not be modified, limited nor abrogated either by an act of the legislature (Congress or State Legislature) or by a ruling of some judge. Part of the problem that we are in is a result of unlawful attempts by legislatures or judges to modify or abrogate Common Law.

While, in England, this Law was derived from feudal tenures in real property as held by a pyramid of proprietors holding their rights from the King (or Crown) on down the line, the American Revolution destroyed any and all allegiance to the British Crown, including the rights of property in land, and all feudal tenures and dues were overthrown. All Rights of property in land in the United States became ALLODIAL TITLES in Allodial Freehold, under no lord or overlord whatsoever, even the authority of the Colony or State.

This is the reason why our founding fathers considered that they had made every man a

"King" on his own property.

In England, William Pitt summarized the concept of private property under Common Law, as follows:

> *"The poorest man may, in his cottage, bid defiance to all the forces of the Crown. It may be frail; its roof may shake; the wind may blow through it; the storms may enter; the rain may enter; but the King of England cannot enter; all his forces dare not cross the threshold of the ruined tenement."*

As a result of all of this, the Common Law of the States is founded and grounded upon substantive titles in real property, and no mere legislative enactment by Congress or State Legislature nor judicial ruling by Federal or State Courts can operate to deprive the People of their Rights at Law, including their Rights inherent in their Allodial Land Titles and to be Merchants and/or Traders at Law on the cash basis, and their Rights to access to Courts of Law and to a jurisdiction where their Rights are protected.

As contrasted with the Common Law of England, the system of law as practised on the Continent of Europe is called Civil Law, or Roman Civil Law, which is derived from the Law of the Ecclesiastical Chancellors. This is partly the ancient law of Rhodes, the law of merchant traders upon commercial documents. The Civil Law is prosecuted by the Chancellor; he is not an impartial referee of the dispute.

This Civil Law of Roman origin has never been part of the Laws of England and has been declared not of the Laws of the Realm by the Parliament and by many experts of England in jurisprudence, such as Coke, Blackstone and Sir John Fortescue.

> *"The Common Law is absolutely distinguished from the Roman or Civil Law systems."*
>
> People v Ballard
155 NYS 2d 59

The Roman Civil Law has always been outside of Common Law, operating on SUMMARY PROCESS, in gross violation of our RIGHTS TO DUE PROCESS.

As English society developed over the years, situations were met in the Common Law for which the Courts could provide no relief by any precedent. The controversies did not involve property, or substance. The parties thus had no other recourse than to go to the King. And when they did, he delegated his first minister to solve these problems. The minister was called a Chancellor (the same title as used on the Continent) and the relief granted was called Equity. This "Equity" meant what would be fair if the Common Law principle were extended and applied to the case at hand, as the Chancellor, in his discretionary judgment, chose to do.

There thus developed in England and America two distinct systems of law and courts, each having a peculiar and particular application and jurisdiction. Equity is a jurisdiction in which the individual does not have any Rights , and one to which the individual can be subjected only if he volunteers or gives his informed consent.

In Equity there are no jury trials. The powers of the Common Law jury to hear and decide questions of both Law and Fact are exercised by the Chancellor. However, there may be "advisory juries" to advise the Chancellor of certain facts, but they are not permitted to hear any arguments regarding the Law. (Does this sound familiar today?) The controversies are decided by the Chancellor, who, besides being the Chief Prosecutor, (or Inquisitor, if you will), can go to any source he chooses, even to his own "conscience", to prove or justify his decision. In Equity, the parties do not have any _Rights_; the Constitution is stated by the Chancellor to be "frivolous"; and any so-called "rights" in his Court are actually "privileges" granted by the Chancellor, which he can also take away.

During the past century, the Congress of the United States and the Legislatures of the several States, as well as the Judges, have presumed to exercise the authority to "merge" the procedures of Law and Equity; this is authority they do not have, yet this, too, is part of the problem we face.

When we realize that a Court of Common Law proceeds "according to the course of the Common Law", and that the parties have a _Right_ to trial by a Common Law jury, where the jury exercised the authority to hear and decide questions of _both_ Law and Fact, we can then _know_ that if we are in a Court where the procedures have been "merged" with Equity, then we can _know_ that we are _not_ in a Court of Common Law ! !

The Constitution of the State of Iowa, Article V, Section 6, states, in part, as follows:

"The District Court shall be a court of law and equity, which shall be distinct and separate jurisdictions, ..."

Obviously, they have not been lawfully merged, and we do not have to accept the idea that they have been merged.

We must realize that the principles of Common Law and of Equity are those as distinguished and defined in England, before the adoption of the Constitution of the United States of America. Any modifications in definition or practise of either Law or Equity in England since the adoption of the Constitution of the United States of America have no significance, bearing or authority in the United States, since we are no longer under the jurisdiction of either Parliament or the Judges of England ! ! Yet there are those in this country who claim that Equity jurisdiction (otherwise known as Chancery jurisdiction) in this country is the same in nature and extent as Equity jurisdiction in England ! !

Where the Constitution of the United States of America, or the Constitution of the State of Iowa, or of any State, mentions "law", it means "Common Law"; it does not mean any other "kind" of law ! ! In addition to the above mentioned jurisdictions of Law (meaning Common Law) and Equity, which are the only _Judicial_ jurisdictions authorized either by the Constitution of the United States of America, or by the Constitution of the State of Iowa, or of any State, as drafted in conformance thereto, and being second thereto, there is also a _private_ , _political_ jurisdiction which is operative only on those who _volunteer_ into it's _private_ domain, _outside_ of the Constitution. It is known as Law Merchant (_lex mercatoria_) the _private_ rule of the bankers and merchants.

Law Merchant is neither Law nor Equity, but is only _raw_ , _private_, _political_ power, alien and illegal to our Constitution whatsoever, and operates _outside_ of the Constitution.

The Law Merchant is an independent, parallel system of law, like Equity or Admiralty. The Law Merchant is not even a modification of the Common Law; it occupies a field over which the Common Law does not and never did extend. Common Law deals with the Money of Substance belonging to the People (Gold and Silver Coins); while the Law Merchant deals with the law of Bills, Notes and Checks, (in other words, with negotiable instruments and commercial paper).

Our Declaration of Independence charges that America had been progressively subjected to "a jurisdiction foreign to our Constitution" (meaning the unwritten English Constitution). This foreign jurisdiction was a jurisdiction of lawless *ad hoc* Equity out of the Roman Civil Law under the stark cover of such obscenities as the Writs of Assistance (which our Courts of today also claim to have the authority to issue) which allowed <u>summary plundering of the colonists' wealth and substance</u> TO THE ADVANTAGE OF the East India Company which controlled the Parliament. (as today, it allows the summary plundering of the American citizens' wealth and substance TO THE ADVANTAGE OF the banks and other financial institutions which control the Congress and State legislatures). It has been recognized and stated for over one hundred years that "we have the best Congress that money can buy" ! !

These Writs, even as only one wrong perpetrated by the commercial interests in the Parliament, were given authority by an Equitable jurisdiction called a <u>debt action in assumpsit</u> . This action, which gave satisfaction pursuant to the customs of the Law Merchant, (having been voluntarily entered into), had been an old debt action triable in a Court of Common Law (merely as a courtesy of the Common Law Courts, and not inherently a part of Common Law) (and triable by a Common Law Jury, as a protection to the Defendant), until Lord Mansfield, Chief Justice of the Kings Bench, in 1760, arbitrarily and on his own authority, denied trial by jury in <u>debt actions in assumpsit</u> AND REMOVED THAT ACTION FROM THE Courts of Common Law into the Courts of Equity, where a trial by jury could not be had, and where there was merely a summary proceeding with no semblance of a "due process of Law".

This case, known as

<u>Moses v MacFerian</u>
2 Burroughs 1005

and is the case that sparked the American Revolution and caused Thomas Jefferson to say that English law since that date should not be used over here.

It was this Equitable <u>debt action in assumpsit</u> which the Seventh Amendment of the Constitution of the United States was specifically meant to outlaw, by specifically providing that "In suits at Common Law, where the value in controversy shall exceed twenty dollars, the right of trial by jury shall be preserved, ..." The significance of this is pointed up by the fact that any controversy involving Money (Gold and Silver Coins) in an amount greater than twenty dollars, or <u>any property such as real estate</u> can only be tried in a Court of Common Law with the right of trial by jury ! ! This means that <u>any Mortgage Foreclosure action</u> can be tried <u>only</u> in a Court of Common Law, and that the State Legislature has no Constitutional authority to provide, by statute, that mortgage foreclosure actions shall be Equity actions ! ! This means that Sheriff's Sales as a result of these Equitable Mortgage Foreclosure actions are <u>null and void</u> ! ! And that the Sheriffs have participated in criminal confiscation of real property in violation of the Constitution and of their oaths of office ! !

So, it can be seen that <u>summary and arbitrary confiscation of income and property</u> is nothing new in American tradition and history <u>out of an illicit (meaning unlawful and unconstitutional) Equitable jurisdiction</u>. It is precisely this Equitable jurisdiction wherein the Chancellor enforces the <u>combination of unconstitutional Executive and Legislative Equity</u> which is the jurisdiction foreign to our Constitution referred to in the Declaration of Independence. This is precisely what our American Revolution was all about and what our Bill of Rights prevents.

It is also a measure of the extent that the Bankers, and their stooges, the lawyers and Judges, as well as the politicians of both major political parties, have betrayed the Public Trust and have attempted to place us in a Dictatorship of Unelected Rulers ! !

Thus it can be seen that there is a direct similarity of our political/legal situation today with what it was in the years immediately preceding the Revolution of 1776. Only today we have a written Constitution that spells our our Rights and our freedoms, whereas two hundred years ago they did not ! ! !

The Common Law Jury members (acting as judges of the Law) were sworn to "Do equal law, and execution of Right, to all the King's subjects, rich and poor, without having regard to any person" and that they will deny no man Common Right; but they were NOT sworn to obey or execute any statute of the King, or of the King and Parliament. Indeed, they are virtually sworn NOT to obey or execute any statutes that are against "Common Right", or contrary to the Common Law, or "Law of the Land"; but to certify the King thereof" . . . . that is, to notify the King that his statutes are against the Common Law; . . . . and then proceed to execute the Common Law, notwithstanding such legislation to the contrary. The words of the oath on this point are these:

"That we deny no man Common Rights by (virtue of) the King's letters, nor none other mans', nor for none other cause: and in case any letters come to you contrary to the Law, (that is, the Common Law) that ye do nothing by such letters, but certify the King thereof, and proceed to execute the Law, (that is, the Common Law), notwithstanding the same letters."

In Federalist Papers #48, Alexander Hamilton wrote in part, "No legislative act contrary to the Constitution can be valid." "The Constitution is, in fact, and must be regarded by judges as a fundamental law."

The Sheriff is a servant of the People; upon taking office he takes an oath to uphold the Constitution and keep the peace.

In American Jurisprudence, on Sheriffs, Police and Constables, we find the following:

"Origin of Office. The office of sheriff is an ancient one, dating back to at least the time of Alfred, King of England, and the holder thereof has always been the chief executive officer and conservator of the peace in his shire or county. He is a county officer representing the executive or administrative power of the state within his county. In this country, the office is generally an elective one, and anciently in England, sheriffs were elected by freeholders of the county, although gradually, it became the custom for the Crown to appoint the Sheriff."

Abraham Lincoln stated the following on February 12, 1865:

"The people are the rightful masters of both Congress and the Courts. Not to overthrow the Constitution, but to overthrow the men who pervert the Constitution."

The general misconception is that any statute passed by legislators bearing the appearance of law constitutes the law of the land. The U. S. Constitution is the supreme Law of the Land, and any statute to be valid, must be in agreement. It is impossible for both the Constitution and a statute violating it to be valid. One must prevail, and that is the Constitution.

In Volume 16, American Jurisprudence, 177, we find the following:

"The general rule is that an unconstitutional statute, though having the form and name of law, is in reality no law, but is wholly void, and ineffective for any purpose; since unconstitutionality dates from the time of its enactment, and not merely from the date of the decision so branding it. An unconstitutional law, in legal contemplation, is as inoperative as if it had never been passed. Such a statute leaves the question that it purports to settle just as it would be had the statute not been enacted.

"Since an unconstitutional law is void, the general principles follow that it imposes no duties, confers no rights, creates no office, bestows no power or authority on anyone, affords no protection, and justifies no acts performed under it . . . .

"A void act cannot be legally consistent with a valid one. An unconstitutional law cannot operate to supersede any existing valid law. Indeed, insofar as a statute runs counter to the fundamental law of the land, it is superseded thereby.

"No one is bound to obey an unconstitutional law and no courts are bound to enforce it."

The Constitution guarantees the right of a freeholder to protect his property from Criminal Trespass.

Civil Law or Equity Law is the law of the ruler: Common Law is the law of the People.

It is the sworn duty of the Sheriff to obey and uphold the Constitution and to protect the property and <u>Rights</u> of the freeborn, Sovereign individuals of the County.

County Sheriffs must be advised of the instances where unlawful acts of officials or agencies of government are committed. It is the duty of the Sheriff to protect the local citizens from such unlawful acts, even when they are committed "under color of law".

There is no lawful authority for Judges and the Courts to direct the law enforcement activities of a County Sheriff. The Sheriff is accountable and responsible <u>only to the citizens who are inhabitants of his County</u>. He is under Oath of Office, and need not receive unlawful Orders from Judges or the Courts. He is responsible to protect citizens, <u>even from unlawful acts of officials of government</u>. He should not allow his office to be used as an unlawful "lackey" of the Courts.

Since the formation of our Republic, the local County (or Parish) has always been the seat of government for the body politic (the People). A County (or Parish) government is the highest authority of government in our Republic as it is closest to the body politic (the People) who are, in fact, THE GOVERNMENT.

The Common Law of the States is founded and grounded upon substantive titles in real property, and no mere legislative enactment by Congress or State legislature, nor judicial ruling by Federal or State Courts can operate to deprive the People of their <u>Rights</u> at Law, including the <u>Rights</u> inherent in their <u>Allodial Land Title Rights</u>.

The Constitution of the United States of America, Article III, Section 2, authorizes Courts of Law and Courts of Equity; Judicial Equity is authorized; but nowhere does the Constitution of the United States of America authorize a single bit of either Federal Executive branch of government Equity jurisdiction, or Federal Legislative branch of government Equity jurisdiction.

The Constitution of the State of Iowa, as drafted in conformance to the Constitution of the United States of America, and being second thereto, Article V, Section 6, authorizes Courts of Law and Courts of Equity; Judicial Equity is authorized; but nowhere does the Constitution of the State of Iowa authorize a single bit of either State Executive branch of government Equity jurisdiction or State Legislative branch of government Equity jurisdiction.

The Federal Bill of Rights was drawn and adopted to guarantee an estoppel (or bar) to the abhorrent Federal Executive and Legislative Equity jurisdiction, and therefore, the State Bill of Rights is also a guaranteed estoppel against any actual or de facto abhorrent State Executive and Legislative Equity jurisdiction; this is an abhorrent and oppressive Equity, because it purports to be able to administer, adjust and deny said Common Law Rights without first pursuing the appropriate remedy at Common Law and thus denying due process.

In other words, State government, both Executive branch and Legislative branch, must be at Law, and may not impose any form of Equity jurisdiction upon the People, by compulsion or otherwise, without their knowledge and informed consent; that such enactments are nullities and do not exist at Law, because the Rights of freeborn, Sovereign individuals would be violated if they were to be forced to obey them.

If an agency of the government, including the court, would act as if it were Principal, and Freeman, as against it's true Principal, the People, this would be an inversion of the legal principle of Sovereignty of the People, and by so acting, this agency of the government, including the court, would be a pretender to the power, and as a pretender, it's acts would be a nullity and would not exist, at Law; that is to say, that it would be null and void, and of no force and effect, at Law; that, in fact, it would not be government at all, but would be a private, criminal operation, imposing a rule of force, fraudulently pretending to be government, since, in this country, the only legitimate function of government is to protect the Rights and freedoms of the People.

Each freeborn, Sovereign individual has the authority and the Right to deny and to disavow all Equity jurisdiction, and to refuse to acquiesce to the jurisdiction of Courts of Equity, or to Equity jurisdiction of any Executive or Legislative branch of government agency or agent, State or Federal.

The Constitution of the United States of America, Article IV, Section 4, guarantees a Republican Form of government to every State.

The definition of a "Republic" is as follows:

"**Republic**: A state in which the sovereign power resides in a certain body of the people (the electorate), and is exercised by representatives elected by, and responsible to, them; "

Webster's Collegiate Dictionary, Fifth Edition .

The Courts of Iowa are nullities, and do not exist, either at Law or in Equity, because unelected State Judges have no jurisdiction, at Law or in Equity, over any one or any thing, being in direct violation of each freeborn, Sovereign individual's Right to a Republican Form of Government; his Right to have an Elected Judge; and his Right to Separation of Powers, because the Governor, as Chief Executive of the State, has no Judicial Power to delegate to an appointee.

The Governor of this State is not a Chancellor, nor are any officials appointed under him authorized to exercise any Judicial powers; there can be no delegated power in Chancery Law to be executed under the alien, outlawed and illegal Roman Civil Law, unless acquiesced to by the freeborn, Sovereign individual.

That evil and alien jurisdiction, the de facto Equity jurisdiction of the Roman Civil Law, allows judges to enforce the unlawful summonses of IRS agents, Highway Patrol Officers, city policemen, building inspectors, OSHA agents, FDA agents, and the agents of all other equally unlawful regulatory bodies of so-called government, who attempt to impose a jurisdiction in which the Rights of freeborn, Sovereign individuals are violated.

That evil and vicious Roman Civil Law allows the 'judges' to have people arrested, jailed, and property taken away from them, or their property to be criminally trespassed upon and destroyed; all without a Common Law Trial by Jury, or just compensation, or due process of Law.

Under the Common Law, no bureaucrat can dictate what happens to your liberty or your property. The only entity that can determine punishment (pass sentence) upon a freeborn, Sovereign individual is a lawfully constituted Common Law Jury.

Aiding and abetting the IRS and similar agencies in enforcing their unlawful summonses and assessments constitute an enforcement of the alien and evil Roman Civil Law.

Aiding and abetting the Highway Patrol Officer, the city policeman, the meter maid, the building inspector, in enforcing traffic tickets and other unlawful summonses constitute an enforcement of the alien and evil Roman Civil Law.

Compelling a freeborn, Sovereign individual to do anything, except upon the verdict of a Common Law Jury, constitutes an enforcement of the alien and evil Roman Civil Law.

Thomas Jefferson has been credited with the warning how the judicial branch of government would usurp the authority of the Executive and Legislative branches of government and turn the country into a judicial dictatorship.

On June 5, 1933, as a result of a prearranged banking crisis, the Congress of the United States passed House Joint Resolution No. 192, suspending the Gold Standard (they did not abolish it), which means they disestablished the fixed content of the Gold Dollar and took away the Law jurisdiction of the U. S. Standard Dollar Lawful Money. In effect, the entire country, every State and every freeborn, Sovereign individual, became insolvent and was effectively put into bankruptcy, making it impossible for each State and each individual to either _pay_ their debts, at Law, or to be _paid_, at Law. This was, in actuality, a criminal act of usurpation of the sovereignty of the People, by Congress.

Instead of being able to demand payment at Law, or to make payment in Standard Gold Dollars, or the equivalent Treasury currency, redeemable on demand, at Par, everyone was forced on to the credit of the private banks, the Federal Reserve Banks and the commercial banks, and began to pass around their debt instruments, as money, making use of their debt-claims for the money, and thereby, by the operation of House Joint Resolution No. 192, into an alien and unlawful Federal Executive Equity Jurisdiction, known as _lex mercatoria_, or the Law Merchant, which is the _private_ rule of the bankers, and from which jurisdiction our forefathers fought, and won, a revolution to be free, and from which jurisdiction our Constitution and Bill of Rights protects us.

When you can _pay_ your debts in Standard Gold Dollars, you operate on a cash basis in a Federal Common Law jurisdiction based on Article I, Section 10, clause 1, of the Constitution of the United States of America regarding tender _in payment of_ debts. This is the General Federal Common Law jurisdiction deriving from the Union, which the Bill of Rights was designed to protect, particularly the Seventh Amendment which guarantees the _Right_ of Trial by Common Law Jury in suits at Common Law where the value in controversy shall exceed twenty dollars. But, when you pass around evidences of debt as if it were the money itself, you are passing around the debt-claims for the money, and you no longer have a jurisdiction at Law, where the individual has access to his _Rights_, but you are in an entirely different court, or jurisdiction, you are in an Equity jurisdiction, one in which the individual does _not_ have any _Rights_. And this is the practical effect which Congress intended to bring about by passing House Joint Resolution No. 192. Even one hundred years ago it was stated that "we have the best Congress that money can buy".

By the operation of House Joint Resolution No. 192, individuals, and States, have been compelled to "perform services", in order, not to pay (because no one could "pay" anymore; there was no money with which to "pay"), but to "discharge obligations" to pay.

What is called "fractional reserve banking", with irredeemable paper, creates multiple demands upon a common substance. With multiple demands, no one can ever satisfy all his claims and no one can ever "pay" at Law in substance, that is, with Standard Gold Dollars, but instead, can only "perform services" as evidence of his willingness to "discharge the obligation to pay". Payment, as such, is thus forever postponed; one only promises the payment.

Overnight, the entire country was placed in an entirely new regime of Equity, which never "pays" a thing but only compels services forever to the private banks, and the debts to private bankers constantly increases, the interest obligations, known as "debt service", constantly compounds and the performance of services in order to "discharge the obligation to pay" this interest are never-ending, being a greater and greater burden upon ourselves and our children, and our childrens' children.

In other words, a feudalistic real property law, in the guise of Equitable discharge of obligations to tender in Equity and not "pay" at Law, was instituted in violation of our Allodial Property Rights, and compels individuals into a feudalistic peonage, or involuntary servitude to the private banks (Federal Reserve Banks, National Banks, State Banks), in violation of the 13th Amendment to the Constitution of the United States of America. Because of the jurisdiction of the Law Merchant, we are not under Common Law, we do not have access to our Right to a Common Law Jury, and as a result our property can be, and every day is, taken without due process of Law. If we do not "perform the services" our property is taken from us by Equity courts imposing the Law Merchant.

The Sheriff, in unknowing and unthinking acceptance of this situation, has become the "bag man" for a bunch of private criminals, and thereby is committing crimes himself, and is therefore a criminal, because it is a crime to violate Constitutional Rights and his oath of office to support and defend the Constitution of the United States of America and the Constitution of his own State, it being drafted in conformance thereto, and being secondary thereto.

The Banks, including the Federal Reserve Banks and the National Banks, are incorporated by the State and operate under Banking Statutes (you will notice I do not use the word Laws) which allow, or at least do not prohibit, the creation of "demand deposits" or "checkbook money", which is not really money, but is actually credit, or debt, created on the spot out of thin air on two levels -- one by the Federal Reserve Banks (they write checks on themselves, thereby creating Federal Reserve Credit "out of thin air", in order to "purchase investments", such as U. S. Government Securities, which then become part of the National Debt, and provide the banking system with new Reserves); on the strength of these newly purchased Securities, they are able to obtain from the Treasury, newly printed Federal Reserve Notes, to cover the new checks when they are cashed, and they only have to tender about two cents for each new Federal Reserve Note; they are practically given the new paper Notes and they still hold the Bonds, which are part of the National Debt, and collect interest on them; the second level by the local commercial bank which creates bank credit, denominated "demand deposits", every time they make a loan. The Federal Reserve (a private Anglo-German-American owned corporation) creates public credit (National Debt), while the commercial banks create private credit (private debt) when they make a loan.

The Federal Reserve Note, at least the one issued in accordance with Title 12, United States Code, Section 411, which requires that they "shall be obligations of the United States" and shall be redeemable on demand . . ., has a double jurisdiction. It is what you may call a legal tender for an equitable interest. That means it passes at Law as money, being a legal tender, but the only interest it passes along is a mere demand or promise. Hence, though it is "legal" or at Law, it never pays the gold because of House Joint Resolution No. 192, which illegally and criminally prohibited payment of the U. S. Standard Dollar Lawful Money, at par, and thus at Law.

It should be noted that Congress did not (could not) take away our Rights to use bank notes at Law, or demand deposits at Law; they just took away our money. We have a Right to take a twenty dollar bill, which means a bill for twenty dollars, into a bank and demand a twenty dollar gold piece. Congress did not take that Right away; since we have unalienable Rights which cannot be taken from us or be forced to give them up; Congress just took away the gold. This was and is a criminal usurpation of the Sovereignty of the People on the part of Congress; and the State of Iowa, and each State, by allowing it to happen at the time, and by continuing to allow it to happen to this date, has become party to this crime against the People.

Instead of going into bankruptcy, everyone, including the States, was provided with the opportunity to use the new Federal Reserve Notes, called (incorrectly) "lawful money" grounded in perpetual debt of the "eligible paper" which formed the assets of the Federal Reserve and the National Banks. These are also known as "units of monetized debt". Everyone thus became the creditor/debtor of everyone else, since no one has paid or been paid for anything since that infamous day of June 5, 1933, and thus, overnight, became liable for specific performance on the basis of a debt action of assumpsit under the private Law Merchant, operating outside of the Constitution and imposing an Equitable jurisdiction, one in which no one has any rights, where one can be compelled summarily to deliver his property without trial-by-common law jury. And the debts to the private bankers keep mounting ever higher.

A freeborn, Sovereign individual cannot be forced into perpetual debtorship and involuntary servitude, that is, feudalistic performance on behalf of, and for the benefit of, any person, real or juristic, against his Thirteenth Article of Amendments to the Constitution of the United States of America, and cannot be compelled, by Law, to accept, or to give informed consent to accept, an Equitable jurisdiction foreign to his Bill of Rights.

Article III, Section 2 of the Constitution of the United States of America, states in part:

"The Judicial Power shall extend . . . . . to all Cases of Admiralty and Maritime jurisdiction; . . . . ."

At the very beginning of government under the Constitution, Congress conferred on the federal district courts exclusive cognizance "of all civil causes of admiralty and maritime jurisdiction, ... ; saving to suitors, in all cases, the right of a common law remedy, where the common law is competent to give it; . . ." (1 STAT 77, Section 9 (1789))

As this jurisdiction is held to be exclusive, the power of legislation on the same subject must necessarily be in the national legislature and not in the state legislatures.

Congress enacted the Limited Liability Act on March 3, 1851. It is codified at Title 46, United States Code, Sections 181-189, as amended in 1875, 1877, 1935, 1936 and the Act of 1884. it intended to cover the entire subject of limitations, and to invest the U. S. District Courts with exclusive original cognizance of all cases of admiralty and maritime jurisdiction, exclusive of the States. This means that the States do not have any jurisdiction in admiralty and maritime matters, at all .

Admiralty and maritime jurisdiction comprises two types of cases: (1) those involving acts committed on the high seas or other navigable waters, and (2) those <u>involving contracts and transactions connected with shipping employed on the seas or navigable waters.</u> In other words, the second type of case must have a direct connection with maritime commerce.

Suits in admiralty traditionally took the form of a proceeding <u>in rem</u> against the vessel, and, with exceptions to be noted, such proceedings <u>in rem</u> are confined exclusively to federal admiralty courts, because the grant of exclusive jurisdiction to the federal courts by the Judiciary Act of 1789 has been interpreted as referring to the traditional admiralty action, the <u>in rem</u> action, <u>which was unknown to the common law</u> .

State courts are forbidden by the Constitution to have Admiralty jurisdiction. While State courts are permitted to <u>handle and try</u> Admiralty cases if the suitor desires, <u>it must be an Admiralty matter to begin with</u> and it must involve property, otherwise there would not be a common law remedy. In other words, the common law courts would not be competent to handle it. More than this, it would need to be tried in a common law court, following common law procedures (not Equity procedures) with a trial by a common law jury.

Therefore, any attempt by a State court to impose a judgment <u>in rem</u> is in violation of the Constitution and is null and void. When a sheriff attempts to enforce a judgment <u>in rem</u> he is attempting to impose the alien and unlawful Roman Civil Law, in violation of his oath of office, and he is thereby committing a criminal act.

The American people are beginning to catch on to and realize the nature of the Dictatorship of Unelected Rulers that is being set up in this country, and they are not going to stand for it.

As the issues become clarified, each public official will need to make a decision: shall he be on the side of the Constitution and protect the <u>Rights</u> and freedoms of the People, as required by his oath of office; or shall he be a party to the criminal usurpation of the Sovereignty of the People ?

The Sheriff is a key person in all of this: he can either be a tool of the evil forces who have set this up and provide the oppressive force that binds the Innocent victims to the chains of slavery, all in the name of "doing his duty", or he can be the instrument of liberation of the People by preventing the imposition of the unconstitutional Equitable jurisdiction (the Roman Civil Law) upon the victims and their property and protecting their <u>Rights</u> and freedoms.

Social Security - Health Care
An Economic Solution

A possible solution to <u>a portion</u> of the current economic crises in the United States may be found in an analysis and restructuring of the Social Security system. Since the current conditions are considerably different from those when this system was put in place we may envision changes that would make it a basis for a more comprehensive and beneficial program.

This system was established via the Federal government as a method of dealing with and handling private individuals' financial security situations mostly focused on retirement. However when this system was created there were different general and specific economic conditions and tremendous new changes have since taken effect in the marketplace.

During the time this system was established and put into place there was a very depressed financial market and jobs were extremely scarce. It must be pointed out there were not near as many businesses providing the quantity nor variety of jobs in those days either. Today we have a much different scenario. There are hundreds of businesses now in place for each of the few then in existence. There are millions of people successfully self-employed where there were very few then. There have been created dozens of new and different ways of managing capital that were not then existent either. Some of these new financial systems have proven to be extremely successful in managing individuals' excess capital to a point where retirement is a real and viable situation whereas the current government managed Social Security system is at the point of collapse and those receiving its monthly piteous returns may be considered poor indeed should they be unfortunate enough to be relying solely on those poorly managed contributions.

The existing Social Security system may be modified by taking the Federal government out of the middle from between the individual contributors and the capital fund managers. After all the Federal government has little if any business being financial advisors to individual investors. This can be done in a variety of common sense and acceptable ways.

<u>THE INDIVIDUAL MUST RETAIN THEIR RIGHT TO FREE CHOICE</u>. This establishes and insures a sense of personal responsibility for their own lives. Which choices may include but not be limited to something like the following choices:
1) Opt for personal management of their own funds.
    a) Similar to the IRA accounts, early withdrawals are restricted.
2) Opt to have a private money management firm to manage their growing capital fund.
    a) For those lacking financial self-confidence.
3) Opt to have their local county (elected financial advisor) oversee their funds:
    a) Invested by the county.
    b) Invested by a private money management firm watched over by the county.
    c) Managed by a relative or friend.
4) Portion of the contributions may go to cover (at contributors' discretion):
    a) Health insurance premiums.
    b) Liability auto insurance premiums.
    c) Set asides for:
        1) Education
        2) Retirement, housing.

3) Living expenses
5) Community support
   a) Charitable contributions
   b) School support
   c) General Community support (roads, etc.)

The standard method of deduction at the source may still apply. But at such deduction source some of the above options and even other options <u>must be</u> chosen by the individual contributor. The funds belong to them after all and not the government.

THIS METHOD BRINGS BACK TO THE INDIVIDUAL:
1) A sense of being more in control of their own lives than they now feel.
2) Personal responsibility for themselves and their families.
3) Direct involvement with their own destiny and that of their local county and city.
4) Develop an awareness and communication between neighbors.

THIS METHOD BRINGS BACK TO THE LOCAL COMMUNITY:
1) An ever growing capital investment fund which will naturally find its way into the community through its banks.
2) Create a meaningful and responsible involvement between the local governments and its citizens.
3) Develop accountability and responsibility within the local governing representatives.
4) Develop a sense of partnership between the citizens and the government.
5) Greater sense of responsibility to the individuals who pay for the communities projects.

THE LOCAL COMMUNITIES MUST ASSUME ACCOUNTABILITY TO THEIR CITIZENRY AND THEMSELVES - because the local citizenry is the local government. Which is really another way of saying all the individuals making up a given community must assume full responsibility for who and what they are individually and collectively. The idea of copping-out responsibility to a larger and further away impotent bureaucracy is old fashioned and does not work - witness the mess that has been created via federalism since the 1930s.

Local financial advisory boards can be established composed of professional and elected representatives. These boards can help those who may not trust themselves sufficiently to manage their own affairs and opt for advisory assistance.

The Social Security system together with all the capital it controls and debts it owes belongs to you, me and our neighbors. Get involved - - Don't be shy and don't sit back and let a nameless and faceless (and brain dead) bureaucrat waste any more of our resources while at the same time deciding our future for us - at their whim. Who are THEY to decide OUR fate ?

As an individual's contributions accumulate over a lifetime these funds can amount to truly awesome proportions. There is no reason whatsoever that a person contributing over their lifetime cannot enjoy an abundant retirement. Capital, ordinarily, doubles every seven years. An ordinary citizen, contributing to Social Security all during their working years, should have accumulated several hundreds of thousands of dollars to enjoy an income from. If they haven't done this it is solely due to mismanagement by Federal Government employees; i.e., our employees poorly managed and overseen from the Federal level.

The major point of this article is to remove this mismanagement. Dismantle the centralized and mismanaged system and make it local. **<u>Put the whole thing back into the hands of its owners.</u>**

This is the only solution.

Political "isms" Defined

by Dale Pond

Anarchy: Absence of government or governmental restraint; a state of society without government or law; political social disorder due to absence of governmental control; in general, disorder due to want of a controlling and regulating agency.

Authoritarianism: Favoring the principle of authority as opposed to that of individual freedom.

Capitalism: An economic system in which the means of production and distribution are for the most part privately owned and operated for private profit.[2]

Communism: A theory of system of social organization based on the holding of property in common, actual ownership beign ascribed to the community as a whole or to the state; a theory or system by which the state controls the means of production and the distribution and consumption of industrial products.

Constructionist: 1) One who contrues laws, etc., or one who advocates a particular construction. 2) One who interprets literally a law or body of writins, especially the U.S. Constitution or the Bible.[2]

Democracy: 1) Government by the people; a form of government in which the supreme power is vested in the people and exercised by them or their elected agents. 2) A state in which the supreme power is vested in the people and exercised directly by them rather than by elected representatives. 3) The common people of a community as distinquished from any privileged class.

Dualism: The state of being dual or consisting of two parts; division into two; also, any system or theory based on a dual principle or involving a duality of principles.

Equalitarianism: The opinions or principles of equality among men.

Fascism: Any authoritarian, anti-democratic, anti-communist system of government in which economic control by the state, militaristic nationalism, propaganda, and the crushing of opposition by means of secret police emphasize the supremacy of the state over the individual.[2]

Fatalism: The doctrine that al lthings are subject to fate or inevitable predetermination; also the acceptance of all things and events as inevitable.

Hedonism: The doctrine that pleasure or happiness is the highest good.

Hegemonic: Leadership; predominance; especially leadership or predominant influence exercised by one state over others, as in a confederation.

Libertarianism: One who maintains the doctrine of the freedom of the will (opposed to necessitarianism); also, one who advocates liberty, especially with regard to thought or-conduct.

Materialism: The philosophical theory which regards matter and its motions, as constituting the universe, and all phenomena including those of mind, as due to material agencies; also, any opinion or tendency based on purely material interests; devotion to material rather than spiritual objects, needs, and considerations.

Matriarchy: A form of social organization, as in certain primitive tribes, in which the mother (not the father) is head of the family, and in which descent is reckoned in the female line, the children belonging to the mother's clan.

Monarchy: Supreme power or sovereignty wielded by a single person; also, a government or state in which the supreme power is actually or nominally lodged in a monarch (being known as an absolute or despotic monarchy when the monarch's authority is not limited by the laws or a constitution of the realm, and as a limited or constitutional monarchy when the monarch's authority is so limited).

Monism: The doctrine of one ultimate substance or principle, as mind (idealism) or matter (materialism) or something that is neither mind nor matter but the substantial ground of both.

Necessitarianism: The doctrine of the inevitable determination of the will by antecedent causes, as opposed to that of the freedom of the will. The action of the will is a necessary *effect* of antecedent causes; will not a causative agent.

Oligarchy: A form of government in which the power is vested in a few; also, a state so governed; also, the ruling few collectively.

Plutocracy: The rule or power of wealth or of the wealthy; a government or state in which the wealthy class rules; also, a class or group ruling, or exercising power or influence, by virtue of its wealth.

Republicanism: The commonwealth or state; also a state in which the supreme power rests in the body of citizens entitled to vote and is exercised by representatives chosen directly or indirectly by them; also, any body of persons, etc., viewed as a commonwealth.

Socialism: A theory or system of social organization which aims at securing better distribution and more effective production of wealth by the vesting of the ownership and control of the means of production, capital, land, etc., in the community as a whole; also, a system of measures of socialistic character, especialy for the benefit of the working class, established and directed by the existing state or government.

Theocracy: A form of government in which God, or a diety is recognized as the supreme civil ruler, and his laws are taken as th statute-book of the state, or as the foundation of the established polity, hence, a system of government by priests claiming a divine commission.

Totalitariansim: Of or pertaining to a centralized form of government in which those in control grant neither recognition nor tolerance to parties [or individuals] of differing opinions.

Triarchy: Government by three persons; a set of three joint rulers; a triumvirate; also, a country divided into three governments, or group of three countries or districts each under its own ruler.

Tribal: Any aggregate of people united by ties of race and blood, community of customs and traditions, adherence to the same chiefs or leaders.

REFERENCES

1) The New Century Dictionary, Appleton-Century Crofts, Inc.; New York, 1948.

2) Funk & Wagnalls Standard Dictionary; Funk & Wagnalls CO., NY, 1962

THE COMMERCE CLAUSE

by Richard Knutson

Regarding the article, "Who Should Decide Whether Nuclear Reactors Are Safe?" by Richard Webb in Issue No. 6 of The Threefold Review.

Webb's inquiry as to who has authority to determine the safety of nuclear reactors touches on the fundamental question of how Congress has been able to pass legislation that breaches the Constitutional contract.

Webb posits that authority over nuclear safety is more a local question and suggests it should at most be a State matter rather than a Federal one. He contends that Congress has no authority through the "welfare clause" of the "commerce clause". His argument against the "welfare clause" is substantive but it is immaterial to the question at hand.

Congress does use the "commerce clause", but not in the way Webb interprets it. Webb contrasts "commerce and "manufacture" and contends that nuclear energy is manufactured. He then cites judicial cases which address the difference and points to questions which center on constitutional interpretation. This, however, is not the real crux of the matter.

Through Article 1, Section 8 of the constitution, Congress was given unlimited control over commerce. Any activity that falls within the realm of commerce can be regulated in any way the Congress sees fit. A corporation, by definition, is "An artificial person or legal entity created by or under the authority of the laws of the state." It is an "artificial person" created for the express purpose for conducting business in commerce. A corporation is formed by those who want to achieve limited liability while they seek profit and gain in commercial activity. Limited liability is a privilege that can only be extended by the state. Because a corporation is a creature of the state, it can be regulated in any way its creator deems necessary.

The point as to whether the nuclear industry is engaged in manufacture or commerce is immaterial. The fact that the companies of the nuclear industry are incorporated is how the Congress gains power and control over them through the commerce clause. Whether this is a good thing or a bad thing is another matter. It is a fact, albeit one that was not always so in this country, but was established step by step. The practice of incorporation is so complete that not only are most all industries incorporated but the States as well.

As to Webb's final point regarding "extremely profound implications". As he implies, it is here that one's concern truly should be. Webb considers the constitutional issues he has raised to be of significance. However, he fails to see there is no question to as what Congress can or cannot do according to the Constitution. His concern over the limitation of Congress' powers is well founded, yet his search for said limitations is not to be found in the categorical interpretation of the contract.

The terms and conditions of the Constitution were intended to be the limitations sufficient and necessary to prevent the United States from becoming a tyrannical central power among the several States. As it turns out, the limitations were insufficient as the Founders did not anticipate the advent of the corporation.

That, in brief, summarizes the answer to Webb's inquiry as to where Congress gets its authority. It leaves out the particulars and doesn't address come of the broader issues which have contributed to political and economic plight of our country. But the "extremely profound implications" are worth pursuing. To further understand how this tyranny has gradually engulfed us, we have to trace the development of the political and economic power over the last hundred years.

Given that business and industry are under the thumb of Congress, one may then wonder how Congress has been able to exercise more and more influence over every individual's activities.

The current vogue is to make the Feds a first string player in a grand conspiracy to enslave the population. This is a convincing perspective, and to a certain degree true. However, most overlook the key mechanism that makes it possible and, at the same time, makes it appear as if the population is in the process of being enslaved. The mechanism is in the desires of the people and the Fed's effort to respond to them. The message the people are giving to the "conspirators" is "We need to be protected from ourselves." Along with it comes "We want to be secure in our possessions and liberty." This presents the government with a paradox. On one hand they are constrained by the Constitution to respect the individual's freedoms (life, liberty, and the pursuit of happiness) while on the other they are being pressed to be in a position of protector and intermediary.

The sense of personal security is a problem every individual faces that can only be solved by the individual. If someone else is to be responsible for one's feeling secure, that someone will, at some time, have to make provision for being able to act in the stead of the insecure individual. It is no different for the government. If it is going to be responsible for the sense of security of the people in their day to day affairs, it must be able to exercise it's authority down into the day to day affairs of each and every person. The problem is that the Republican form of government doesn't lend itself to such a task. It assumes the individual will be responsible and capable in the conduct of daily life. It is only prepared for the exception and relies on conscientious, responsible people ready to step forward as witnesses and jurors to take care of the rare errant individual. The Republican form of government is slow moving and relies on trust among the constituency for it's effectiveness. People are expected to protect themselves. That's why they have the right to bear arms. A God fearing man is not going to shoot his neighbor for sport. Nor is he going to take his neighbor's cow or the fruit of his neighbor's labor. The Republican form of government is geared to make and enforce laws that the people will follow out of their own moral uprightness. It is intended to protect the rights of the individual, but not the individual. If the majority of the people want personal protection, then the government has the not so glorious task of being a protector of people instead of the protector of the rights of people. Sure, it still makes and enforces law, but the nature of the laws it makes and enforces is different than would be when it protects rights instead of people. "Rights" laws are general in character and prodigious in number.

As a Republic is not responsive to the people's desire for personal security, a legislative democracy (which responds more readily to the majority) is more practical. But, the legislative democracy is only operative in the political sphere. There needs to be a common ground in which people and politics interact. This is the economic sphere. By being able to set and enforce economic policy, the government has both the ball and the field upon which the protection game is played. All that remains is to make everyone a player and then make sure they all follow the rules.

The ball is money and the field is commerce. Once the government has control of the ball, it then has but to get everyone on the field. That is, everyone must use government money and be engaged in commerce. Commerce is an economic activity that is governed by civil law. Civil law is a body of law that developed out of Roman law. Civil law lends itself to enforcing policy set by a central power. By way of contrast, trade is the counterpart of commerce and common law is the counterpart of civil law. Although this is a bit of an over simplification, it will get one by for the purposes of this inquiry. The difference between trade and commerce, like the differences between common law and civil law, are nominal with regard to appearances. In both trade and commerce, one exchanges something for goods and services. But, in commerce, one is a player while, in trade, one is not. Since all need to be players if the government is going to be in the protection game, it was practical that the distinction be allowed to be obscured.

In order to keep the players on the field, there needed to be a contract. The right to contract is a natural right that is protected by the government, in so far as it protects the natural rights of the people. Unlike a civil right, the government cannot enforce the right to contract. It cannot require an individual to enter into or break a contract. But, it can enforce one's right to do so. As all contracts are equal before law, in so far as they are contracts, any contract an individual makes is on par with the Constitution. Thus, if one makes a contract that waives rights protected by the Constitution, they have no recourse to protection from the Constitution. Thus, if one wants to play in the protection game, one must enter into a commercial contract and set aside the Constitutional contract.

Every individual who participates in the Social Security system has declared (unknowingly) that they are engaged in commerce. The signed application for a Social Security account is evidence of the contract between an individual and government. One's birth certificate is the foundation document for said application. Few people realize the implications of this. The terms and conditions of this contract are well publicized: they are the Statutes At Large of Congress. These statutes only apply to political or economic entities under the jurisdiction of the Federal government. Federal statutes may or may not apply to individuals. In order for them to apply, the individual must establish a political or economic connection with the Federal government. In exchange for receiving (or at least being able to receive) the benefits of government, i.e., welfare, unemployment benefits, social security, etc., one agrees to obey the statutes of Congress. By participating in these programs, one is acting in a corporate capacity in commerce. And since Congress has unlimited powers over corporate activity in commerce, they can do anything they wish to control it.

To traverse the labyrinth of how this has come to pass requires a large ball of Ariadne's thread. First, one must bear in mind that the Constitution is a two-party contract between the States as a collective and the Federal government. Geographically, the Federal government is seated in the District of Columbia. The District of Columbia is a separate state that is unique from the States of the Union as it is vested, according to the terms and conditions of the Constitution, with limited sovereign powers that are not enjoyed by any of the States of the Union. These powers were deemed necessary in order to have a central power which could protect the States from international interference and to conduct national affairs without convening the States on each point of national policy. These same terms and conditions were also intended to limit this central power so that it could not gain supremacy over any one or all of the States of the Union. This functioned according to intent until after the 17th Amendment. At that time when Senators were no longer appointed by the States the Republic became a legislative Democracy. As time went on the powers of Congress broadened to the extent that the States ability to represent their interests as independent sovereign powers became nominal. What was 48 united sovereign States and a Federal state representing the States independent and common interests and the peoples common interests became a Federal state representing the people of 48 nominal states. Thus, the States that were to protect the individual from the United States (the Feds) became partners with the Feds.

To see how the individual has gained Federal representation without the intermediate agency of the State, is revealed in the changes in the State constitutions. One of the most visible changes is the qualifications of Electors (voters). From the aftermath of the Civil War until the 17th Amendment, voter qualification changed from a white freeman to a "citizen of the United States" in nearly all the State constitutions. This may not seem of consequence, but the qualifications for the right of suffrage reveals the legislative body who is representing them. If we look at the changes in the Pennsylvania State constitution, for instance, we find there have been several constitutional conventions since the original constitution of 1776.

The original voter qualifications in 1776 were:

Section the Sixth: "Every freeman of the full age of twenty-one years, having resided in the state for the space of one whole year next before the day of election for representatives, and paid public taxes during that time, shall enjoy the right of an elector: Provided, always, that sons of freeholders of the age of twenty-one years shall be [i]ntitled to vote although they have not paid taxes."

In 1790, they became:

Article III, Section 1: "In elections by the citizens, every freeman of the age of twenty-one years, having resided in the State two years next before the election, and within that time paid a State or county tax, which shall have been assessed at least six months before the election, shall enjoy the rights of an elector: Provided, That the sons of persons qualified as aforesaid, between the ages of twenty-one and twenty-two years, shall be entitled to vote, although they shall not have paid taxes."

And in 1838, they became:

Article III, Section 1: "In elections by the citizens, every white freeman of the age of twenty-one years, but a citizen of the United States, who had previously been a qualified voter of this State and removed therefrom and returned, and who shall have resided in the election-district and paid taxes as aforesaid, shall be entitled to vote after residing in the State six months: Provided; That white freemen, citizens of the United States, between the ages of twenty-one and twenty-two years, and having resided in the State one year and in the election-district ten days as aforesaid, shall be entitled to vote although they shall have not paid taxes."
However, if we look in the constitution of 1874, we find:

Article VIII, Section 1: "Every citizen twenty-one years of age possessing the following qualifications, shall be entitled to vote at all elections subject, however, to such laws requiring and regulating the registration of electors as the General Assembly may enact.
   1. He or she shall have been a citizen of the United States at least one month.
   2. He or she shall have resided in the State one year (or, having previously been a qualified elector or native born citizen of the State, he or she shall have removed therefrom and returned, then six months) immediately preceding the elections."

And, finally, if we look at the constitution of 1968, we find:

Article VII, Section 1: "Every citizen 21 years of age possessing the following qualifications, shall be entitled to vote at all elections subject, however, to such laws requiring and regulating the registration of electors as the General Assembly may enact.
   1. He or she shall have been a citizen of the United States at least one month.
   2. He or she shall have resided in the State 90 days immediately preceding the election."

(Notice the above laws make clear reference to both, individually, the State (of Pennsylvania) and the United States being the Federally organized national government.)

There is more of a story here than is going to be commented on. For now we want to notice in 1838 the "citizen of the United States" was someone who could vote in Pennsylvania and not be a Pennsylvania Citizen. This apparently curious circumstance is clarified when it is realized that a "citizen of the United States" was one who resided in the

District of Columbia. At that time, State Citizenship was the focus. National citizenship was a secondary consideration, if it was considered at all. There was no defined national citizen. The "Citizen" referred to in the Constitution of the United States was a State Citizen. The term "United States" applied to the District of Columbia as its function was that of representing the whole. It wasn't until the 14th Amendment that the term "citizen of the United States" was defined. It then became necessary to distinguish between the "citizen of the United States" who lived in one of the States of the Union and the one who lived in the District of Columbia. The need to make the distinction was not forthcoming, as it turns out because there was a multitude of new "citizens of the United States" living in nearly every State of the Union due to the 13th and 14th Amendments. Furthermore, all of the State Citizens became candidates for "citizens of the United States" by virtue of the same legislation. There is still great debate in some quarters about the difference between a "Citizen" and the "citizen of the United States". It is not without foundation. However, few recognize there is no longer a State citizenship of the quality to be found before the 17th Amendment. If a Citizen is such by virtue of his citizenship in a State which has no representation in Congress, how can he be a Citizen? The status may still be there, but access to it is well nigh impossible.

The change in voter qualifications is the most visible indicator to show how we all have become Federal citizens. National Citizenship was once incidental. It was a logical extension of being a State Citizen in a union of sovereign states that were united to form a single nation. State Citizenship became an endangered species with the advent of the "citizen of the United States" and is now virtually extinct. So, what has this to do with the authority of Congress? Prior to the 17th Amendment, a Citizen was not within the jurisdiction of the United States (the Federal government, i.e., Congress) by virtue of citizenship in their State. But, by becoming a "citizen of the United States" one could become a subject of the Federal government. I call this the political "avenue of access" to the individual. Being a "citizen of the United States" means one could be approached directly by Congress without Congress having to go through the State. This was one of the very things the States were originally trying to prevent when the contract with the Federal state (the Constitution) was written.

To see how Federal access to the individual was accomplished economically, one has to look at the contract. It is in the "commerce clause" that we find the avenue of access. The political access, as we have seen from the above, was subtle. The economic access is even more so. As we all know, the activity of commerce is wrought with corporations. Corporations are commercial entities created by a political entity (the state). Political entities are created out of the activity of men. As political entities, both the Federal state and the several States have the power to create corporations. The several States are incorporated. They are the corporate creations of the Federal state. The Federal state got its power in Article I, Section 8, Clause 3 (the Commerce Clause). This power was granted to them by the several States on the behalf of the collective sovereignty of the people. Thus, the Federal state, a political entity, gained access to total economic power over the several States. All corporations created by the States are also under the power of the Federal state. An individual who is in any way associated with a corporation is under the same power. It may be either direct or indirect. If one is an officer, partner or board member of a corporation, it is direct. If one is an employee or contractor, it is indirect. That is the economic "avenue of access" of the Federal state to the individual living in one of the several States.

The political and economic "avenues of access" are linked together in the Federal income tax program and the Federal Insurance Contributions Act program. The details of this connection would take us too far from the context we have been following were we to elaborate on it. However, the binding cord of these programs is the use of the "paper of account" of the Federal state. This paper is in the form of a dollar. It is called a "Federal Reserve Note". This note is offered as a privilege of being a "citizen of the United States". It serves the same function as the dollar it displaces but it lacks substance. It is a note on the credit of the Federal government of the United States. With it one may buy anything they normally would with a real dollar. Only they don't have to pay for it. The debt accumulated by the use of these notes will be born by all until such time the Federal government will settle it's account with it's creditors. These "dollars" are tickets to ride on the titanic ship of state that will carry it's passengers on a record breaking voyage across the sea of uncertainty.

The crucial issue is where do "we the people" seek our protection and maintain our faith. This nation owes it's origin to the individual's quest for a political community where one could establish "life, liberty and the pursuit of happiness" with "justice for all" under God. It was never intended for the state to be between the individual and God. We had, and still do have, the choice, as freemen and creatures of God, to reside (seek protection and have faith) with the State or with God. We have taken the protection of God to be a given and choose to also be protected by the State.

The separation of church and state is an established doctrine that intends to eliminate either from interfering with the affairs of the other. The state is prohibited from interfering with the individuals' practice of religion. The church is prohibited from interfering with the affairs of state. History is replete with the transgressions by both sides. The state cannot be justifiably condemned as its actions are in response to its creator, the collective of individuals, who contracted it into existence. The fault lies with the people. Whether they elect to appoint a king or establish a government to protect them, they are opting for the displacement of the protection offered by God. God offered his protection with a covenant between Himself and all the people of the planet. Although He used the term Israel (which means "those of God"), He was not excluding anyone. If there was any question of His intention, it was settled with the establishment of the New Covenant. The Bible is the documented evidence of His covenant. It is a contract. A contract everyone enters into when they are born. It states explicitly in its terms and conditions that no other contract shall be made that place any other being or beings between the individual and Himself. That includes making a contract with a state for the purpose of granting the power of personal protection. The state has no power over nature. It cannot legislate the weather, nor can it outlaw earthquakes. It's power of protection is limited to the political and economic affairs of men. It has not power to reduce or extend the unalienable rights granted by God. It can only offer civil rights in their place. The right to contract is unalienable. The state can recognize that right but cannot enforce it. When an individual enters into a contract with the state, he leaves the realm of unalienable rights and enters the realm of civil rights. He is no longer an individual only under God, but also a person under government. The government of this country was intended to be a servant not a guardian. The choice in this country is still with the individual. He can he a ward of Congress or a child (ward) of God. Whether Congress has sought guardianship or has had it pressed upon it by the desires of the people is a question every individual will have to settle for himself. Either way, he can elect to reinstate his relation to God if he so chooses. The only thing that stands in his way is his contract with Congress. Whether he breaches it or rescinds it is his choice. Either way, he is in breach of his contract with God until he does.

We are a nation of wealth. Wealth that has been derived from the bounty of God. We have mortgaged that wealth to powers of our own making in a quest for security in a world ruled by unseen powers that are appointed by God to bring us into an awareness of wisdom. Out of that awareness He would have us unite ourselves with the Love He gave the world in the person of His "only begotten Son".

The wealth is still with us, the Prodigal son, we need only to recognize the source of that wealth and acknowledge the contract that prescribes the terms and conditions by which that wealth will be made over to us. It is a choice to be made in freedom; voluntarily, knowingly and intentionally. However, we can also choose the wealth being offered by the state.

"That which seems to be wealth may in verity be only the gilded index of a far-reaching ruin; a wrecker's handful of coin gleaned from a beach to which he beguiled an argosy; a camp followers' bundle of rags unwrapped from the breasts of goodly soldiers dead; the purchase-pieces of potter's fields, wherein shall be buried together the citizen and the stranger."

John Ruskin, Unto this Last, 1862.

The U. C. C. Connection
Free Yourself From Legal Tyranny

This is a slightly condensed, casually paraphrased transcript of tapes of a seminar given in 1990 by Howard Freeman. We prepared it in order to make available the knowledge and experience of Mr. Freeman in his search for an accessible and understandable explanation of the confusing state of the government and the courts. It should be helpful to those who may have difficulty learning from lectures. Also it should help those who want to develop a deeper understanding of the information, without having to listen to three or four hours of recorded material.

The frustration many feel about our judicial system can be overwhelming and frightening and cause fear based on a lack of understanding and knowledge. Those of us who have chosen a path out of bondage and into liberty face, eventually, the seemingly tyrannical power of a governmental agency and the mystifying awesome power of the courts. We learned that we must "get a good lawyer", that is becoming harder to find, if impossible. When defending ourselves from government, we find that the lawyers quickly take our money and then tell us, as the ship is sinking, "I can't help you with that – *I'm an officer of the court.*"

Ultimately, the only way for us to have a "snowball's chance" is to understand the rules of the "game" san to come to an understanding of the true nature of the Law. The lawyers have established and secured a virtual monopoly over this sphere of knowledge by implying that the subject is just too difficult for the average person to understand, and by creating a separate vocabulary out of English words of otherwise common usage. While it may, at times, seem hopelessly complicated, it is not that difficult to grasp. Are lawyers really as smart as they would have us believe? Besides, anyone who has been through a legal battle

against the government with the aid of a lawyer has come to realize that lawyers know *procedure, not law.*

> Then answered one of the lawyers, and said unto him, master, thus saying thou reproachest us also. And he said, woe unto you also, ye lawyers! For ye made men with burdens grievous to be born, and ye yourselves touch not the burdens with one of your fingers... Woe unto you, lawyers! For ye have taken away the key of knowledge; ye entered not in yourselves, and them that were entering in ye hindered.
>
> (Luke 11:45-52)

Mr. Freeman admits that he is not a lawyer and as such, he has a way of explaining law to us that puts it well within our reach. Consider also that the framers of the Constitution wrote in language simple enough for the people to understand, specifically so that it would not have to be interpreted.

So again we find, as in many other ways, the "buck stops here!" It is *we* who must take the responsibility for finding and putting to good use the TRUTH. It is *we* who must claim and defend our God-given rights and freedom from those who would take them from us. It is *we* who must protect ourselves, our families and our posterity from intrusion by those who live parasitically from the labor, skill and talents of others.

To these ends, Mr. Freeman offers a simple. hopeful explanation of our plight and a *peaceful method* of dealing with it. Please take note that this lecture represents one chapter in his book, which he continues to refine, expand, and improve. It is, as all bits of wisdom are, a point of departure from which to begin our own journey of discovery, so that we all might pass on to others greater knowledge and hope, and to God the gift of lives lived in peace, freedom and praise.

"I send you out as sheep in the midst of wolves, be wise as a serpent and harmless as a dove."

INTRODUCTION

When I beat the IRS, I used Supreme Court decision and if I had tried to use these in court, they would have convicted me. I was a member of a patriotic group and studied Supreme Court cases. I concluded that the Supreme Court had declared that I was not a person required to file an income tax return. That tax was an excise tax on *privileges granted* by the government. So I quit filing and paying income taxes, and it was not long before they came down on me with a heavy hand. They issued a Notice of Deficiency, which was a fantastic sum. The biggest temptation was to go in with their letter and say, "Where in the world did you ever get that figure?" They claimed I owed them some $60,000. Even if I had been paying taxes, I never had that much money. How could I have owed them that much?

Never Argue The Amount Of Deficiency

Fortunately, I had just a little bit of information: NEVER ARGUE THE FACTS IN A TAX CASE. If you're not required to file, you should not care whether they say you owe sixty dollars or sixty thousand dollars. If you are not required to file, the amount doesn't matter. Don't argue the amount – that is a *fact* issue. Usually, when you get a Notice of Deficiency, it is for some fantastic amount. The IRS wants you to run in and argue about the amount. The minute you say "I don't owe that much," you have agreed that you owe something and you conceded jurisdiction.

Just don't be shocked at the amount on a Notice of Deficiency, even if it is ten million dollars! If the law says that you are not required to file or pay income tax, the amount doesn't matter. By arguing the amount, they will just say that you must go to tax court and decide what the amount is to be. When you walk into tax court, the *law* issues are already decided. You are only there to decide how much you owe – they will not listen to arguments of law.

So I went to see the agent and told him that I wasn't a taxpayer and didn't need to file. He said, "You are required to file, Mr. Freeman." Yet I had these Supreme Court cases, and I started reading them to him. He said, "I don't know anything about law, Mr. Freeman, but the Code says that you must file, and you're going to pay that amount or you're going to go to tax court." I thought that someone there ought to know something about law, so I asked to talk to his superior. I went to him and got out my Supreme Court cases, but he wouldn't listen to them. "I don't know anything about law, Mr. Freeman..." Finally I got to the Problems Resolution Officer, and he said the same thing. He said that the only person above him was the District Director. So I went to see him. When I got to his office, they had phoned ahead, and his secretary said that he wasn't there. But I heard someone in his office, and I knew he was in there.

I went down the elevator, around the corner to the Federal Building and into Senator Simpson's office. There was a girl there at a desk, and she asked if she could help me. I told her my problem. I said that I really thought the District Director was up there. I asked her to call the IRS and tell them that it was Senator Simpson's office calling and to ask if the District Director was in. I said, "If you get him on the phone, tell him that you are from the Senator's office and you have a person whom you are sending over to speak with him – if he can wait just five minutes." It worked. He was there, and I ran back to his office. His secretary met me when I came in and said, "Mr. Freeman, you're so lucky – the Director just arrived."

The Director was cordial and offered me coffee and cookies while we sat and talked. Then he asked me what I wanted to talk to him about. (If you ever have someone say to you, "I'm from the government and I'm here to do you a favor," watch out! So we turn that around and approach them the same way). "So," I said, "I thought you ought to know that there are agents working for you who are writing letters over your name that you wouldn't agree with. Do you read all the mail that goes out of this office over your signature?" The Director said, "Oh, I couldn't read everything

– it goes out of here by the bagful." That was what I thought and I said, "There are some of your agents writing letters that contradict the decisions of the Supreme Court of the United States. And they're not doing it over their name, they're doing it over your name."

He was interested to hear about it and asked if I had any examples. I just happened to have some with me, so I got them out and presented them to him. He thought it was very interesting, and asked if I could leave this information with him, which I did. He said he would look it over and get in touch with me in three days. Three days later he called me up and said, "I'm sure, Mr. Freeman, that you will be glad to know that your Notice of Deficiency has been withdrawn. We've determined that you are not a person required to file. Your file is closed and you will hear no more from us." I haven't heard another word from them. That was in 1980, and I haven't filed since 1969.

The Supreme Court on Trial

I thought sure I had the answer, but when a friend got charged with Willful Failure to File an income tax return, he asked me to help him. I told him that they have to prove that he willfully didn't file, and I suggested that he should put me on the witness stand. He should ask me if I spoke at a certain time and place in Scott's Bluff, and did I see him in the audience. He should then ask me what I spoke of that day. When I got on the stand, I brought out all the Supreme Court cases I had used with the District Director. I thought I would be lucky to get a sentence or two out before the judge cut me off. Instead I was reading whole paragraphs, and the judge didn't stop me. I read one and then another, and so on. Finally, when I had read just about as much as I thought I should, the judge called a recess of the court. I told Bob I thought we had it made. There was just no way that they could rule against him after all that testimony. So we relaxed.

The defense presented its case and decided to rest after my testimony. We showed that Bob was not required to file, and that the Supreme Court had upheld this position. Then the prosecution presented its closing statements. We were sure we had won. But, at the very end,

the judge spoke to the jury and told them, "you will decide the facts of this case and I will give you the law. The law required this man to file an Income Tax form; you decide whether he filed it." What a shock! The jury convicted him. Later some members of the jury said, "What could we do? The man had admitted that he had not filed the form, so we had to convict him."

When the trial was over I went around to the judge's office and he was just coming in through his back door. I said, "Judge, by what authority do you overturn the standing decisions of the United States Supreme Court? You sat on the bench while I read that case law. Now how do you, a District Court Judge, have the authority to overturn decisions of the Supreme Court?" He says, "Oh, those were old decisions." I said, "Those are standing decisions. They have never been overturned. I don't care how old they are; you have no right to overturn a standing decision of the United States Supreme Court in a District Court."

Public Law vs. Public Policy

He said, "Name any decision of the Supreme Court after 1938 and I'll honor it, but all the decisions you read were prior to 1938. He went on, "Prior to 1938, the Supreme Court was dealing with Public Law; since 1938, the Supreme Court has dealt with Public Policy. The charge that Mr. S was being tried for is a Public Policy Statute; not Public Public Law, and those Supreme Court cases do not apply to Public Policy." I asked him what happened in 1938. He said that he had already told me too much – he wasn't going to tell me any more.

1938 and the Erie Railroad

Well, I began to investigate. I found that 1938 was the year of the Erie Railroad vs. Tompkins case of the Supreme Court. It was also the year the courts claim they blended Law with Equity. I read the Erie Railroad case. A man had sued the Erie railroad for damages when he was struck by a board sticking out of a boxcar as he walked along beside the tracks. The district court had decided on commercial (Negotiable Instruments) Law; that this man was not under any contract with the Erie Railroad, and therefore he lacked standing to sue the company. Under the Common Law (Natural Law), he was damaged and he would have had the right to sue.

This overturned a standing decision of over one hundred years. Swift vs. Tyson in 1840 was a similar case, and the decision of the Supreme Court then was that in a case of this type, the court would judge by the Common Law (Natural Law) of the state where the incident occurred – in this case Pennsylvania. In the Erie Railroad case, the Supreme Court now ruled that all federal cases will be judged under the Negotiable Instruments Law. There would be no more decisions based on the Common Law at the federal level. So here we find the blending of Law with Equity.

This was a puzzle to me. As I put these new pieces together I reasoned that all our courts since 1938 were Merchant Law courts and not Common Law courts. There were still pieces missing from the puzzle.

A Friend in Court

Fortunately, I made a friend of a judge. Now you won't make friends with a judge if you go into court like a "wolf in black sheep country." You must approach him as though you are the sheep and he is the wolf. If you go into court as a wolf, you make demands and tell the judge what the law is and how he should uphold the law, or else. Remember the verse: "I send you out as sheep in wolf country; be wise as a serpent and harmless as a dove." We must go into court and be wise and harmless, and not make demands. We must play a little dumb and ask questions. Well, I asked lots of questions and boxed the judges into a corner where they had to give me victory or admit what they didn't want to admit. I won the case, and on the way out I had to stop by the clerk's office to get some papers. One judge stopped and said, "You're an interesting man, Mr. Freeman. If you're ever in town, stop by, and if I'm not sitting on a case we will visit."

America is Bankrupt

Later, when I went to visit the judge, I told him of my problem with the Supreme Court cases dealing with Public Policy rather than Public Law. He said, "In 1938, all the higher judges, the top attorneys, and the U.S. Attorneys were called into a secret meeting and this is what we were told: 'America is a bankrupt nation. It is owned completely by its creditors. The creditors own the Congress, they own the Executive, they own the Judiciary and they own all the State Governments. Take silent judicial notice of this fact, but never reveal it openly. Your court is operating under Admiralty Jurisdiction – call it anything you want, but do not call it "Admiralty."'

Admiralty Courts

The reason they cannot call it Admiralty Jurisdiction is that your defense would be different in Admiralty Jurisdiction from your defense under the Common Law. In Admiralty, there is no court that has jurisdiction unless there is a valid international contract in dispute. If you know it is Admiralty Jurisdiction, and they have admitted on the record that you are in an Admiralty Court, you can demand that the international maritime contract, to which you are supposedly a party, and, which you supposedly have breached, be placed in evidence.

No court has Admiralty or Maritime Jurisdiction unless there is a valid International Maritime Contract that was breached.

So you say, innocent like a lamb, "Well, I never knew that I got involved with an international maritime contract, so I deny that such a contract exists. If this court is taking jurisdiction in Admiralty, then place the contract in evidence, so that I may challenge the validity of it. What they would have to do is place the national debt into evidence. They would have to admit that the International Bankers own the whole nation, and that we are their slaves!

Not Expedient

The bankers said it is not expedient at this time to admit that they own everything and could foreclose on every nation of the world. The reason they don't want to tell everyone that they own everything is that there are still too many privately owned guns. There are uncooperative armies and other military forces. So until they can gradually consolidate all armies into a WORLD ARMY and all courts into a single WORLD COURT, it is not politic to admit the jurisdiction under which the courts are operating.

When we understand these things, we realize that there are certain secrets they don't want to admit and we can use this to our benefit.

Jurisdiction

The Constitution of the United States mentions three jurisdictions in which the courts may operate: Common Law, Equity Law, and Admiralty or Maritime Law.

Common Law

Common Law (Natural or Constitutional Law) is based on God's Laws as originally presented by Moses. Anytime someone is charged under the Common Law, there must be a damaged party. You are free under the Common Law to do anything you pleases, as long as you do not infringe on the life, liberty, or property of someone else. You have a right to make a fool of yourself provided you do not infringe on the life, liberty, or property of someone else. The Common Law does not allow for any governmental action which prevents a man from making a fool of himself. For instance, when you cross state lines, you will probably see a sign which says, "BUCKLE YOUR SEAT BELTS – IT'S THE LAW." This cannot be Common Law because who would you injure if you did not buckle up? Nobody. This would be compelled performance. But *Common Law cannot compel performance.* Any violation of Common Law is a CRIMINAL ACT, and is punishable.

Equity is law which compels performance. It compels you to perform to the exact letter of any contract that you are a party too. So, if you have compelled performance, there must be a contract somewhere, and you are being compelled to perform under the obligation of that contract. Now this can only be a civil action – not criminal. In Equity Jurisdiction you cannot be tried criminally, but you can be compelled to perform to the letter of a con-

tract. If you then refuse to perform as directed by the court, you can be charged with contempt of court, <u>which is a criminal action</u>. Are our seat belt laws Equity Laws? No, they are not, because you cannot be penalized (imprisoned) or punished for not keeping to the letter of a contract.

Admiralty or Maritime Law

This is a civil jurisdiction of Compelled Performance which also has Criminal Penalties for not adhering to the letter of a contract, but this only applies to International Contracts. Now we can see what jurisdiction the seat belt laws (and all traffic laws, building codes, ordinances, tax codes, etc.) are under. Whenever there is a penalty for failure to perform (such as willful failure to file), that is Admiralty or Maritime Law and there must be a valid international contract in force.

However, the courts don't want to admit that they are operating under Admiralty or Maritime Jurisdiction, so they took international law or Law Merchant and adopted it into our codes. This is what the Supreme Court decided in the Erie Railroad case, that the decisions from the non will be based on commercial law or business law and that it will have criminal penalties associated with it. Since they were instructed not to call it Admiralty Jurisdiction, they now call it Statutory Jurisdiction.

Courts of Contract

You may ask how we got into a situation where we can be charged with failure to wear seat belts and be fined for it. Isn't the judge sworn to uphold the Constitution? Yes, he is. But you must understand that the Constitution in Article I, Section 10, gives us the unlimited right to contract, as long as we do not infringe on the life, liberty, or property of someone else. Contracts are enforceable, and the Constitution gives two jurisdictions where contracts can be enforced: Equity and Admiralty. But we find them being enforced in Statutory Jurisdiction. This is the embarrassing part for the courts, but we can use this to box the judges into a corner in their own courts. We will cover this later.

Contracts Must be Voluntary

Under the Common Law (Natural Law), every contract must be entered into knowingly, voluntarily, and intentionally by *both* parties or it is void and unenforceable. These are characteristics of a Common Law contract.

There is another characteristic. It must be based on *substance*. For example, contracts used to read: "For one dollar and other valuable considerations, I will paint your house, etc." That was a valid contract, the dollar was a genuine, silver dollar. Now, suppose you wrote a contract that said: "For one Federal Reserve Note and other considerations, I will paint your house, etc." and suppose, for example, I painted your house the wrong color. Could you go into a Common Law court and get justice? No, you could not. You see, a Federal Reserve Note is a "colorable" dollar as it has no *substance*, and in a Common Law jurisdiction that contract would be unenforceable because the Federal Reserve Note is not *substance*.

"Colorable: That which is in appearance only, and not in reality, what it purports to be; hence counterfeit, feigned, having the appearance of truth." <u>Black's Law Dictionary</u>, 5th ed.

Colorable Money and Colorable Courts

The word "colorable" means something that appears to be genuine, but is not. Maybe it looks like a dollar, and maybe it spends like a dollar, but if it is not redeemable for lawful money (silver and gold) it is colorable. If a Federal Reserve Note is used in a contract, then the contract becomes a colorable contract, and colorable contracts must be enforced under a colorable jurisdiction. So by creating Federal Reserve Notes, the government had to create a jurisdiction to cover the kinds of contracts which use them. We now have what is called Statutory Jurisdiction, which is not a genuine Admiralty Jurisdiction. It is colorable because we are using colorable money. Colorable Admiralty is now known as Statutory Jurisdiction. Let's see how we came under this Statutory Jurisdiction.

Uniform Commercial Code

The government set up a colorable law system to fit the colorable currency. It used to be called the Law Merchant or the Law of Redeemable Instruments, because it dealt with paper which was redeemable in something of substance. But, once Federal Reserve Notes had become unredeemable, there had to be a system of law which was completely colorable from start to finish. This system of law was codified as the Uniform Commercial Code, and has been adopted in every state. This is colorable law, and is used in all the courts.

I explained one of the keys to this mess earlier, which is that the country is bankrupt and we have no rights. If the master says "Jump!" then the slave had better jump (compelled performance) because the master has the right to cut off his head. As slaves (we are compelled to perform), we have no rights. But the creditors or masters had to cover that up, so they created a system of law called the Uniform Commercial Code. This colorable jurisdiction under the Uniform Commercial Code is the next key to understanding what has happened.

Contract or Agreement

One difference between Common Law and the Uniform Commercial Code is that in Common Law, contracts must be entered into: (1) Knowingly; (2) Voluntarily; and (3) Intentionally. Under the U.C.C., this is not so. First of all, written contracts are unnecessary. Under this new law, "agreements" can be binding and if you only exercise the benefits of an "agreement" it is presumed or implied that you intend to meet the obligations associated with those benefits. If you accept a benefit offered by government, then you are obligated to follow, *to the letter*, each and eery statute involved with that benefit. The method has been to get everybody exercising a benefit and they don't even have to tell the people what the benefit is. Some people think it is the drivers' license, the marriage license, or the birth certificate, etc. I believe it is none of these.

Compelled Benefit

I believe the benefit being used is that we have been given the privilege of discharging debt with *limited liability*, instead of actually paying off debt *en toto* with substance. When we pay a debt, we give substance for substance. If I buy a quart of milk with a silver dollar, that dollar bought the milk, and the milk bought the dollar; substance for substance. But if I use a Federal Reserve Note to buy the milk, I have not paid for it. I still owe for the milk. I have incurred debt. There is no substance in the Federal Reserve Note. It is worthless paper (because it cannot be reasonably be used for anything else) given in exchange for something of substantive value. We have been "given" a way to escape this endless accrual of debt albeit with plenty of strings. Congress offers us this escape in the form of a *benefit*; debt money, created by the Federal United States, can be spent all over the continental United States; it will be legal tender for all *debts*, public and private, and the limited liability is that you cannot be sued for not paying your debts when you "pay" a debt using this colorable money.

So now they have said, "We're going to help you out, and you can just discharge your debts instead of paying your debts."When we use this "closeable" money to discharge our debts, we cannot use a Common Law court. We can only use a colorable court. We are completely under the jurisdiction of the Uniform Commercial Code – we are using non-redeemable negotiable instruments and we are discharging debt rather than paying debts.

Remedy and Recourse

Every system of civilized law must have two characteristics: Remedy and Recourse. Remedy is a way to get out from under the law. The Recourse provides that if you have been damaged under the law, you can recover your loss. The Common Law, the Law of Merchants, and even the Uniform Commercial Code all have remedy and recourse, but for a long time we could not find it. If you go to a law library and ask to see the Uniform Commercial Code they will show you a tremendous shelf completely filled with the Uniform Commercial Code. When you pick up one volume and start to read it, it will seem to have been intentionally written to be confusing. It took is a long time to discover where the Remedy and Re-

course are found in the U.C.C. They are found right in the first volume, at 1-207 and 1-103.

Remedy

"The making of a valid Reservation of Rights preserves whatever rights the person then possesses, and prevents the loss of such rights by application of concepts of waiver or estoppel." (UCC 1-207.7)

It is important to remember when we go into a court, that we are in a commercial, international jurisdiction. If we go into court and say. "I DEMAND MY CONSTITUTIONAL RIGHTS!", the judge will most likely say, "You mention the Constitution again, and I'll find you in contempt of court!" Then we don't understand how he can do that. Hasn't he sworn to uphold the Constitution? The rule here is: you cannot be charged under one jurisdiction and defend yourself under another jurisdiction. For example, if the French government came to you and asked where you filed your French income tax of a certain year, do you go to the French government and say "I demand my Constitutional Rights?" No. The proper answer is: "THE LAW DOES NOT APPLY TO ME. I AM NOT A FRENCHMAN." You must make your reservation of rights under the jurisdiction in which you are charged, not under some other jurisdiction. So in a UCC court, you must claim your Reservation of Rights under UCC 1-207.

UCC 1-207 goes on to say...

"When a waiveable right or claim is involved, the failure to make a reservation thereof, causes a loss of the right, and bars its assertion at a later date." (UCC 1-207.9)

You have to make your claim known early. Further, it says:

"The Sufficiency of the Reservation: any expression indicating an intention to reserve rights is sufficient, such as "without prejudice"". (USS 1-207.4)

Whenever you sign any legal paper that deals with Federal Reserve Notes, write under your signature: "Without Prejudice UCC 1-207.4)" This reserves your rights. You can show, at UCC 1-207.4, that you have sufficiently reserved your rights.

It is very important to understand just what this means. For example, one man who used this in regard to a traffic ticket was asked by the judge just what he meant by writing "without prejudice UCC 1-207" on his statement to the court? He had not tried to understand the concepts involved. He only wanted to use it to get out of the ticket. He did not know what it meant. When the judge asked him what he meant by signing in that way, he told the judge he was not prejudice against anyone... The judge knew that the man had no idea what it meant, and he lost the case. You must know what it means!

Without Prejudice UCC 1-207

When you use "without prejudice UCC 1-207" in connection with your signature, you are saying, *"I reserve my right not to be compelled to perform under any contract or commercial agreement that I did not enter knowingly, voluntarily and intentionally. I do not accept the liability of the compelled benefit of any unrevealed contract or commercial agreement."*

What is the compelled performance of an unrevealed commercial agreement? When you use Federal Reserve Notes instead of silver dollars, is it voluntary? No. There is no lawful money or alternative, so you have to use Federal Reserve Notes; you have to accept the benefit. The government has given you the benefit to discharge your debts with limited liability, and you don't have to pay your debts. How nice they are! But if you did not reserve your rights under 1-207.7, you are compelled to accept the benefit, and are therefore obliged to obey every statute, ordinance, and regulation of the government, at all levels of government; federal, state and local.

If you understand this, you will be able to explain it to the judge when he asks. And he will ask, so be prepared to explain it to the court.

You will also need to understand UCC 1-103, the argument and recourse. If you want to understand this fully, go to a law library and photocopy these two sections from the UCC. It is important to get the Anderson, 3rd edition. Some of the law libraries will only have the West Publishing version, and it is very difficult to understand. In Anderson, it is broken down with decimals into ten parts and, most importantly, it is written in plain English.

Recourse

The Recourse appears in the Uniform Commercial Code at 1-103.6, which says:

> "The Code is complimentary to the Common Law, which remains in force, except where displaced by the code. A statute should be construed in harmony with the Common Law, unless there is a clear legislative intent to abrogate the Common Law."

This is the argument we use in court. The Code recognizes the Common Law. If it did not recognize the Common Law, the government would have had to admit that the United States is bankrupt, and is completely owned by its creditors. But, it is not expedient to admit this, so the Code was written so as not to abolish the Common Law entirely. Therefore, if you have made a sufficient, timely, and explicit reservation of your rights at 1-207, you may then insist that the statutes be construed in harmony with the Common Law.

If the charge is a traffic ticket, you may demand that the court produce the injured person who has filed a *verified* complaint. If, for example, you were charged with failure to buckle your seat belt, you may ask the court: "Who was injured as a result of your failure to 'buckle up'?" However, if the judge won't listen to you and just moves ahead with the case, then you will want to read to him the last sentence of 1-103.6, which states: (2) Actually, it is better to use a rubber stamp, because this demonstrates that you had previously reserved your rights. The simple fact that it takes several days or a week to order and get a stamp shows that you had reserved your rights before signing the document. Anderson Uniform Commercial Code, Lawyers' Cooperative Publishing Co. The Code cannot be read to preclude a Common Law section. Tell the judge, "Your Honor, I can sue you under the Common Law, for violating my rights under the Uniform Commercial Code. I have a remedy, under the UCC, to reserve my rights under the Common Law. I have exercised the remedy, and now you must construe this statute in harmony with the Common Law. To be in harmony with the Common Law, you must come forth with the damaged party."

If the judge insists on proceeding with the case, just act confused and ask this question: "Let me see if I understand, Your Honor, has this court made a legal determination that sections 1-207 and 1-103 of the Uniform Commercial Code, which is the system of law you are operating under, are not valid law before this court?"

Now the judge is in a jam! How can the court throw out one part of the Code and uphold another? If he answers, "yes", then you say: "I put this court on notice that I am appealing your legal determination." Of course, the higher court will uphold the Code on appeal. The judge knows this, so once again you have boxed him in.

Practical Application in Traffic Court

Just so we can understand how this whole process works, let us look at a court situation such as a traffic violation. Assume you ran through a yellow light and a policeman gave you a traffic ticket.

1) The first thing you want to do is to delay the action at least three weeks. This you can do by being pleasant and cooperative with the officer. Explain to him that you are very busy and ask if he could please set your court appearance for about three weeks away. At this point we need to remember the government's trick: "I'm from the government. I'm here to help you." Now we want to use this same approach with them.

2) The next step is to go to the clerk of the traffic court and say, "I believe it would be helpful if I talk to you, because I want to save

the government some money (this will get his attention). I am undoubtedly going to appeal this case. As you know, in an appeal, I have to have a transcript, but the traffic court doesn't have a court reporter. It would be a waste of taxpayer's money to run me through this court and then to have to give me a trial *de novo* in a court of record. I do need a transcript for appealing, and to save the government some money, maybe you could schedule me to appear in a court of record."

3) When you get into court, the judge will read the charges; driving through a yellow light, for instance, and this is a violation of ordinance XYZ. He will ask, "Do you understand the charge against you?"

4) "Well, Your Honor, there is a question I would like to ask before I can make a plea of innocent or guilty. I think it could be answered if I could put the officer on the stand for a moment and ask him a few short questions. Judge: "I don't see why not. Let's swear the officer in and have him take the stand."

5) "Is this the instrument that you gave me?" (hand him the traffic citation).
   Officer: "Yes, this is a copy of it. The judge has the other portion of it."
   "Where did you get my address that you wrote on this citation?"
   Officer: "Well, I got it from your driver's license."

(Number (4) above is very important to get into the record, clearly stating that you do not understand the charges. With that in the record, the court cannot move forward to judge the facts. This will be covered later on.)

Hand the officer your driver's license. "Is this the document you copied my name and address from?"
   Officer: "Yes, this is where I got it."
   "While you've got that in your hand, would you read the signature that's on that license?" (The officer reads the signature) "While you're there, would you read into the record what it says under the signature?"
   Officer: "It says, 'Without Prejudice, UCC 1-207'.
   Judge: "Let me see that license!" (He looks

at it and turns to the officer). "You didn't notice this printing under the signature on this license when you copied his name and address onto the ticket?"

Officer: "Oh, no. I was just getting the address. I didn't look down there."

Judge" "You're not very observant as an officer. Therefore, I'm afraid I cannot accept your testimony in regards to the facts of this case. This case is dismissed."

6) So, the judge found a convenient way out. He could say that the officer was not observant enough to be a reliable witness. He did not want to admit the real nature of the jurisdiction of his court. Once it was in the record that you had written "Without Prejudice UCC 1-207" on your license, the judge knew that he would have to admit that:

a) You had reserved your Common Law rights under the UCC;

b) You had done it sufficiently by writing "Without Prejudice UCC 1-207" on your driver's license.

c) The statute would not have to be read in harmony with the Common Law, and the Common Law says the statute exists, but there is no injured party; and

d) Since there is no injured party or complaining witness, the court has no jurisdiction under the Common Law.

7) If the judge tries to move ahead and try the facts of the case, then you will want to ask him the following question: "Your Honor, let me understand this correctly. Has this court made a legal determination that it has authority under the jurisdiction that it is operating, to ignore two sections of the Uniform Commercial Code which have been called to its attention?" If he says yes, tell him that you put the court on notice that you will appeal that legal determination, and that if you are damaged by his actions, you will sue him in a Common Law action under the jurisdiction of the UCC. This will work just as well with the Internal Revenue Service. In fact, we can use the UCC with the IRS before we get to court.

Using the Code with the IRS

If the IRS sends you a Notice of Deficiency, this is called a "presentment" in the Uniform Commercial Code. A "presentment" in the UCC is very similar to the Common Law. First, we must understand just how this works in the Common Law. Suppose I get a man's name from a phone book, someone I have never met, and I send him a bill or invoice on a nice letterhead that says, "For services rendered: $10,000.00." I send this by certified mail at the address taken from the telephone book. The man has to sign for it before he can open it, so I get a receipt that he received it. When he opens it, he finds a bill for $10,000.00 and the following statement: "If you have any questions concerning this bill or the services rendered you have thirty days to make your questions or objections known."

Of course, he has never heard of me, so he just throws the bill away and assumes that I'm confused or crazy. At the end of thirty days, I go to court and get a default judgement against him. He received a bill for $10,000.00, and was given thirty days to respond. He failed to object to it or ask any questions about it. Now, he has defaulted on the bill and I can lawfully collect the $10,000.00. That's Common Law. The UCC works on the same principle. The minute you get a Notice of Deficiency from the IRS, you must return it immediately with a letter that says:

The presentment above is dishonored (Your name) has reserved all of his rights under the Uniform Commercial Code at UCC 1-207. This action should be all that is necessary, as there is nothing more that they can do. In fact, I recently helped someone in Arizona who received a notice of Deficiency. The man sent a letter such as this, dishonoring the "presentment." The IRS wrote back that they could not make a determination at that office, but were turning it over to the Collections Department. A letter was attached from the Collections Department that said they were sorry for the inconvenience they had caused him and that the Notice of Deficiency had been withdrawn. So you see that if it is handled properly, these matters are easily resolved.

Impending Bankruptcy

On my way here, I had a chance to visit with the Governor of Wyoming. He is very concerned that if he runs for office this November, there won't be a State of Wyoming at the end of four years. He believes that the International Bankers might foreclose on the nation and officially admit that they own the whole world. They could round up everybody in the state capitol building, put them in an internment camp and hold them indefinitely. They may give them a trial, or they may not. They will do whatever they want. As I explained earlier, it has not been convenient to foreclose on the nation, until they could get everything ready. This is where the Federal Emergency Management Agency comes in. It has been put in place without anyone really noticing it.

FEMA

FEMA, or the Federal Emergency Management Agency, has been designed for America when it is officially declared bankrupt. That would be a national emergency. In a national emergency all Constitutional Rights and all law that previously existed, would be suspended. FEMA has created large concentration camps where they will put anyone who might cause trouble for the orderly plan and process of the new regime to take over.

Even a governor could be thrown into one of these internment camps, and kept there indefinitely. The mechanism is all in place now, and FEMA is just waiting to declare a national emergency. Then even state governments could be dissolved. Anybody who might oppose the new regime could be imprisoned until a new set of laws could be written and a new government set up. The Governor knows all this, and he is very concerned. He doesn't want to be in office when all this happens.

When I visited with him and I told him that there are certain actions we should take right now. I think we should consider the fact that, according to the Uniform Commercial Code, Wyoming is an accommodation party to the national debt. In order to understand this statement we must realize that there are two separate entities known as the United States.

The Rothschild Influence

When America was founded, the Rothschilds were very unhappy because it was founded on the (Christian) Common Law. The Common Law is based on substance, and this substance is mentioned in the Constitution as gold or silver. America is a Constitutional Republic, a union of the States under the Constitution. When Congress was working for the Republic, the only thing it could borrow was gold or silver, and the Rothschild banks did not lend gold or silver. Naturally, they did not like this new government. The Rothschilds had a deal with the King of England. He would borrow paper and agree to repay in gold. But these United States, with their Constitution, were an obstacle to them, and it was much to the Rothschild's advantage to get the colonies back under the King. So the Rothschilds financed the War of 1812 to bring America back under England. Of course, it didn't work, so they had to find another way.

The Missing Thirteenth Amendment

If the British could not defeat America and bring it directly under its heel then the army was to do the next best thing. There was at that time a 13th amendment circulating among the colonies for ratification. It was absolutely of utmost importance that this amendment be subverted and made to disappear before it became general public knowledge.

This amendment was referred to as the "title of nobility" amendment and was introduced for ratification in 1810. It was eventually ratified by sufficient colonies to be made law in 1819.

The Flaw in the Constitution, Two Nations in One

It was around the time of the American Civil War that they discovered a flaw in the Constitution. The flaw was Article I, Section 8, Clause 17. Remember that there are two nations called "United States." What is a nation? If you would agree with this definition: Whenever you have a governing body, having a prescribed territory containing a body of people. Is that a nation? Yes. We have a governing body in the Republic, "the three branches of government." There are the legislative, the executive, and the judicial branches. There is a prescribed territory containing a body of people. This is a Constitutional Republic.

But Article 1, Section 8, Clause 17 gave Congress, which is the legislative branch of the three branches government, exclusive rule over a given territory known as the District of Columbia, containing a body of people. Here we have a nation within a nation. This is a legislative democracy within a Constitutional Republic.

When Congress was a part of the Constitutional Republic, it had the obligation of providing a medium of exchange for us. Its duty was to coin gold or silver. Anyone who had a piece of gold or silver could bring it in and have it freely minted into coin. This was the medium of exchange for the Republic. But, in the Legislative Democracy (over Washington D.C.), Congress is not limited by the Constitution. Congress has exclusive rule over the District of Columbia. The legislators can make the law by a majority vote, and that makes it a democracy; they have the authority to have administrative agents to enforce their own law; and they have courts in the legislative branch of government, to try their own law. Here we have the legislature making the law, enforcing the law and trying the law, all within the one branch of government. This is a one-branch government within a three branch government.

Under the three-branch government, Congress passes law which has to be in harmony with the Constitution. The executive enforces the law passed by the Congress, and the judiciary tries the law, pursuant to the Constitution.

The Three-branch Constitutional Republic, and the One-branch legislative democracy are both called the United States. One is the federal United States, and the other is the continental United States.

Are You a United States Citizen?

If you say that you are a United States citizen, which United States are you referring to?

Anyone who lives in the District of Columbia is a United States citizen. The remaining population in the fifty states is the national citizenry of the nation. We are domiciled in various sovereign states, protected by the constitutions of those states from a direct rule of Congress over us. In the democracy, anyone who lives in those states known as Washington D.C., Guam, Puerto Rico, or any of the other federally held territories is a citizen of the United States (D.C.).

We must be careful with our choice of words; we are not citizens of the United States. We are not subject to Congress. Congress has exclusive rule over a given territory, and we are not part of that territory. Where did Congress get the authority to write the Internal Revenue Code? It is found in Article I, Section 8, Clause 17 of the Constitution. To pass that law, they only needed a majority vote. There is no other way that they could pass laws directly affecting individuals. Title 26, the Internal Revenue code, was passed as law for another nation (remember our definition of 'nation'), but Title 26 is not consistent with the Bill of Rights. If you try to fight the IRS, you have no rights-the Code does not allow you any of your constitutional rights. It simply says, "You failed to file an income tax form. You failed to perform in some specific manner."

Remember, under the Common Law, you are free to do whatever you want, as long as you do not infringe upon the life, liberty, or property of anyone else. If you do not want to perform, you don't have to. The only way you can be compelled to perform under the Constitution in the the continental United States, is when you have entered a contract and have failed and fulfill our obligations. But if you are not under a contract you can not be compelled to perform. How can you be compelled to file an income tax form, or any form? You can't!

When Congress works for the Republic, every law it passes must be in harmony with the Constitution and the Bill of Rights, but when Congress works for the Legislative Democracy, any law it passes becomes the law of the land (remember, Congress has exclusive legislative control over federal territory). If you are charged with willful failure to file an income tax 1040 form, that is a law for a different nation. You are a non-resident alien to that nation. It is a foreign corporation to you. It is not the Republic of the continental United

States coming after you, it is a foreign nation, a legislative democracy of a foreign nation coming after you.

If you get a Notice of Deficiency from the IRS, it is a presentment from the federal United States, and then you can use the UCC to dishonor it, and you can also mention that you are among the national citizen of continental United States, and you are a non-resident alien to the federal United States. You never lived in a federal territory and never had any income from the federal United States. Furthermore, you cannot be required to file or pay taxes under the compelled benefit of using the Federal Reserve Notes, because you have reserved your rights under the Common Law through the Uniform Commercial Code at 1-207.

Original Intent of the Founders

The Founding Fathers would never have created a government that was going to push them around! There were 13 sovereign States, They were nations, and they joined together for protection from foreign enemies. They provided a means by which the union of the sovereign states could fend off foreign enemies. But they never gave the congress of the federal United States direct rule over any citizen of any state. They were not going to be ordered around by that government they set up.

Federal Region

The Supreme Court has declared that Congress can rule what Congress creates. Congress did not create the States, but Congress did create federal regions. So Congress can rule the federal regions, but Congress cannot rule the States. How have we been tricked into federal regions?

The Zip Code Trick

Remember how the government always comes to us and says, "I'm from the government and I'm here to help you." The government went out into the various states and said, "We don't want you to have to go to all that trouble of writing three or four letters to abbreviate the name of the state, such as Ariz. for Arizona. Just write AZ, instead of Ariz. Or

you can just write WY for Wyoming instead of Wyo. So all of the states of the union have got a new two-letter abbreviations. Even a state such as Rhode Island has a new abbreviation. It is RI, instead of R.I. They have just left off the periods. When you use a two-letter state abbreviation, you are compelled to use a zip code, because there are so many states, for example, which start with M. ME is Maine, MI is Michigan. How many people dot every "I" or make an "I" that looks like an "E"? With MA, MO, MN, MS, etc., and some sloppy writing, and you could not tell one from another. So, we have to use the zip code in order to tell them apart. But if you wrote Mich., or Minn., or Miss., there would be no real problem telling which state it was.

There is no harm in using the zip code, if you lawfully identify your state. I found out that no state legislature has met to lawfully change the abbreviation of the state from the old abbreviation to the new. Therefore, if you do not use the lawful abbreviation for your state, but use the shorter new abbreviation, you have to use the zip code. Look on page 11 of the Zip Code Directory, and it will tell you that the first digit of your zip code is the federal region in which you reside. If you use AZ for Arizona, you cannot use the state constitution to protect you because you did not identify your state. You used the zip code, which identifies which federal region you live in. And Congress may rule directly federal regions, but it cannot rule the citizens of any state.

Accommodation Party

Let's look at the way in which the states have become the "accommodation party" to the national debt. There are many people I have talked with, including the Governor, who are very concerned about this problem, and who knew that it could soon become a real problem.

If America is declared a bankrupt nation then, there will be a national emergency. The Federal Emergency Management Agency will take over, and anyone who opposes the new government of the creditors can be sent to a detention camp in Alaska, or somewhere else. We will have no rights whatsoever. They have already set up prison camps with work camps nearby so the people can be used for slave labor. It could be the governors, legislators, and other leaders who would be hauled away to Alaska, while the people now disenfranchised from power would likely be chosen to run the new government. This could all happen very soon, as the national debt is so large as to be unpayable. Even the interest on the debt is virtually unpayable. As I explained, the national debt, more than three trillion dollars, is not owned by the Continental United States. It is the federal United States that had authority to borrow bank credit. When Congress worked for Continental United States it could only borrow gold or silver, so the national debt was borrowed in the name of the federal United States. The federal United States has been bankrupt since 1938, but the federal United States had to trap the States into assuming the debt obligation of the federal debt. In the Uniform Commercial Code, we find the term, "accommodation party." How did the states become the accommodation party to the federal debt?" The federal government, through our money system, made the states deal in "Federal Reserve Notes, which means that everything the states do is colorable. Under the colorable jurisdiction of the Uniform Commercial Code, all of the states are the accommodation party to the federal debt. Now the concern is to find out how we can get out of this situation. I told the Governor that in the Common Law and the Law of Merchants, that's the International Law Merchant, there is a term called no-Interest contract. A no-interest contract is void and unenforceable. What is a no-interest contract?

No-Interest Contract

If I were to insure a house that did not belong to me, that would be a no-interest contract. I would just want the house to burn down. I would pay a small premium, perhaps a few hundred dollars, and insure it for $80,000 dollars against fire. Then I would be waiting for it to burn so I could trade my small premium for $80,000. Under the Common Law and under international law of the Law Merchant, that is called a no-interest contract, and it is void and unenforceable in any court.

Unconscionable Contracts

In the Uniform Commercial Code, no-interest "contracts" are called unconscionable contracts. The section on unconscionable contracts covers more than forty pages in the Anderson Code. The federal United States has made the states an accommodation party to the federal debt, and I believe we could prove this to be an unconscionable contract. We should get some litigation into the courts before the government declares a national emergency, claiming that this state has no lawful responsibility for the national debt, because it became an accommodation party to this debt through an unconscionable contract. If we have this litigation before the courts under International Law, when the nation is declared bankrupt, the creditors would have to settle this matter first, and that would delay them. They would want the new government to appear to be legitimate, so that they could not just move right in and take over the state, as the case would be heard in an International Court. This action is very important.

Questions and Review

Note: These are some of the questions that were asked after the main lecture. Some are restatements of material presented earlier, but they contain very valuable information that is worth repeating.

Courtroom Technique

Question: How did you "box in" the Judge? This is easy to do if you don't know too much. I didn't know too much, but I boxed him in. You must play a little dumb. If you are arrested and you go into court, just remember that in a criminal action, you have to understand the law or it is a reversible error for the court to try you. If you don't understand the law, they can't try you. "5 UCC Y3-415. "Accommodation Party." One who signs commercial paper in any capacity for purpose lending his name to another party to instrument. Such a party is a surety. Surety is, "One who undertakes to pay money or do other act in the event that his principal fails therein." In any traffic case or tax case you are called into court and the judge reads the law and then asks, "Do you understand the charges?"

Defendant: No, You Honor, I do not.

Judge: "Well, what's so difficult about that charge? Either you drove the wrong-way on a one-way street or you didn't. You can only go one way on that street, and if you go the other way it's a fifty dollar fine. What's so difficult about this that you don't understand?"

Defendant: Well, You Honor, it's not the letter of the law, but rather the nature of the law that I don't understand. The Sixth Amendment of the Constitution gives me the right to request the court to explain the nature of any action against me, and upon my request, the court has the duty to answer. I have a question about the nature of this action.

Judge: Well, what is that? What do you want to know?

Always ask some easy questions first, as this establishes the fact that they are answering. You ask:

Defendant: Well, Your Honor, is this a Civil or a Criminal Action?

Judge: It is a criminal. (If it were a civil action there could be no fine, so it has to be criminal.)

Defendant: Thank you, Your Honor, for telling me that. Then the record will show that this action against   (your name) is a criminal action, is that right?

Judge: Yes.

Defendant: I would like to ask another question about this criminal action. There are two criminal jurisdictions mentioned in the Constitution: one is under the Common Law, and the other deals with International Maritime Contracts, under and Admiralty Jurisdiction. Equity is Civil, and you said this is a Criminal action, so it seems it would have to be under either the Common Law, or Maritime. Law. But what puzzles me, You Honor, is that there is no *corpus delecti* here that gives the court a jurisdiction over my person and property under the Common Law. Therefore, it doesn't appear to me that this court is moving under the Common Law.

Judge: No, I can assure this court is not moving under the Common Law.

Defendant: Well, thank you, Your Honor, but now you make the charge against me even more difficult to understand. The only other criminal jurisdiction would apply only if there was an International Maritime Contract involved. I would have to a party to it, and it would have to be breached. Too, the court would have to be operating in an Admiralty Jurisdiction.

I don't believe I have ever been under any International Maritime contract, so I would deny that one exists. I would have to demand that such a contract, if it does exist, be placed in evidence, so that I would have the chance to contest it. But surely, this court is not operating under an Admiralty Jurisdiction.

You just put the words in the judges mouth.

Judge: No, I can assure you, we're not operating under an Admiralty Jurisdiction. We're not out in the ocean somewhere. We're right here in the middle of the State of (any state). No, this is not an Admiralty Jurisdiction.

Defendant: Thank you Your Honor, but now I am more puzzled that ever. If this charge is not under the Common Law, or under Admiralty-and those are the only two criminal jurisdictions mentioned in the constitution-what kind of jurisdiction could this court be operating under?

Judge: It's Statutory Jurisdiction.

Defendant: Oh, thank you, Your Honor. I'm glad you told me that. But I have never heard of that jurisdiction. So , if I have to defend under that jurisdiction, I would need to have the Rules of Criminal Procedure for Statutory Jurisdiction. Can you tell me where I might find those rules?

There are no rules for Statutory Jurisdiction; so the judge will get very angry at this point and say:

Judge: If you want the answers to questions like that, you get yourself a licensed attorney. I'm not allowed to practice law from the bench.

Defendant: Oh, Your Honor, I don't think anyone would accuse you of practicing law from the bench if you just answered a few questions to explain to me the nature of this action, so that I might defend myself.

Judge: I told you before, I am not going to answer any more questions. Do you understand that? If you ask any more questions in regards to this, I'm going to find you in contempt of court! Now if you can't afford a licensed attorney, the court will provide you with one. But if you want those questions answered, you must get yourself a licensed attorney.

Defendant: Thank you, Your Honor, but let

me just see if I got this straight.

This court has made a legal determination that it has authority to conduct a criminal action against me, the accused, under a secret jurisdiction, the rules of which are known only to this court and licensed attorneys, thereby denying me the right to defend in my own person?

He has no answer for that. The judge will probable postpone the case and eventually just let it go. In this way, you can be as "wise as a serpent and as harmless as a dove, but you must not go into court with a chip on your shoulder and as a wolf in "black sheep" country. Remember Jesus' words, "I send you out as sheep in wolf country, be wise as a serpent, and harmless as a dove." Sheep do not attack wolves directly. Just be an innocent little lamb who just can't understand the charge. Remember, too, they can't try you criminally if you don't understand the charge. That would automatically be a reversible error on appeal.

The Social Security Problem

If I were a young man, 18 to 20 years old and just starting out in my first job, I would not want Social Security. With my signature on the application I would write, "Without prejudice" UCC 1-207, and I would reserve my Common Law rights." But why wouldn't I want Social Security today? I got into the Social Security system in the 1930's, and I paid into it dollars that had good purchasing power. Now I'm getting a promised return in Federal Reserve Notes which have considerable less value. For example, in 1940, you could buy a deluxe Chevrolet for 800 dollars. With today's Federal Reserve Notes, that won't buy the rear fenders and trunk on a new Chevrolet. It I were a young man, I would not want to put Federal Reserve Notes into Social Security now, and get back something later like the German mark after World War I, when it took a billion to buy a loaf of bread. They will give you every Federal Reserve Note back that they promised you, but it might not buy anything.

Assurance

Under the Uniform Commercial Code, you have the right with any agreement, to demand a guarantee of performance. So, don't go to them and say, "I want to rescind my Social Security number," or "refuse to take it." Just take it easy and say, "I would be happy to get a Social Security number and enter into this contract, but I have a little problem. How can I have assurances before I enter into this contract that the purchasing power of the Federal Reserve Notes I get back at the end of the contract will be as good as the ones that I pay in at the beginning? They can't guarantee that, and you have a right under the UCC to assurance of performance under the contract. So tell them, "Well, I can not enter this contract unless the government will guarantee to pay me at the end of the contract with the same value Federal Reserve Notes that I'm paying in. Both may be called Federal Reserve Notes, but you know that these Federal Reserve Notes don't hold their value. I want assurance on this contract that the Federal Reserve Notes that I get in my retirement will buy as much as the ones that I'm giving you now in my working years." They can't make that guarantee. If they won't give you that guarantee, just say, "I'd be glad to sign this, but if you can't guarantee performance under the contract, I'm afraid I cannot enter the contract."

Now, did you refuse or did they refuse? You can get the sections of the Uniform Commercial Code which grant the right to have assurance that the contract you have entered will be fulfilled properly; that the return will equal the investment, and you can reject the contract using the Code. Using their own system of law, you can show that they cannot make you get into a contract of that nature. Just approach them innocently like a lamb. It is very important to be gentle and humble in all dealings with the government or the courts. Never raise your voice or show anger. In the courtroom, always be polite, and build the judge up, call him 'Your Honor.' Give him all the 'honor' he wants. It does no good to be difficult, but rather to be cooperative and ask questions in a way that leads the judge to say the things you need to have in the record.

The Court Reporter

In many courts, there will be a regular court reporter. He gets his job at the judges pleasure, so he doesn't want to displease the judge. The court reporter is sworn to give an accurate transcript of every word that is spoken in the courtroom. But if the judge makes a slip of the tongue, he turns to his court reporter and says, "I think you had better leave that out of the transcript. Just say it got a little too far ahead of you, and you couldn't quite get everything in." So this statement will be missing from the transcript. In one case, we brought a licensed court reporter with us and the judge got very angry and said, "This court has a licensed court reporter right here, and the record of this court is this court reporter's record. No other court reporter's record means anything in this court."

We responded with, "Of course, Your Honor, we're certainly glad to use your regular court reporter. But you know, Your Honor, sometimes things move so fast that a court reporter gets a little behind, and doesn't quite keep up with it all. Wouldn't it be nice if we had another licensed court reporter in the courtroom, just in case your court reporter got a little behind, so that we could fill in from this other court reporter's data. I'm sure, Your Honor, that you want an accurate transcript. (I like to use the saying: give a bad dog a good name, and he'll live up to it!) The judge went along with it, and from that moment on, he was very careful about what he said.

These are little tricks to getting around in court. This is how to be "wise as a serpent and harmless as a dove" when we enter a courtroom. There are others using the same information presented here who end up in jail, handcuffed and hit over the head, because they approach the situation with a chip on their shoulder. They try to tell the judge what the law is and that he is a no-good scoundrel and so on. Just be wise and harmless.

UCC 1-207 Review

It is so important to know and understand the meaning of "Without prejudice" UCC 1-207, in connection with your signature, that we should go over this once more. It is very likely that a judge will ask you what it means. So please learn and understand this carefully: The use of "Without prejudice' UCC 1-207," in connection with my signature indicates that I have reserved my Common Law right not to be compelled to perform under any contract that I did not enter into knowingly, voluntari-

ly, and intentionally. And furthermore, I do not accept the liability associated with the compelled benefit of any un-revealed contract or commercial agreement.

Once you state that, it is all the judge needs to hear. Under the Common Law, a contract must be entered into knowingly, voluntarily and intentionally, by both parties, or it can be declared void and unenforceable. You are claiming the right not to be compelled to perform under any contract that you did not enter into knowingly, voluntarily and intentionally. And you do not accept the liability associated with the compelled benefit of any unrevealed contract or agreement.

The compelled benefit is the privilege to use Federal Reserve Notes to discharge your debts with limited liability rather than to pay your debts with silver coins. It is a compelled benefit, because there are no silver coins in circulation. You have to eat, and you can only buy food with the medium of exchange provided by the government. You are not allowed to print your own money, so you are compelled to use theirs. This is the compelled benefit rendered by government, so that you will be obligated, under an implied agreement, to obey every statute, ordinance and regulation passed by government, and at all levels; federal, state and local.

Conclusion

The editor of this transcript has taken great liberties in putting this on paper, in an effort to make it readable and compact. He wishes to offer his gratitude to Howard Freeman for the opportunity to work with information so vital to our survival as dignified, unenslaved, human beings. He must also ask Mr. Freeman's forgiveness for any errors committed in getting this in print. Its purpose, as already stated, is to make this knowledge available to as many people as will take the time and trouble to read it. It is meant to be supplemental to Mr. Freeman's recorded lectures; not a substitute. Indeed, there is no substitute for hearing him present this material in his own words. It is not just the law and the facts that are important here, but the way they are used. His many reminders of Jesus; commission to be "...like sheep among wolves..." cannot be overstated, and is certainly good advice to us in all dealings, not just in court or with the government. Hearing him explain this in his own words brings to life the practical application and usefulness of being "wise" and "harmless." In fact, after being introduced to this approach, it becomes hard to imagine that any other way of defending oneself from the government would be effective.

It goes without saying that none of this information is offered as legal advice. For that, as you know, you must "get yourself a licensed attorney." Having said that, I feel obliged to point out that one of the most difficult aspects of dealing with a licensed attorney, even a good one, may be knowing just whose side he is on (he is, after all, an officer of the court!) So, for those of us who have concluded that having an attorney means that you will soon be "chained, gagged, and lead to the gallows," this information may be indispensable. For the extraordinary challenges of appearing in court in one's own person, pro per, there are few reliable sources of information. Learning to defend oneself, that is, being responsible instead of turning over one more part of our lives to "professionals" may be the only way to have any chance of digging ourselves out of this pit of legal tyranny.

Perhaps the greatest problem we face in education today is the matter of widespread legal illiteracy. Naturally, there will always be a number of people who just don't care about these issues who either:

1) Have a soft life which is supported and maintained by this secret system of law and the institutions which have grown up around it ("I can make a bundle buying these IRS seized homes cheap and reselling them') or--

2) Don't believe that anything can be done about it ('you can't fight city hall',) or

3) Simply don't have the energy or inclination to do anything about it ('that's nice, but let's see what's on TV'.)

See UCC 1-201. General Definitions (3) "Agreement" means the bargain of the parties in fact as found in their language or by implication from other circumstances including course of dealing or trade or usage of trade or course of performance...

To those good 'citizens' all this effort may seen useless, or even threatening. But it is this writer's view that God did not intend for us to spend our lives in statutory slavery for the benefit of a handful of secret world manipulators, even if the 'masters' grant us some token pleasures and diversions. Human dignity requires much more than entertainment. The door is there and the key exists; we must find it and we must use it to return to freedom!

Let us discover the mistakes we have made, let us find the truth, let us apply it with meekness and wisdom and let us gently but firmly reclaim the precious freedom which we have so foolishly given up.

For More Information

I encourage anyone interested enough to read this far, to obtain a set of tapes of Howard Freeman and listen to them carefully. A donation of $4.00 per tape would be appropriate. This information was taken from tapes #'s 90-30; 90-32 and 90-33; which may be ordered from:

America's Promise Ministries
P.O. Box 157
Sandpoint, Idaho 83864

The next set of tapes from 1991 are #'s: 1004; 1005; and 1006, and contain vital material not found in this transcript.

Declaration for Redress of Grievances

by Dale Pond

We The People, in order to establish a more perfect, peaceful and harmonious society in which We live, petition Our city, county, state and federal governments for redress of the following negative conditions in which We now find Ourselves. The power of Our government is derived from, by and for Us, The People and it is We The People who wish compliance to Our will, by all levels of Our government in all things lawfully its duty, as We The People, determine that duty to be. We are Our government and We do recognize and choose to uphold the following:

1) Our local(2) and city, state and federal police act without humane concern and in complete disregard of the nation's Constitution and Our Rights under that Constitution and with disrespect and inconsideration of Ourselves.

2) Our city, county, state and federal employees(1) have forgotten they actually and in truth work for Us, The People and not for an authoritarian boss or imposed set of rules, laws, regulations or guidelines. Nor are Our governing agencies separate and distinct from Us, The People but We are in actuality those same, governing Ourselves, through those of Us thusly employed in Our behalf.

3) Our city, county, state and federal employees(1) now act and have their very existence within the evil Civil or Equity (3) Law which is totally outside of the provisions of Our nation's Constitution and amended Bill of Rights.

4) Our city, county, state and federal employees(1) now act as though the rule of law is greater than God, country or Us The People and they impose and force, in an inhumane way, these self-created laws upon Us, The People,in a way in which we have little or no recourse of corrective actions.

5) Our city, county, state and federal employees(1) have allowed themselves to be manipulated by specially interested parties to cause to have laws passed in their favor which have nearly always been to the detriment the rest of Us, The People.

6) Our city, county, state and federal employees(1) have caused Us, The People, to support them and their actions even when these actions have been contrary to Our own benefit such as hiring and maintaining on the payroll criminals(5), protecting and harboring criminals, engaging in wars without consent of Us, The People, creating and forcing upon Us laws and situations contrary to Our desires and in short behaving in a totalitarian manner contrary to any accepted form of representative government.

7) Our city, county, state and federal employees(1) have failed to protect and enforce Our Constitution in their own actions and behaviors and that of others when proposing and enacting the evil Civil or Equity Law which is nothing other than slavery or blind adherence to a centralized authority that does not recognize the sovereign individuality of each of Us, The People.

Thus we can all see that the state of affairs in Our beloved society has degenerated to a point where We The People deem it necessary to petition all of Our government sectors for redress and proper corrective measures be adopted. These being:

1) All of Our local, state and federal employees must swear upon penalty of perjury an oath to know, support and protect Our Constitution.

2) All of Our local, state and federal employees must swear upon penalty of perjury an oath to know, support and protect We The People in our persons, rights and property.

3) All of Our local, state and federal employees must swear upon penalty of perjury an oath to eliminate, in every way possible, the evil Civil or Equity(3) Law now employed throughout Our society.

4) The Federal Reserve Act of 1913 was illegally adopted and shall be made null and void and all actions taken because of such evil villainy be made as though they never were and all of Our property taken from Us because of this law be returned to Us. Our federal government shall reassume forthwith its rightful duty and responsibilities under the original Constitution, Article I, Section 8, Paragraph 5, as stated therein.

5) All of Our local, state and federal employees must swear upon penalty of perjury an oath that each and every individual person in this country is a Child of God(4) and is to be treated as such and not as has grown to be the custom like a piece of property or chattel or source of income.

6) All of Our local, state and federal employees must swear upon penalty of perjury an oath to henceforth refer to all police as "Peace Officers" or "Keepers of the Peace" and never again as "Law Enforcers" or "Enforcers of the Law" because We The People desire to live in a lawful and peaceful society and not one in which the evil Civil or Equity law is forced upon Us.

7) All of Our local, state and federal employees must swear upon penalty of perjury an oath to henceforth refer to all Our elected officials as "Representatives" and never as "Law Makers" because it is not they who make the law but We The People make the laws through them, acting as Our agents and in and for Our behalf.

8) All of Our city, and/or local police forces not operating or existing directly under the locally elected county sheriff shall be caused to be brought under the elected sheriff's authority and never again shall a police force be created or maintained that is not directly responsible and responsive to Us, The People.

9) All of Our federal military personnel and associated properties shall cease to be under the federal authority, except in case of war. Our military personnel and properties shall be brought under the authority of Our respective states in which it finds itself and made part of that states' militia as written in Our Constitution.

10) That any violation of Our Constitution and Bill of Rights be classified as a misdemeanor in the first instance and a felony in subsequent instances.

11) That all of Our federal agencies which have activities throughout the nation's states be broken up into individual and sovereign parts within each of Our states equally. These separate authorities of Our's must then learn to work together respecting such sovereignty and authority of themselves and Ourselves in each state. This act is to re-establish the original sovereignty of Our states and Our peoples free of coercion from centralized power structures which are in reality too far removed from Us, The People.

12) That the current form of Our income tax and the evil, destructive IRS be abolished altogether. In its place shall be a flat tax of 6% of total gross income per person without deductions of any kind. This 6% tax shall be paid directly to Our local county government to use as We The People deem fit for Our benefit. These county revenues shall be equally distributed: one fourth to support Our local county government; one fourth to support our state governments; one fourth to support Our much smaller federal government and one fourth to be invested so that one day We The People shall eliminate taxing Ourselves altogether.

13) That all of Our courts of law shall be, by default, Constitutional courts, and not Equity courts as is now the case. Judges of said courts shall administer the Constitutional law and never again the evil Civil or Equity Law as is now being done.

14) That the current and unacceptable practice of Our federal government to blackmail Our state and Our local governments, through the threat of withholding Our funds in order to establish compliance in any action, cease. The power of Our federal government is derived from Us, The People and it is We The People who wish compliance to Our will, by Our federal government in all things lawfully its duty, as We The People, determine that duty to be.

(1) Employees herein is understood to be any employee, agent, contractor, hire, appointee or elected person or legal entity.

(2) Local is herein understood to be village, city (incorporated or not) and county.

(3) See attached addendum.

(4) God being defined as those creative and universal forces which have made and maintain all that there is in the universe.

(5) Criminals are those who behave contrary to accepted standards of law. The law has become contrary to standards of Common Sense and thus few people can decipher the meaning or intent of the evil Civil or Equity Law. Thus what may be legal is not necessarily right.

OUR INDIVIDUAL COMMON LAW RIGHTS

by Howard Fisher

Another Constitutional issue that each of us needs to understand is the issue of Individual Common Law Rights of We the People of the United States of America. This directly concerns the <u>limits of authority</u> of all branches of government over each of us as individuals: the Authority of the Executive, Legislative and Judicial Branches of Government.

As stated in the Declaration of Independence, we are endowed by our Creator with certain <u>Unalienable Rights</u>, that among these are Life, Liberty and the Pursuit of Happiness.

Thomas Jefferson placed great emphasis on the concept of Rights. He said we did not bring the English Common Law, as such, to this continent; we brought the <u>Rights of Man</u>. The reason why he said that is that it is from the Common Law controversies, all of which involved property, that all of our <u>Rights</u> have come to be recognized in the Law.

In a legal sense, Property is a bundle of Rights, a bundle of Powers, wherein one claimant to these Rights possesses these Rights to the exclusion of all other claimants to these Rights, as these Rights pertain to the possession, occupancy and use of a specific piece of property.

So, at Common Law, <u>Rights</u> is the name of the game.

The Bill of Rights was added to the Constitution of the United States of America because the Founding Fathers believed these Amendments should be added to avoid misconstruction of the provisions of the Constitution of the United States of America <u>by Judges</u> and to avoid an abuse of powers <u>by Judges</u> of the sort that had already, at that time, taken place in England and from which abuse of powers we had just fought, and won, a revolution to be free. (See the Preamble to the Bill of Rights. The original Constitution has it, and in some sources which print the Constitution, this Preamble is included.) This abuse had been committed <u>by Judges</u> who were not tied down by any <u>written</u> Constitution in England, and who had started to whittle away at the Common Law Rights in England and the Colonies, by their decisions, with the cooperation of the statutes passed by the Parliament and enforced by the Crown. This is precisely the combination of Executive and Legislative Equity (otherwise known as Roman Civil Law) which our Bill of Rights prevents and protects us from.

The Constitution of the State of Iowa has its Bill of Rights, comprising Article I. The first two sections deserve special emphasis :

Section 1. All men are, by nature, free and equal, and have certain inalienable rights -- among which are those of enjoying and defending life and liberty, acquiring, possessing and protecting property, and pursuing and obtaining safety and happiness.

Section 2. All political power is enherent in the people. Government is instituted for the protection, security, and benefit of the people, and they have the right, at all times, to alter or reform the same, whenever the public good may require it.

So the Constitution of the State of Iowa expressly includes the Right of acquiring, possessing and protecting Property, although it is high on the Priority List of Common Law Rights. This is an example of a Constitution **securing** Rights which come from the Common Law.

Back in 1921 someone wrote:

"It is not the Right of property which is protected, but the Right to property. Property, as such, has no rights ; but the individual -- the man -- has three great Rights, equally sacred from interference :

the Right to his LIFE; the Right to his LIBERTY; the Right to his PROPERTY. .. .

The three Rights are so bound together as to be essentially one Right. To give a man his life but deny him his liberty, is to take from him all that makes life worth living. To give him his liberty but take from him the property which is the fruit and badge of his liberty, is to still leave him a slave."

Thomas Jefferson said :

"Our rulers can have no authority over [our] natural rights, only as we have submitted to them. **The rights of conscience we never submitted. We are answerable for them to our God.** The legitimate powers of government extend to such acts **only as are injurious to others."**

This points up the significance of the requirement of the proceedures of the Common Law that there be an injured party, that the injured party make a sworn complaint as to the injury that has been done to him by the alleged Defendant. That unless this is done, the Court does not have jurisdiction over the Defendant.

We have been told, from childhood, that we have unalienable Rights, **and we do ! !** Unalienable means that they cannot be taken from us, and that we cannot be forced to give them up. There are those who point out that, strictly speaking, we cannot even **give them up voluntarily**. However, if we submit to those who would **rule** over us, it is true that our Rights were not taken from us -- as Thomas Jefferson said, -- **we have submitted to their rule**. We have **allowed ourselves** to become their slaves. There is one important fact concerning slavery, of any sort, the institution of slavery **depends upon the cooperation of the slaves ! !** Without the cooperation of the slaves, there can be no slavery.

In Common Law Courts our Rights are protected. The Rules and Procedures of the Common Law Courts were established to protect our Property Rights -- to make it difficult for Property to be taken from someone without Due Process of Law. The Right to require that an injured party swear under oath as to damage or injury that he claims that you caused to him; the Right to a *Corpus Delicti* : The body of the offense: " the essence of the crime." : Under the Common Law, the Courts do not have an **automatic jurisdiction**. The Common Law Rules and Procedures specify certain steps, or procedures, which must be done, and certain things which must not be done -- all as a protection to the Rights of the Accused. And, as we have pointed out previously, Rights are inherent in Property, and Property is inherent in Rights. We have the Right to have our controversy, once the Common Law Court has acquired jurisdiction, tried before a Common Law Jury of our Peers, wherein the Jury has the authority to **hear and decide** questions of both Law and Fact. There is no monkey business of pretending that arguments involving the Law must be held outside of the hearing of the Jury and that their supposed only function is to hear and decide questions of Fact presented in evidence and that the Judge will tell them what the Law is ! !

As evidence that the Founding Fathers operated under the Common Law, in addition to the wording of the Constitution of the United States of America, the following was included in the instructions to the Jury in the first case ever tried before the United States Supreme Court, as a court of original jurisdiction, which means that a Trial by Jury was held in front of the Supreme

Court, with Chief Justice John Jay presiding:

"It is presumed, that juries are the best judges of facts; it is, on the other hand, presumably, that the courts are the best judges of law. But still both objects are within your power of decision. You have a right to take upon yourselves to judge both, and to determine the law as well as the fact in controversy. "

STATE OF GEORGIA vs. BRAILSFORD , 3 Dall I (1794)

Our Property Rights are inseparable from our individual Rights and our individual Rights are inseparable from our Property Rights. Both types of Rights are protected in the Procedures and Due Process of the Courts of Common Law.

The Bill of Rights in both Constitutions have to do with matters that the governments, both of the United States and of the State, have to do with matters that the government, and its agents and agencies, have no authority over at all to enact statutes, or to issue rules and regulations, binding on the individual, dealing with such Rights as are included in the Bill of Rights. It should be emphasized that the Ninth Amendment includes all of the Common Law Rights which are not listed, or enumerated, anywhere else. In other words, the Bill of Rights are prohibitions against government at any level over the individual.

The Constitution authorizes Courts of Law and Courts of Equity. When the Constitution says Law, it means Common Law, because that's what the Founding Fathers meant when they said Law. In Courts of Law your Rights are protected by the Constitution and the Rules and Procedures of the Common Law, known as Due Process of Law; and the Bill of Rights was adopted to avoid misconstruction and abuse of powers, by the Judges; but in Courts of Equity, by the nature of Equity jurisdiction, you don't have any Rights.

THE DOLLAR AS MONEY DEFINED

Looking at an old Federal Reserve Note (1934 series not in abundant circulation) and reading the data thereon, it states:

"This note is "legal tender" for all debts public and private and is redeemable in "lawful money" at the United States Treasury or at any Federal Reserve Bank." (Emphasis added)

It plainly states that the note is "legal tender" but then says that it is redeemable in "lawful money". Therefore Federal Reserve Notes are "legal tender" but not "lawful money". The Federal Reserve Note is apparently evidence of some right to recover, as printed at the bottom of the front side of the note, just under the picture, are the following words:

"WILL PAY TO THE BEARER ON DEMAND"
"ONE HUNDRED DOLLARS"

This becomes obvious when looking at the United States Code. which, in talking about Federal Reserve notes, says:

"They shall be redeemed in lawful money on demand at the Treasury Department of the United States, in the city of Washington, District of Columbia, or at any Federal Reserve Bank." (emphasis added) U.S.C.A., Title 21, Sec 411.

Therefore, "ONE HUNDRED DOLLARS" or ONE DOLLAR is something different from a Federal Reserve Note or it would not state on the note that the note is redeemable in "DOLLARS."

It appears that Federal Reserve Notes are simply a medium of exchange used in place of, in lieu of, or as temporary substitutes for that which should be redeemable for "lawful money" of the United States ---- "DOLLARS." "Lawful Money" of the United States is not Federal Reserve Notes, as "lawful money" can only be "DOLLARS." A DOLLAR is a "UNIT" of measure and is so defined:

"A silver coin of Spain and of the United States, of the value of one hundred cents of four shillings and a sixpence sterling. (emphasis added) American Dictionary of the English Language, Noah Webster, 1828.

The DOLLAR means "lawful money" of the United States. (103 U.S. 792)

"The gold coins of the United States shall be one DOLLAR piece, which at the standard weight of 24.75 grains shall be the unit of value..." (emphasis added) 31 U.S.C.A. 314.

A DOLLAR then is a coin that has value. In other words a DOLLAR is something of value -- not something that represents something of value, nor an implied evidence of value. A coin has value as it is made from a substance that of itself has value. A coin is defined as:

"Money stamped; a piece of metal, as gold, silver, copper, or other metal, converted into money by impressing on it marks, figures or characters." Webster's, 1828, Vol I, page 40

A coin then, of stamped gold or silver, is money. Money is defined as:

"Coin, stamped metal; any piece of metal usually gold, silver, or copper stamped by public authority ,...among modern commercial nations, gold, silver, and copper are the only metals used for this purpose. Gold and silver containing great value in a small compass, and being therefore of easy conveyance, and being also durable and little liable to diminution by use, are the most convenient metals for coin or money, Which is the representative of commodities of all kinds, of lands, and of every thing that is capable of being transfered in commerce." Webster's Vol II, page 18

This definition is further substantiated in law dictionaries which define money as:

"Gold and silver coins. The common medium of exchange in a civilized nation."
Bouvier's Law Dictionary, 1870, page 192.

"In usual and ordinary acceptation it means gold, silver, or paper money used as circulating medium of exchange, and does not embrace notes, bonds, evidence of debt...Lane v Railey, 280 Ky 319..." (emphasis added) Black's Law Dictionary, 4th Ed. page 115

"In its strict technical sense, 'money' means coined metal, usually gold or silver, upon which the government stamp has been impressed; it indicates its value." (emphasis added) Black's, supra

Interestingly enough, in this definition it can be plainly seen that money is coined gold and silver (DOLLARS) having a value, and cannot be NOTES or other evidences of debt.

A DOLLAR is defined as: "The money unit of the United States...established under the confederation by a resolution of Congress, July 6, 1785. This was originally represented by a silver piece only; the coinage of which was authorized by the act of Congress of Aug. 8, 1786. But the coinage was not effected until after the passage of the act of April 2, 1792, establishing a mint." Bouvier's, p. 496

That act was passed after the Constitution was in force and effect and is 1 U.S. Statute at Large, 246 which states: "That there shall be from time to time struck and coined at the said mint, coins of gold, silver, and copper of the following denominations, values and descriptions,... "DOLLARS or UNITS -- each to be of the value of a Spanish milled dollar as the same is now current, and to contain three hundred and seventy one grains and four sixteenth parts of a grain of pure, or four hundred and sixteen grains of standard silver.

"That the money of account of the United States shall be expressed in dollars or units... and that all accounts in the public offices and all proceedings in the courts of the United States shall be kept and had in conformity to this regulation." (emphasis added) All DOLLARS are specific "units" of gold and silver coins having a fixed "value" based upon their weight content of gold and /or silver in grains and are "Lawful money" of the United States. This is further substantiated by the United States Code which states: "Lawful money shall be construed to mean gold or silver coin of the United States." (emphasis added) U.S.C.A., Title 12, Section 152.

The "DOLLAR" means lawful money of the United States. 103 U.S. 792.

Lawful money of the United States is quite a different thing from legal tender or other lawful currency for the United States. Federal Reserve Notes are a legal tender for but not of the United States. It can be said that all DOLLARS are legal tender but not all legal tender is DOLLARS, Federal Reserve Notes cannot be "Lawful money" of the United States.

Federal Reserve Notes and other forms of Lawful currency are not the topic of this paper but it should suffice to say that anything could serve as a currency for the United States (such as Federal Reserve Notes) but there is only one form of "lawful money of the United States" and that is the DOLLAR, expressed in a unit of weight in grains of gold and silver contained in coin. Since Federal Reserve Notes are not gold and silver coins, have no fixed value, and are not even redeemable in silver or gold dollars, Federal Reserve Notes are not dollars or even evidence of dollars. The so called modern Federal Reserve Note is quite different from the one mentioned in the beginning of this Notice, as current Federal Reserve Notes only state: "This note is legal tender for all debts, public and private" (There is not even a period after this statement, proving the statement is not complete.) There is no mention of the note being redeemable in "lawful money at the United States Treasury or at any Federal Reserve Bank" and it makes no promise to "PAY TO THE BEARER UPON DEMAND" DOLLARS in the amount printed on its face. There is a vast difference between the two notes as one is redeemable in something of value (lawful money) and the other is redeemable in nothing except more Federal Reserve Notes. Therefore, Federal Reserve Notes have no value except what they may bring in the market place from day to day.

MONEY OF ACCOUNT OF THE STATE OF IDAHO

Article 1, Section 10, of the United States Constitution states:

"No State shall...make any Thing but gold and silver Coin a Tender in payment of Debts."

The State of Idaho has fulfilled this Constitutional requirement by declaring only gold and silver coin to be a tender in payment of all debts in Idaho as follows: "Money of account defined --- the money of account in this state is the "dollar", cent and mill, and all public accounts and the proceeding of all courts in relation to money must be kept and expressed in money of the above denominations." Idaho Code 28-42-401

Therefore, "money of account" of the State of Idaho conforms to the Constitutional mandate as the DOLLAR is the "unit" of measuremant of gold and silver coins having a fixed value based upon the weight of the coins expressed in grains of gold or silver. As expressed in Idaho Code 28-42-403 and the United States Statute at Large, 1792, quoted above, this court can only issue judgements expressed in money units called DOLLARS --- being gold and silver coins. Since the state cannot and the Federal government is not currently coining any DOLLARS, DOLLARS are not available to any person; therefore, no person can pay any debt arising from a judgement of the court.

Since there are no DOLLARS available to the Accused to pay the debt judgement of the court, the court has no capacity to enforce the judgement and therefore lacks the ability to effect a remedy. Since the court cannot enforce its judgement in DOLLARS, it has no jurisdiction in this case and the case should be dismissed.

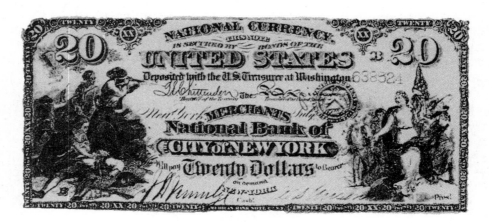

STATUS OF CITIZENS

The most significant identity an individual can have is his status in the world of law. From his position and standing in relation to the state flows his entire capacity to do, create, and exist at his highest level.

In the United States, a citizen has rights which are constitutionally guaranteed, not to be restricted by government.

But there are natural rights and there are rights created by government, the difference being manifested in the status of the person in question. The natural rights, or rights at the common Law, are those belonging to natural persons -- those people who are citizens in the United States and who possess the power of political action. These inalienable rights of men, as the Declaration of Independence calls them, are absolute in our governmental system, not to be infringed or abridged by any office or process of the governing powers. Only Natural persons or mortal man has political rights. These "institutory" powers are where we shall focus; the created rights held by subjects of franchise, or other privileges granted by the state, are of another nature and not in the same class with the rights of men.

All law in America is based on the status of the individual. All legislation, judicial actions, and administrative policy is based on status, for there are different classes of citizens and subjects. (For example, under the 14th Amendment, "equal protection" is applied to corporate "persons" as "citizens," even though, strictly speaking, they are simply subjects.) Though a law be termed "general" and not special, it must be decided by the court as to whom it will apply. The application of laws, or statutes (as they really are only expressions of the law) is basically unknown as to the fullest extent of their range. Only in individual cases can it truly be determined according to the facts surrounding the respective case.

Therefore, the status of the party must be determined before the Court should proceed and before the Court can make an intelligent decision. How can status be determined if it is not pleaded? How can it be pleaded except by statements of fact, and of the constitutional application and intent of the particular statute in the case? The way to determining law is to plead all the facts in a case in such a way as to show the status of the parties, and therefore, the rightful scope of the statute.

Where fundamental rights are in question, there shall be no rule making or legislation which would abrogate them." (Miranda vs. Arizona) Among the most important rights the people hold are those protected by the Bill of Rights, but these are only a scant few of all the capacities, abilities and potentials of any one human being. The Bill of Rights was only a statement, brief and definite, that the Founders considered the Constitution to be a strictly expressed grant of political power by the people to a governmental structure designed to protect their rights first and foremost, and never, under any pretense, to violate any right held by the people.

Perhaps the right of greatest importance, of greatest value to the free citizen of these United States in his association with his fellow man and his government, is the absolute ownership of property. From this absolute dominion, said Thomas Jefferson, flows all free society, and without it, of course, comes dictatorship and oppression. If the owner of the property shall not have unconditional control and use of it --- who shall? If the owner shall not reap the profits of the use of property, who shall? Who shall have the fruits of labor? Should it be the man whose right it is to labor? Who, but a freeman, can claim this right?

America was founded on this principle; that no taking of property could occur without just compensation. That is, if government should proceed to demand from the citizen some of his wealth, it shall be only in return for a just service, duly warranted, that was rendered him bygovernment.

As the constitutional protection of rights is a joint effort between the citizen and his government, this protection is a voluntary one, arising from the consent of the individual, and he must pay for his own government, to whatever extent it serves him.

Whereas a corporation holds its wealth in franchise, or at the grace of government, it can therefore be taxed on the holding or the profits of that property. However, a natural person has an inalienable right to acquire and possess all the subjects of property, land, goods, etc. (Art. I, Sec. I, Idaho Constitution), and not be hindered nor have his rights regulated by his government. A tax on an act is regulation of that act.

A tax which is based on the supposed value of a property specie, is a tax on the holding of the property. While taxation to pay for constitutional government is a demand on the possessions of a citizen, the just tax can only be for the services rendered to that citizen according to his particular status in law. To put it in general terms, the natural person has the least taxation upon him, while the corporation must bear the most. "For the natural person owes nothing to the state except for the protection he receives therefrom." (Hale v. Henkel) As Rights of property are natural rights, the Natural Person does not owe his government the returns or benefits of his possessions; the corporation does.

Contingent to the right to possess is the right to acquire. Acquiring property in a thing is often done with lawful money; a medium of exchange for all transactions. Without money, men would be severely hampered in their right to acquire.

Fundamental rights of property, therefore, include the right to have and use a lawful medium of exchange.

But what if the medium has no purchasing power? What if it will not pay debts? How can a man buy when he cannot pay the debt in the transaction?

The basic question in property rights is Quid pro quo, or something for something. This is the basic principle of all transactions of the market place, or between private parties. If a man give nothing and receive something, he has robbed his neighbor, and still owes him.

Money must convey property in something, else it is only a mutual debt. Debt is not a satisfactory proposition to everyone, so debt cannot be a medium of exchange. Article I, Section 10, of the Constitution states: "No state shall make any Thing but gold and silver coin a tender in payment of debt." (Roger Sherman's addition). The founders intended this to be the end of the question of money: gold and silver coin. At the state level, taxation is for duly constituted government, process in the courts, and all other legal transactions of the government. The protection of property rights are also secured in the states, by guaranteeing that no state can enforce collection of taxes or any discharge of debt in anything but gold or silver coin; that is, payment with specie which transfers legal title to property. This clause binds the states down. They are bound to operate at the Common Law.

History is rife with examples of the subterfuges and resulting oppression and slavery from paper "money". The Founding Fathers wished, once and for all, to bar the door against this oft repeated debauchery of the people's wealth. They knew that no surer way to destroy a nation and the quality of life for all its people exists than the insidious horror of paper money, for it drives out the gold, and gives the power of government into the hands of the few (George Bancroft). Such, though, has been the situation in the United States since 1933. In fact, the door that opened on the economics of totalitarianism, was with the founding of the Federal Reserve System in 1913.

The results of leaving behind the monetary system established by the Constitution have been disastrous, as could be expected. Jefferson warned against paper money and central banks. Washington considered it crime of the first water to allow a printing of bills of credit. The results have been farreaching and insidious, reaching into every facet of life, and overturning, in due time, the very relationship of citizen and government!

For the overturning of the monetary system from one of specie to one of irredeemable paper has brought about the replacement of the Common Law by custom. It is well known that the merchant traditionally dealt in bills and notes, based upon customs called Law Merchant. He had his own "law" because he dealt not in substance (coin), but in promises, or "the potentiality of substance". Therefore, he was barred from the process of the Common Law courts.

Today, however, as there is no constitutional economic system, everyone is deemed a merchant in equity, or in the custom of merchants; this newer status brought on by his dealings of a mercantile nature. What happened to the Common Law? It went out with the gold standard. Why, Congress bragged of "suspending" the Constitution itself in 1933 when they repudiated the gold standard dollar and all such obligations in House Joint Resolution 192 (now 31 USC 463).

Is it possible that there was a plan, or several plans, as to the kind of laws which could be promulgated upon this "new society" where supposedly no one operated at the Common Law any more?

Of course it is possible, for HJR 192 opened the door for infinite application of the Law Merchant at the Federal level, and the regulatory Roman civil law at the state level. And with the bounds of the Common Law removed from all business transactions, all business fell into the class of privilege, just as merchants had always operated. The incredible growth of regulatory law, taxes, and bureaus has been based upon the new "status" created by Congress in a statement of policy, to the end that all persons operate under corporate capacity and, therefore, can be taxed and regulated as such.

And true enough, the natural person who does not deal in banks and credit is rare today; almost everyone has given up the status of citizen at Law for the "convenience" of transacting business in credit. This is essentially the privilege of limited liability for the payment of debts. This is a corporate privilege not existing at the Common Law; therefore the jurisdiction over these acts is one of a commercial nature.

But does this mean that there are no citizens who can and do operate at law? This leads to the question of the Constitution.

Is the Constitution a statute enacted by Congress? Or is the Constitution the people's government and the Supreme Law of the Land?

If a statute, then it pertains to only a class of persons, who, by reason that there is no lawful money today, are, in fact, extinct.

If the Constitution be the Supreme Law of the people, by the people, and for the people, then it is the birthright of all citizens of the United States, never to be repealed or undermined by Congress. If a birthright, then it is recoverable at any time, for like the Prodigal Son, a citizen may choose to leave behind a life of the alien and return home to the law of his fatherland -- the Constitution.

In this day of economic strife and destruction, the proposition of changing one's economic status might be increasingly desirable to a citizen. How is he to do this? Through the establishment of a central bank and the repudiation of payment of debts by Congress, the American people were placed upon credit of the Federal Reserve System. As credit does not pay debts at Law, andbecause there is no lawful money in circulation today with which to pay debts, the citizen is, in fact, an insolvent upon bank credit, using credit to transact business. Not even the Federal Reserve Note can pay a debt, for it is legal tender for debts and not in payment of debts. (Note: Article I, Section 10, says "No state shall make any Thing but gold and silver coin a tender in payment of debts.")

Yet acts of congress cannot violate the Constitution. And the fact is that congress has attempted to overthrow the Bill of Rights and negate the property rights of every American by removing from the people their sovereign medium of exchange mandated by the Constitution itself.

The Congress, on June 5, 1933, bragged of "suspending the Constitution" itself by repudiating payment of debts. This act, in conjunction with acts of the President, deluded the people into giving up their gold coin in exchange for paper intended to be irredeemable henceforward. As a congressman of the day remarked, these acts had for their design the establishment of a new form of government.

By creating a new status of insolvency nationwide, the congress opened wide the door for a new system of law; regulatory, commercial law promulgated by administrative agencies, bureaus, and courts at both federal and state levels. For all persons of the insolvent class or, in other words, all those dealing totally without lawful money in their business affairs, there is a body of customs and usages termed law merchant, or mercantile equity, long used by merchants since the 13th century to expedite disputes in commercial contracts. The custom of merchants is largely enacted under the terms and principles of the Civil Law in the states by the legislatures.

How does this affect the status of a citizen in the court? Due to the economic situation, it is assumed that all persons operate on credit and that the common Law is nowhere applicable. All are assumed to be "merchants in equity," and thereby governed by the "general commercial law."

This brings us to the Erie R. R. v. Tompkins case of 1938. It was a landmark case because it overturned the 96 year old doctrine of Swift v. Tyson. Stated in Erie, "there is no general federal common law," meaning that there is no base of common law generic to the states. This decision was a direct ratification of HJR 192, passed five years earlier, and effects a repudiation of the basic principle of the Constitution, that the people as one created for themselves as Americans a general law and a supreme law, binding upon every government official in the United States, both state and federal. It is the birthright of every natural person who is a citizen of these United States, never to be abrogated, repudiated, diminished, or "suspended" by the governmental offices it created, or by any other office created under "commercial law."

In fact, Erie implied that the "commercial law" or law merchant, was the province of the state as common law! This travesty of decisional law is the central issue today for anyone wishing to maintain a status of citizen at law, for it necessitates a statement of repudiation by the person himself. This could be called an equity disclaimer statement.

"This natural person is by all intents and purposes a merchant and trader at law on a cash basis, without recourse to Standard Lawful Money, and enjoys no privilege of limited liability for the payment of debts. I deny all jurisdictions of mercantile equity brought on by HJR 192 of

June 5, 1933, expressly Law Merchant, Roman Civil Law, and Admiralty Law, and demand all of my rights at the Common Law."

A statement of this sort is the beginning pleading in any case today in order to establish the Common Law status of the party in court. As mentioned above, the application of laws is the court's function. If the status of one of the parties is a bar to the action, then it must be so pleaded, by stating the facts surrounding the case, and the facts surrounding the law.

For instance; in the Traffic courts, the statement of status is one of the facts surrounding the case. Then, a pleading that the magistrate's court lacks jurisdiction over a freeman is a fact surrounding the law, for they try quasi-criminal cases upon the "traffic code" where there is no crime. How can the citizen injure the state by exercising his right to travel? He cannot. (Interesting note: "Traffic" is found to be one of the definitions of "commerce." Another is "transport of persons." Therefore, it is plain to see that the "traffic code" is but the regulatory "custom of merchants" for those involved in commerce. A drivers license is, then, evidence of a commercial contract with the state seal upon it! "Code" means a body of regulatory law.)

A law which contemplates compelling all persons to purchase a driver's license is null and void as it violates the status of the citizen. No law can be made which would effect a change of status to the detriment of rights. What, then, do we think of HJR 192? What if the state attempts to impose licensure of occupations or activities?

These laws are intended to operate upon the privileged person, being a corporation or otherwise enfranchised individual. There is another fact to surround the law -- intent of the lawmakers. In Idaho law, that is the decisional law of Idaho's highest court, if there is a question between an application of a statute which would be unconstitutional and one which would not, the choice must be in favor of the lawful application so as to preserve the statute. Therefore, in the individual case, it is far wiser to plead that the application of a certain statute in that case would violate rights, than to plead that the statute is unconstitutional; for, one can easily see, the statute may have an application in some other case, making it a constitutional law. It is assumed in our law that the legislators were aware of their limits and intended no violation of the supreme law in any enactments.

To whom does a statute apply? That is the question for the court's judgement. Policemen on the street, or bureaucrats or agents cannot decide for themselves, and they should be so instructed. The courts are the forum for redress of grievance, and let the word transmit to the legislature of its ignorance.

Federal Citizen or Sovereign Citizen?

North American Freedom Council

There is a distinct separation of American citizen and citizen of the United States. Notice the words employed in this sentence and their relationship to each other as I quote from General Rules of Pleading, R 8 page 80:

"Residence is not the equivalent of citizenship; and wherever jurisdiction is predicated upon the citizenship (or alienage) of the parties, an allegation that a party is a resident of a certain state or foreign country is not a sufficient allegation of citizenship. (cite omitted) An allegation that a party is an American citizen is insufficient, for a person may be an American citizen but not a citizen of a state. Similarly, an allegation that a person is not a citizen of the United States is an insufficient allegation of alienage." See discussion under § 1332 PO, 75 [1-3], [1-4].

So you have to understand this fact and where you stand in relation to that entity called the "Unites States" in tax law. In other words, substitute American for nonresident alien whenever you see the term nonresident alien when talking about citizenship. You will now see your "constitutional issues" you have put before the courts (which in reality are commercial corporate tribunals) simply melt away because you have not properly brought before the tribunal the right issues. Remember, under the Erie Doctrine, the trier of the fact UCC 4-503, is making the presumption UCC 1-201 (31), that you are a "United States citizen". Wouldn't that be, "the state of the forum" that you are presumed to be inhabiting? Isn't that a "state" of corporate jurisdiction, not a geographical state jurisdiction? So the phrase nonresident alien, contains two terms and has two meanings. Nonresident, for corporate contract, therefore you are alien to the "state of the forum" and nonresident for geographical and therefore Alien/Stranger to that particular part of the country. See how quickly I changed from citizenship to contract using one word, "nonresident"? Remember the definition of "resident" in Black's Law Dictionary? It does have many meanings doesn't it?

Read 26 USC § 865 (g) over and over until your mind cannot hold any doubt.

(g) UNITED STATES RESIDENT; NONRESIDENT.---For purposes of this section ---
   (1) In General.---Except as otherwise provided in this subsection ---
      (A) UNITED STATES RESIDENT.---The term "United States Resident" means--
         (i) any individual who has a tax home (as defined in section 911 (d) (3) in the United States, and
         (ii) any corporation, partnership, trust, or estate which is a United States person (as defined in section 7701 (a) (30)).
      (B) NONRESIDENT.---The term "nonresident" means any person other than a United States resident.

Are you an individual listed in 911 (d) (3)?

911 (d) DEFINITIONS AND SPECIAL RULES.--For purposes of this section--
   (3) TAX HOME,--The term "tax home" means, with respect to any individual, such individual's home for purposes of section 162 (a) (2) (relating to traveling expenses while away from home). An individual shall not be treated as having a tax home in a foreign country for any period which his abode is within the United States.

Sovereign States or United States?

The definitions used in 26 USC CFR are very clear in defining State and United States. In every definition that uses the word "include", only the words that follow are defining the Term. For example,

26 USC § 3121 (e) (1) "State. The term "State" includes the District of Columbia, the Commonwealth of Puerto Rico, the Virgin Islands, Guam, and American Samoa."

26 USC § 7701 (a) (9) "United States. The term "United States" when used in geographical sense includes only the States and the District of Columbia."

So when the IRS, for example, says citizens of the United States are liable for income taxes that is exactly what they mean. If you are a citizen of the United States you are a citizen of the federal government and not a citizen of the State in which you live. Therefore you are under their jurisdiction. If you are a citizen of a Union State and not of the United States you do not fall under federal jurisdiction. **It is that simple folks. It is and has always been a question of jurisdiction.**

In other words, the state in which you live has adopted the Uniform Commercial Code for its operation. The Uniform Commercial Code is contract law. The state has given up its constitutional sovereignty in exchange for simple administrative contract law. It has become nothing more than a corporation acting under corporate law. This being the case, the state has become a fiduciary under the Federal Government's granted privilege of incorporation. All 'state' employees are technically federal employees beholden to the Federal Government and wholly under the Federal jurisdiction and thus liable for Income Tax, Selective Service, etc. none of which are lawful in any State of the Union not subscribing to federal dictates.

Only a nonresident alien (to the United States or federal government) can be free as a citizen of a Free and Sovereign State in which they live and have their livelihood. The Federal Government does not have lawful jurisdiction in any State of the Union. This is why you see the feds issuing "guidelines" to the various states suggesting such guidelines be adopted. Or using blackmail to force the several states to adopt such guidelines. If the Federal Government had lawful jurisdiction they would not issue guidelines - they would dictate directly to each state - YOU WILL DO SO AND SO OR ELSE!!! This is not the case.

Only citizens under the federal jurisdiction are liable to obey their laws, rules and regulations. To any of the several states, the "United States" is a foreign power to that state. Foreign powers or governments do not have jurisdiction in local affairs. If you pay Income Tax which is a federal assault on your property it is because you agree to pay voluntarily or because you are under their jurisdiction.

What happened in our country that we gave away our own control over our own States to a foreign power - the government residing in Washington, DC? The explanation is an incredible tale that began prior to the Civil War and extends to this day. This story is beyond the scope of this short booklet but may be found in any number of places.

What to do now? If we want to be free there is only one solution. Educate yourself in these matters, educate your neighbors and then determine appropriate courses of action to reinstate your States sovereignty as well as your own as a free man/woman.

Common Law vs. Civil Law Rights

COMES NOW the Accused, In Propria Persona appearing specially and not generally or voluntarily herein, to demand all rights under the Constitution of the United States/Common Law based upon the status of the Accused as a matter of due process of law and to determine what rights the Accused has in this court and what rights will be denied, if any, to enable the Accused to determine what jurisdiction the State is attempting to apply to this person as:

No change in ancient procedure can be made which disrupts those fundamental principles . . . which . . . protect the citizen in his private right and guard him against the arbitrary action of the government." Ex Parte Young, 209 US 123.

When summoned into any court, the first thing a party must do is analyze and identify the nature of the charges, jurisdiction of the court, and the status of the Accused, to determine if the status of the Accused falls within the statute and the jurisdiction of the court.

The State and the Court are obviously proceeding based upon Civil Law statutes, and therefore, are using an Admiralty/Maritime/Equity jurisdiction to proceed rather than the principles and modes of the common law. (See Davison v. New Orleans, 96 U.S. 97; Dartmouth College Case, 4 Wheat 518) Facts supporting this conclusion are:

I JURISDICTION

The Accused recognizes that when jurisdiction is not squarely challenged it is presumed to exist (Burks v. Lasker, 441 US 471). This includes supposed duties, liabilities, and sanctions --- attached by way of statutes --- for violations of said duties. (U.S. v. Grimaud, 220 US 506).

In this Court there is no meaningful opportunity to challenge jurisdiction, as the Court merely proceeds summarily. However, once jurisdiction has been challenged in the courts, it becomes the responsibility of the Plaintiff to assert and prove said jurisdiction. (Hagans v. Lavine, 415 US 533, note 5), as mere good faith assertions of power and authority(jurisdiction) have been abolished. (Owens v. City of Independence, 100 SCt. 1398, 1980).

II THE STATE APPEARS AS THE PLAINTIFF AND AS A PARTY TO THE ACTION:

The state functions in two capacities:

1. In behalf of the "People of the State" in common law actions; and

2. As a person in a corporate capacity to protect and enforce its interests through summary proceedings.

But the state in either capacity is still bound by the U. S. Constitution. (Martin v. Hunter's Lesses, 1 Wheat 304)

Since the Plaintiff is the "State of Idaho", it is acting in its own interest and is, therefore, the person who is allegedly complaining. The State is attempting to bring a personal action and is seeking a remedy for an alleged injury of nonexistent rights, as rights only exist between moral beings. (Bouvier's Law Dictionary, 1914, p. 2960)

III PUBLIC PROSECUTOR

In order for the Court to be properly set in a common law criminal action, there must be a member of:

1. The judiciary (the judge);
2. The executive (the public prosecutor); and
3. The Accused.

In this case the State is proceeding with a city official (city attorney) who is a member of the Judiciary, not an appointed member of the executive branch of state government.

The functions of the city attorney are not even outlined or authorized by Code, and he is neither appointed by nor works for the executive branch of government. Therefore, this person is functioning under a statutory Civil Law jurisdiction and not under the provisions of the Common Law. The governor of the state is not discharging his duty to execute the laws of the state, by and through an appointed prosecutor. Instead, the laws of the State are being prosecuted by a municipal city (judicial) officer. Such judicial proceedings are only found in proceedings under the Civil Law.

IV CHARGE NOT BROUGHT BY COMPETENT AUTHORITY

A principle of the Common Law is that the People are the party of the action in a felonious, or public offense. Public offenses are either felonies or misdemeanors (the offense charged in this case). Misdemeanors comprehend all indictable offenses (1 Bish. Cr. L. Section 624; Bouvier's p. 2222) and, therefore, the charges must be brought forth by the People in the form of a grand jury indictment.

V ARTICLE III, SECTION 2, U. S. CONSTITUTION

The original jurisdiction in this case is with the United States Supreme Court because:

1. The State is a Party;
2. The magistrate court is operating in a jurisdiction alien to the Common Law.

VI STATE IS COMPELLING A PERFORMANCE

The State by statute is attempting to compel a performance and the city attorney and the local police are applying said statutes without having to prove whether or not the statute applies to the Accused.

Due process of law is not necessarily satisfied by any process which the legislature may prescribe. See Abrams v. Jones 35 Idaho 532, 207 P. 724.

There can be no constructive offenses, and before a man can be punished, his case must be plainly and unmistakably within the statute. US v Lacher 134 US 624.

An action under the common law only exists after there has been a loss or a damage, and it cannot compel a performance. The charges against the Accused are because she did not show a drivers license and display license plates. Punishing a person for not doing a thing is tantamount to compelling a person to do the thing. Therefore, the nature of the action and the kind of relief sought is compelling in nature and not an action under the common law.

Under the common law a person cannot be compelled "to purchase, through a license fee or a license tax, the privilege freely granted by the Constitution" Blue Island v. Kozul, 41 N.E. 2d. 515 (As quoted in Murdock v. Pennsylvania (City of Jeanette) 319 U.S. 105, 114.

In addition: "A state may not impose a charge for the enjoyment of a right granted by the Federal Constitution. Thus, it may not exact a license tax for the privilege of carrying on interstate commerce." Mc Goldrick v. Bewind White Co., 309 U.S. 33, 56-58. "Although it may tax the property used in, or the income derived from that commerce, so long as those taxes are not discrimination." Id., p.47

As repeatedly stated, this person is not enfranchised by any state nor engaged in any form of trade, commerce, or industry that makes him subject to any licensing requirement, and therefore, travels on the rights-of-way as a matter of right and "Where rights secured by the Constitution are involved, there can be no rule making or legislation which would abrogate them." Miranda v. Arizona, 384 U.S. 436, 491. Also see Marbury v. Madison, 1803.

The power to tax is the power to destroy and this person claims that the taxing power of the state if it were to pertain to this person in this case would not only control but also suppress and/or abrogate his absolute right to personal liberty (locomotion) as: "The power to tax the exercise of a privilege is the power to control or suppress its enjoyment." Magnano Co. v. Hamilton, 292 U.S. 40, 44-45.

Since the State is attempting to control or suppress the Accused's actions by taxing through the vehicle registration program and operator's license, the state is proceeding in some kind of administrative law not the common law. This type of action is an equitable action brought on by some enfranchisement, license, or contract, which must be shown to establish jurisdiction over this person. As stated by Blackstone: "Let a man therefore be ever so abandoned in his principles, or vicious in his practice, provided he keeps his wickedness to himself, and does not offend against the rules of public decency, he is out of reach of human laws." Blackstone Commentaries, Vol I, p. 113.

Since no such conditions exist in this case, no jurisdiction exists in this Court.

VII COUNSEL

The Accused demands unlicensed Counsel of choice. The right to counsel at a criminal trial is deemed so fundamental to the interests of justice that denial thereof automatically vitiates any conviction obtained (the automatic reversal rule). This is true even though there is no showing of any prejudice or unfairness in the proceedings or even any need for counsel. Gideon v. Wainright, 372 US 335.

A conviction obtained where the accused was denied counsel is treated as void for all purposes. Lack of counsel of choice can be conceivably even worse than no counsel at all, or having to accept counsel beholden to one's adversary. Burgett v. Texas, 309 US 109.

The right to counsel exists not only at the trial thereof, but also at every stage of a criminal proceeding where substantial rights of an accused may be affected. Mempha v. Rhay, 389 US 128.

"A state or federal court which arbitrarily refuses to hear a party by counsel, denies the party a hearing and, therefore, denies him due process of law in a constitutional sense." Reynolds v. Cochran, 365 US 525.

VIII NO COMPLAINT

The state is proceeding without any formal complaint. Since no "proper plaintiff" exists who can bring the action for a violation of rights in a common law action, the state is proceeding on the face of a citation which is a proceeding under a Civil Law jurisdiction (probate or admiralty) of licenses and contracts, and which are not applicable to this natural person.

The Uniform Citation "tickets" fail as complaints for the following reasons:

1. No corpus delicti is established upon the face of the "tickets".
2. No criminal intent is alleged, nor shown by apparent circumstances surrounding this case.
3. No offer of proof is made that defendant is subject to Title 49, Chapters 1, 2, & 3, and thereby subject to these summary proceedings for lesser offenses.

Where no corpus delicti is shown, a conviction cannot be supported.

IX NO INTENT

The formal complaint must allege 2 elements of any crime, to be valid and sustain a case.

Idaho Code 18-114: Union of Act and Intent -- "In every crime or public offense there must exist a union, or joint operation, of act and intent, or criminal negligence."

The Plaintiff does not have to prove intent in this case as the only issue before the Court is whether Petitioner committed the act or not. Experience has proven that in like cases before this court, there is no presumption of innocence. Since intent will not be a matter of fact before the jury, intent must be a matter of law. Therefore, the state legislature has legisled guilt and the Court is proceeding in a summary process under the Civil Law to regulate corporations and regulated industry. (Almeida Sanchez, 413 U.S. 266; Colonnade Catering Corp. v. United States, 397 U.S. 72; United States v. Biswell, 406 U.S. 311) Under the Common Law, "intent" is a matter of status and conduct and must be a matter of fact before the jury, and if not so, the proceedings are alien to the common law.

X COMMON LAW JURY

The Accused demands a common law struck jury of twelve of his peers. A trial by jury at the Common law consists of twelve men, neither more or less. Patton et al v. U.S., 281 US 276.

XI JURY TO DETERMINE THE LAW AS WELL AS FACTS

The Accused demands a jury that would be able to determine the law and evidence in this case as well as the facts. This is a common law right. State v. Croteau, 23 Vt 14, 54; State v. Meyer, 58 Vt 457; Appeal of Lowe, 46 Kan 255; Lynch v. State, 9 Ind 541; Hudelson v. State, 94 Ind 426; People v. Videto, 1 Parker, Gr R. 603; Pleasant v. State, 13 Ark 360; Wohlford v. People, 45 Ill App 188; Commonwealth v. Porter, 51 Mass 263; U.S. v. Watkins, Fed Case No. 16, p. 649 (3 Cranch, C.C. 4411); 4 L.R.A. 675; Beard v. State, 71 Md 275.

XII STATE HAS NOT STATED A CLAIM UPON WHICH RELIEF CAN BE GRANTED

The complaint naming the State of Idaho as Plaintiff, by the word "Plaintiff" alleges a Cause of Action which is: "Matter for which an action may be brought." "A cause of action implies that there is some person in existence who can bring suit and also a person who can lawfully be sued". "When a wrong has been committed, or a breach of duty has occurred, the cause of action has accrued, although the claimant may be ignorant of it".

A cause of action consists of those facts as to two or more persons entitling at least some one of them to a judicial remedy of some sort against the other, or others, for the redress or prevention of a wrong. It is essential to the existence of such facts that there should be a right to be violated and a violation thereof.

In this case, no evidence or testimony can be brought before the court to establish any natural person or persons who have suffered a loss of rights and therefore, there can be no cause of action or criminal causation.

XIII MEANINGFUL HEARING

This Court has repeatedly stated on the record that it will not even read or hear any constitutional issues brought before it much less rule on such issues, therefore the Court has denied the Accused due process of law.

XIV THEORY OF THE CASE

Proceedings in the Court during trial will not allow the Accused to address issues of law nor will Petitioner be allowed to express her theory of the law and the case to the jury. The Accused is restricted by the form of the proceedings to restrict her defense solely upon the basis of whether or not she committed the acts, and substantive issues cannot be related to the jury.

This clearly shows that the jury proposed by the state is not a common law jury but one operating under statutory and judicial restrictions to satisfy the conscience of the king and his court. This type of jury is prescribed in admiralty/ maritime /equity jurisdictions and foreign to the common law.

CONCLUSION

In this case:

1. The Accused is a Free and natural person who has claimed all of her rights at the common law and has denied all other jurisdictions until asserted and proved.
2. The Plaintiff has brought forth charges that, in this case, are not within the jurisdiction of the court.
3. The Court is proceeding in a summary fashion and not according to the rules of procedure of the Common Law.
4. The Plaintiff and the Court are apparently conspiring to defeat the legal/civil rights of the Accused.
5. The Plaintiff and the Court are proceeding in a jurisdiction foreign to the Common law.

REMEDY SOUGHT

Since the action and the proceedings in this case do not conform to the rules and procedures of the common law, the Accused demands that the court to dismiss the charges.

MERCHANT AT LAW

The Accused can find no other term to define his status as a Free and Natural Citizen than that of a Merchant and a Trader at Law on a cash basis.

Merchants and traders, for this application, share one trait; they both deal in goods and merchandise in their business transactions. The unfortunate fact is that since 1933 Americans have all been compelled to speculate on the value of the Federal Reserve Note or, more specifically, evidences of "choses in action" for currency or "cash", not having recourse to the "Standard Gold Dollar Lawful Money" with its standing in the Common Law as payment. The use of "choses in actions" as "legal tender" for debts is but traffic (commerce) in bids against the goods and services of America's market, compelled upon us by an Act of Congress in the form of House Joint Resolution (HJR) 192, June 5, 1933, which suspended the "Gold Standard" and placed a moratorium on the payment of debts, effectively reducing us to merchants in equity.

To state then, as the Accused has, that one is At Law, is to repudiate such acts of Congress and resume the status of the Common Law even though one cannot pay debts At Law with "Lawful Money of the United States." A Free and Natural Person is "without recourse" to such money-of-account and uses the nearest cash substitute for all transactions. Therefore, the status of Merchant/ Trader At Law on a cash basis.

Congress, created by The People through the Constitution, is without power to overthrow the Common Law of Article 1, Section 10, on tender or contract, or the Bill of Rights, which serves as The People's further restrictions on governments. Acts of Congress which effect a derogation or outright overthrow of a citizen's status are patently unconstitutional and void ab initio, nor can any court of the State compel such an implied contract upon citizens at the Common Law.

The Accused then, feels compelled to Notice the Court that the Accused claims this status, so rare today, but absolutely imperative and pertinent to this case. How this affects the Court's jurisdiction in the area of the Person and the ability of the Court to effect a remedy are as follows:

PREVENTIVE OR PENAL REMEDY

Jurisdiction is derived from power and capacity. The fines and payments ordered by the Court are payable or tendered only in the form irredeemable "paper money", sometimes called "Federal Reserve Notes"(FRN's). This paper is redeemable in nothing but more paper and is not substance nor representative of substance. FRN's were not "an attempt to make dollars." (United States v Balklard, 14 Wall 457) They are, in fact, registered bearer bonds, and as such, small change for United States Bonds. Not being a property in possession, they are not dollars. On the other hand, the "Standard Gold Dollar", is or was property (allodium) in possession and is or was substance At Law and usable in payment of debts (rather than payment for debts).

Property is defined as: "The sole and despotic dominion which one man claims and exercises over the external things of the world in total exclusion of the right of any other individual in the universe." (2 Bla. Com 2) "The right to possess, use, etc., (Bouvier Law Dictionary, p.2750)

This absolute property right is best defined in the word "allodium", which is defined as: "an estate held by absolute ownership, without recognizing any superior to whom any duty is due on account thereof." (Bouvier, p.183)

Standard Gold Dollars, being absolute property in possession, are actually "portable lands" inasmuch as they vest the owner with full legal and equitable rights and interests, and are allodial property. However, property is further defined into property in possession, or choses in action.

The truth that there are no dollars in circulation today becomes apparent when we define "choses in action." They are "A right to receive without action..." (Bouvier, p. 483) In order to properly explain this a distinction must be made between the security of the evidence of the debt and the thing due.

A deed, a bill of exchange, or a promissory note may be in the possessionof the owner, but the money or damage due on them are no less "choses in action." This distinction must be kept in mind. The choses in action are the money damages, or the thing owing, the bond or note is but evidence of it. There can, in the nature of things, be no possession on a thing which lies merely in action. I Bouv. Inst. p. 191; First National Bank v Holland, 99 Va 495, 39 S.E. 126, 55 LRA 155; 86 Am St Rep 898.

And, as to the Court's ability to order a fine paid, it should be interesting to note, "In the absence of fraudulant transfer or other such fraud as would positively impede an action At Law and proceeding in garnishment," equity will not subject the choses in action of the debtor to the payment of his debts." Hall v Imp Co, 143 Ala 464, 39 south 285

It is obvious that the "paper currency" here in question, and that contemplated by this Court as "payment" of a fine are, in fact, in operation of the law, but evidences of choses in action.

The difference between the two species of property are carefully explained in Knox v Lee, 12 Wall 522 as follows:

"We will notice briefly an argument presented in support of the position that the unit of money value must possess intrinsic value. The argument is derived from assimilating the Constitutional provision respecting a standard of weights and measures to that conferring the power to coin money and regulate the value. It is said there can be no standard of value which has no value itself. This is a question foreign to the subject before us. The legal tender acts do not attempt to make paper a standard of value. We do not rest their validity upon the assertion that their emission is coinage, or any regulation of the value of money, nor do we assert that Congress can make anything that has no value money. What we do assert is that Congress has power to enact that a government's promises to pay money for the time being equivalent in value to the representative of value determined in the coinage acts..." And, "It is thus clear that a promise of delivery is no delivery, nor upon national currency, even meant to be." Milan v United States et. al., 524 F.2d 629

For more on this subject see Knox v Lee, a portion of which follows:

"No one supposes that these government certificates are never to be paid, that the day of specie payments is never to return, and it matters not in what form they are issued. The principle is still the same. Instead of certificates they may be Treasury Notes, or paper in any other form and their payment may not be made directly in coin but they may be first convertible into government bonds, or other government securities. Through whatever changes they may pass, their ultimate destiny is to be paid."

It should be clear that money is a substance and not a promise, though the promise may be compelled of acceptance, and thus passes as money, contemplating the substance. Such was the law, and the general Federal Common Law at that, during the reign of Swift v Tyson, which lasted until 1938 when the Erie R. R. decision and subsequent decisions expelled the Law Merchant from the Federal Common Law, effectively destroying the Seventh Amendment to the Constitution of the United States and paving the way for the reign of irredeemable paper. Paper redeemable in "Nothing" but more paper became a full reality on March 18, 1968, exclusively on the Federal level, through Public Law 90:269. Yet Article 1, Section 10, Clause 1, of the United States Constitution remains in effect. The Erie R. R. case decision could not destroy the Common Law of the States founded and grounded upon substantive allodial titles in real property. The best it could achieve were the compulsions of record in Milam v United States et. al. supra. Nor can the Courts of any Judicial District, magistrates, or prosecuting attorneys work in collusion with the King's agents (policemen) to destroy the Common Law of the several States in substantive allodial titles.

Land titles in the State of Idaho, as in all States of this union, once glorious and free, are allodial and substantive and not feudal and comtemplative. There is no paramount overlord in any instance. The meaning of this should be known to the learned Courts as in all our law, fundamental property consists in lands and goods as distinguished from franchises, jurisdictional powers, and fiscal immunities or other immunities derived from some civil authority not beholden to The People of the Union. (Article 1, Section 1, Idaho State Constitution)

The States are yet, by Article 1, Section 1O, Clause 1, absolutely forbidden from making anything a tender but gold and silver coin for the precise reason that fundamental property was considered to be substance at the Common Law in every State and not privileges or franchises for the purpose of preservation of substance, and derive from no authority superior to The People who framed the Constitution of the United States and created the States for their own protection against Federal tyranny.

The Accused submits that the legislative authority which enacted codes commanding or prohibiting specific performances such as licensing noncommercial activities, creating traffic codes and the Magistrates' Courts, to try all such nonindictable misdeameanors by summary process, may properly extend to those who volunteer themselves into such juristic beings, paper fiction persons and any other franchises in servitude or other classes of persons like members and subjects. However, such legislation cannot regulate or deny Rights to a Free and Natural Citizen or any traveler At Law.

Legislation cannot compel servitutes in the form of regulation, specific performance nor require any penalty by a chose in action.

Any compelling codes requiring any chose in action are nothing more than a discriminatory punishment upon the Accused who has not the ability to tender a payment At Law making him, in fact, an insolvent before the Court, such status being forced on the Accused by acts of Congress, in abrogation of the Common Law. The fundamental Common Law, which drew its source from The People, is, in this respect, unalterable by acts of a Congress sworn to uphold the Law.

The Court is, therefore, without capacity to render the Accused to be subjected to perpetual indebtedness to the State as Article 1, Section 10, of the Constitution of the United States absolutely forbids this abrogation of the fundamental law of substance. This Accused Citizen, by right of status, cannot be compelled into performances upon a debt that never existed, or upon contract likewise nonexistent by this or any other Court in the land.

Because of the Constitution of the United States, Article 1, Section 10 and an act of Congress, this court possesses no power to effect a remedy and therefore, has no jurisdiction in this case.

RIGHTS OF A FREEMAN

Article 1, Section 3, of the Idaho State Constitution states; "The state of Idaho is an inseparable part of the American Union, and the Constitution of the United States is the Supreme law of the land."

Other State Constitutions also make references concerning the information contained in the above paragraph. The Constitution of the United States states; "This Constitution....shall be the supreme law of the land; and the judges in every State shall be bound thereby..."

There can be no doubt that all judges are bound by the Constitution of the United States which is a part of the Common Law, which nullifies any legislative law or statute that violates the rights of a FREEMAN.

In this country Rights preceed government or the establishment of states, which is an ancient maxim of law. Rights are acknowledged above government or they cease to be Rights and become privileges authorized by the government or state.

The rights governing contracts, money, appearances, pleading, and pleas are more ancient than the history of this country and were well established in the early days of American jurisprudence. It has been the arbitrary rule making on the part of government officials, diligently at work expediting the judicial system into streamlined Courts of Equity and chancery proceedings, which have been abrogating Free and Natural Citizens' Rights and freedoms. "Where rights secured by the Constitution are involved, there can be no rule making or legislation which would abrogate them." Miranda V Arizona, 384, US 436, 491

This Person hereby lays claim to the absolute inalienable rights of contract, freedom, and liberty -- that is, the claim of unrestricted action except so far as the claim of others necessitates restriction -- and the right to free locomotion... There is a monstrous difference in restricting actions of locomotion and prohibiting and commanding actions, or the lack of, and punishing by penalty, fines, and imprisonment persons who fail to comply when the action committed by the Person has not, in fact, caused any loss or damage of another's Life, Liberty, or Property as opposed to those classes of crimes where another's Life, Liberty, orProperty has been damaged or lost. Restriction of various functions on certain classes of commercial travelers and other juristic persons may be necessary; however, penal action is not. A penal action is nothing more than an action or information brought on by an "agent of the king" and in which the penalty goes to the "king" (government). (Bouvier Law Dictionary, P. 2551)

Any FREEMAN who claims his rights cannot be forced to comply with penal offenses. Under the Common Law there can be no constructive offenses. United States V. Lacher, 134 US 624; Todd V. United States, 158 US 282. It should be understood that a constructive offense is nothing more than an act which may or may not be performed; the doing that which a penal law forbids to be done or omitting to do what it commands.

Penal statutes are essentially those actions which impose a penalty or punishment arbitrarily extracted for some act or commission thereof on the part of some person. (Black's Law Dictionary, 5th Ed., P. 1019) Such statutes operate to compel a performance (Black, P. 1020) and inflict a punishment by statute for its violation. (The Strathairly, 124 US 571)

In any appearance of this Free and Natural Citizen, it must be noted that no jurisdiction other than the Common Law will be recognized and executive chancery is specifically denied. This denial includes state codes that are in violation of the rights of man, and in this case a code demanding a specific performance commanding that a certain thing can or cannot be done, making said statute an unconstitutional statute. "Constitutional and legal rights are protected by the Law, by the Constitution; but if government does not create the idea of right or original rights, it acknowledges them; just as government does not create property or values and money, it regulates them. If it were otherwise, the question would present itself, whence does government come? Whence does it derive its own right to create rights? By compact? But whence did the contracting parties derive their right to create a government that is to make rights? We would be consistently led to adopt the idea of a government by just divinum; that is, a government deriving its authority to introduce and establish rights (bestowed on it in particular) from a source wholly separate from human society and the ethical character of man, in the same manner in which we acknowledge revelation to come from a source not human." (Bouvier, P. 2961)

The powers of our government are supposed to be severely limited and this has been best presented by the Chief Justice of the Supreme Court in 1803: "The powers of the legislature are defined and limited; and that those limits may not be mistaken, or forgotten, the constitution is written. To what purpose are powers limited, and to what purpose is that limitation committed to writing, if these limits may, at any time, be passed by those intended to be restrained? The distinction between a government with limited and unlimited powers is abolished, if those limits do not confine the persons on whom they are imposed, and if acts prohibited and the acts allowed are of equal obligation. It is a proposition too plain to be contested, that the constitution controls any legislative act repugnant to it; or, that the legislature may alter the constitution by any ordinary act. "Between these alternatives there is no middle ground. The constitution is either a superior paramount law, unchangeable by ordinary means, or it is on a level with ordinary legislative acts, and, like other acts, is alterable when the legislature shall please to alter it. "If the former part of the alternative be true, then a legislative act contrary to the constitution, is not law; if the latter part be true, then written constitutions are absurd attempts, on the part of the people, to limit a power in its own nature illimitable. "If then, the courts are to regard the constitution, and the constitution is superior to any ordinary act of the legislature, the constitution, and not such ordinary acts must govern the case to which they both apply. "Why does a judge swear to discharge his duties agreeably to the constitution of the United States, if that constitution forms no rule for his government -- if it is closed upon him, and cannot be inspected by him? "If such to be the real state of things, this is worse than solemn mockery. To prescribe, or to take this oath, becomes equally a crime. "It is also not entirely unworthy of observation, that in declaring what shall be the supreme law of the land, the constitution itself is first mentioned; and not the laws of the United States generally, but those only which shall be made in pursuance of the constitution, have that rank". "Thus, the particular phraseology of the constitution of the United States confirms and strengthens the principle, supposed to be essential to all written constitutions, that a law repugnant to the constitution is void; and that courts as well as other departments, are bound by the instrument." Marbury V Madison, 1 C. 137, 176-179 In the United States all three branches of government, state or national, are granted "limited" powers. These powers are granted by "The People." The People are, in fact, individuals including the Accused. The People are principals and authorize agency to the three branches of government. The concept of limited powers of government establishes the fact that the agent is not granted sufficient power in any case to invert the relationship so as to make the individual an agent and the state his principal. Such an inversion would prohibit acts of "free agency" which are privy to a principal and are outside the discretion of an agent. Since our government is a government of self-governing individuals, the individuals have, and must have, the sovereign powers.

If the People, as principals, do not possess the Sovereign powers, they possess no power from which they can convey a limited portion to their agents, the government, and so any government that would act presumably under the Constitution and convert the people from the principals and Sovereigns to agents is, infact, a pretender, a government of pretense, because it does not derive its authority from the people. Therefore, the People would be reduced to agents and are no longer the source of authority. Such a government has destroyed it's source of power through upsurpation; it has become a principal in violation of it's creator's interests. Government is deriving it's authority from some source outside the People in violation of the operation of a Constitutional Republican form of government and, therefore, inverts the relationship of the individual, principal, and the state, agent. This violates the "limited powers" doctrine.

The controlling principle in the Common Law is that no man may order the life, actions, and decisions of another. Each individual being answerable to his Creator for his actions and their consequences, must have the right to choose the acts. The Common Law provides protection guaranteeing man's independent action in all ways, unless there is a responsible swearing to an allegation that he is the probable cause of damage to another's Property, injury to another's Person, or infringement on another's Rights. The oath attending a swearing of charges protects the accused by making the Plaintiff answerable to perjury if falsely brought. Our heritage, the Common Law, requires no performance of the individual. The Common Law demands and secures restitution and punishment for wrongs.

As this pertains to the highways and the use of vehicles. The People own the rights-of-way. The name explains the law. People have "rights" of way.

As it pertains to absolute ownership and use of property. The People own the inalienable Right to possess, carry, move, and use said property in any manner in which they choose so long as those actions do not infringe upon the Rights of others. The accused does not need a grant of privilege to use his own Property (Rights). A state granted privilege cannot be compelled on a Free and Natural Citizen (Freeman) who possesses Rights and powers that antedate the State or the Nation and who gains no immunities from the State and has full liability for his acts.

As it pertains to contracts, this Free and Natural person has the inalianable right to contract with anyone this person pleases, and the government can pass no law "impairing the obligation of contracts,." State granted privileges to juristic persons have their source in the limited powers granted by the natural individuals of the State. The licensing or permit statutes of states require a specific performance. Beyond that licensing asks for more; for some reason it asks for a signature, and that is something the Accused objects to because it is contractual and constitutes a presumed voluntary waiver of Common Law process in criminal actions and a voluntary entry into police courts of chancery. Licensing requires such information that this person considers private, which the licensing agencies do not keep private. The State cannot compel the Accused to waive his Right of privacy. The operation of licensing statutes requires all of these private things which it cannot compel a Free and Natural Citizen (Freeman) to provide, whether or not it is a statute. Cited as proper authority is the following:

"An unconstitutional act is not law; it confers no rights it imposes no duties; affords no protection; it creates no office; it is in legal contemplation, as inoperative as though it had never been passed." Norton v Shelby County, p. 442 "The general rule is that an unconstitutional statute, though having the form and the name of law, is in reality no law, but is wholly void and ineffective for any purpose; since unconstitutionality dates from the time of its enactment, an unconstitutional law, in legal contemplation, is as inoperative as if it had never been passed." 16 Am. Jur. 2d 177 The best definitions that the Accused has obtained of licenses are:

1) "Permission to do something which would otherwise be illegal," and
2) "A grant to use the property in which one possesses no estate."

The People own the "rights-of-way". The name explains the law. Again, the People have "RIGHTS" of way. The Accused does not need a grant of privilege to use his own property (rights). A state granted privilege cannot be compelled on a Free and Natural Citizen (Freeman) who possesses "rights" and powers that antedate the state or the nation and who gains no immunities as from the state and has full liability for his acts. State granted privileges to juristic persons have their source in the limited powers granted to the State by the Natural Persons of the State.

It is only fitting and proper that juristic persons, subjects, members, and artificial persons be totally constrained in their actions, since they are legal fictions and can suffer no penalties of the mind and flesh. They must be controlled through making their creation and their every act a grant of privilege and prescription. No interior conscience, no love of freedom, no pride of independence, no tender hope for a future environment suitable for his offspring that can be relied upon to govern his conduct constructively, exists in a legal fiction, and no freedom or unrestrained action can safely be permitted a juristic person.

The Court should agree that the Accused possesses no legal identity other than "Freeman" and Defendant. If that is the case, it raises questions in the mind of the Accused about understanding the charge and the nature of the charge. In order for the charge to have applicability to the Accused, the Accused would seemingly have to possess some legal juristic identity in which specific performance is required as a juristic person created by the State, or a contractor inviting an exchange of obligations, or an agent, insolvent, bond servant, subject, or trespasser. If the Court sees the Accused as a "Freeman," any charge of failure to specifically perform is unrelated to that sole identity because that identity does not describe a relationship to duty. What Complaint has been brought forward by the Plaintiff stating what act has transpired and how that act caused a damage, injury, or infringement of another Person's Property (Right)?

If a Person does not have a contract, gun permit, a marriage license, a fishing/hunting license, a driver's license, or has not fulfilled any other state requirement ---- is he a trespasser? Has a person then volunteered into administrative law jurisdiction? If a person has a permit, license, or etc.--is he a benefactor? Of whom? Most statutes donot say what benefit a Free and Natural Citizen (Freeman) receives that causes a corresponding duty. Upon what undisclosed benefit does a Citizen owe duty to license himself?

The statute fails to identify the grantor of the privilege. The statute does not say what benefit a Free and Natural Citizen receives that cause any corresponding duty. In addition, the statute contains no evidence of any consideration.

Therefore, said statute is unconstitutional in its operation for what it requires of the Free and Natural Citizen (Freeman). Additionally, statutes such as this are void for vagueness and ambiguity, as they fail to identify the relationship of the parties to an alleged controversy and does not specifically define who is, and who is not subject to said statute. Therefore, the issues in question are not within in the jurisdiction of the Court.

ISSUE OF STATUS AND JURISDICTION

The ownership or possession of lands which, in America, is titled allodium, is attended with the full legal rights to use such property for one's own benefit and advancement. This is embraced by the Declaration of Independence when it mentions the inalienable rights (which became civil rights with the ratification of the Constitution) as absolute Property, along with Life and Liberty. The undiminished rights of property are the freedom of an individual to expand or not to expand his material wealth, or more to the specific terminology of the Declaration of Independence, the pursuit of happiness. A property tax, or direct tax, compels one to produce in order to pay the tax. As all government is derived from the consent of the people, and the Rights of the individual are more sacred than the will of the collective citizenry, the consent of the people is actually individual in essence, and must only extend to the particular situation, or status, of said individual.

Basic government, while hard to define in its full role or duty other than to protect Life, Liberty, and Property other than the individual is, at minimum, the process of the Courts, a County Sheriff, Prosecutor, etc. at the lower levels, and the Constitutionally mandated branches of government with their respective functions.

So much more of what seems to be "government" is simply extensive program and process (jurisdictions) designed to create and then direct businesses in the State, the end result of which is to finally move all society from status to contract, or privilege, in order to construct a "new society or new order" upon more equitable lines of thought and method. This erosion of the substantive law, or in America, the Common Law, a law of privilege and quasi-contract which does not regard the Common Law principle of possession, but instead introduces the use or trust, equitable estates, which are then subject to new and foreign jurisdiction under statute. This could be termed the statute-merchant or statute-staple, and is based upon a presumed enfranchisement of all citizens and subjects in the society. Such a condition is absolutely unconstitutional.

Now we come back to the principle of implied consent, a basic tenet of contract and of government. Implied consent is a principle used in this legislative process of lawmaking. Somehow, it seems, all society has collectively implied its consent to statutes of the civil law. This is because of the virtually universal use of corporate privilege or a derivative, the commercial paper methods of conducting business, a capacity, by society's members, which has occasioned the broad scale "general" legislation in the areas of police powers, taxations and assessments, and regulations of property by municipalities. Such statutory enactments, and the subsequent adoption of procedures and jurisdictions to enforce this "will of the legislature" upon the subjects are strictly limited, or even prohibited by the Constitution. Therefore, status becomes the central issue, and jurisdiction must be decided at every turn. Rights are preserved under the Common Law, which must not depend upon the nearly unlimited will of the legislature.

Of course, the specific subject matter involved is the crucial argument in support of, or in dispute of such legislation and its enforcement or exercise in the Courts. We have the law (Common Law) as decided by previous Court cases as a guide and tentative authority in the issues, but with each new statutory enactment, there can be new principles (issues) or Rights (denial of) involved which have yet to be specifically ruled upon. Therefore we must apply, not only our knowledge and understanding of the law, but our common sense as well, for as Coke stated; "Reason is the soul of the law, and when the reason of any particular law ceases, so does the law itself." (7 Rep. 69)

We (each individual) must decide for ourselves, for we are the principals of government (Idaho Constitution, Art. I, Sec. 2) and cannot enfranchise ourselves, only our business entities, or persons. "Status may yield ground to contract, but cannot itself be reduced to contract." Pallock's Maine's And. Laws, 184 (quoted in Bouvier's Law Dictionary, 1914).

Contracts must include informed consent, less any ministerial process be effectively a denial of due process of law. It is status, and not the kind of contract, which determines due process. Legislative authority cannot subject the fundamental, constitutional rights to any proceeding other than those which satisfy due process, that is the ancient accepted mode of judicial proceedings, the law which hears before it condemns, which proceeds only upon inquiry, and renders judgment only after trial. (See Bilbert v. Elder, 65 Idaho 383,144 P. 2d. 194. (19430, and Abrams v. Jones, 35 Idaho 532 (1922).) Summary or special proceedings are not in the nature of actions at Common Law and are created by personal statutes (see Black's 5th) of the legislature, in foreign and modern civil law.

There can be no doubt that this is but derivative of the jus gentuim of the Roman law, and consistent with the Lex Mercatoria or Law Merchant, the law of commercial contracts. Black's 5th also defines this body of law, statute, or code to be the "statute merchant" or "statute staple" mentioned above. The courts of the staple in the merchant nations of centuries past were merely "trading pits" for the quick and equitable settlement of questions of a purely commercial nature and therefore, absolutely foreign to the Common Law or the municipal law of any land. Such law dealt necessarily in the potentiality of substance, or the promise of payment and not in the possession itself. The object and intent was the expediting of claims arising out of transactions with choses in action (personal property) and done in summary proceedings. It is elementary to any reasonable mind, that the entrance of these modes and principles into the realm of the Common Law and the rights of citizens under the Constitution of the United States, would be an intolerable perversion and eventual abrogation of all freedom in Life, Liberty, and Property as defined by the Declaration and the Bill of Rights.

Personal Statutes create status, but a status other than that of the Free and Natural Citizen at Law under the Constitution. The rights, duties, capacities, or incapacities created are, in fact, franchises or privileges granted by a principal, the legislature, and thereby totally subject to its enactments and procedures. In Idaho, the procedural merger of law and Equity has ordained that all actions prosecuted by the State of Idaho are in criminal forms, but at the same time, actions instituted by the municipal corporations acting as agents for the State upon these statutes, are civil actions. Witness the language of the Idaho Constitution, Art. 5, Sec. I, in defining the civil action: "...for the enforcement or protection of private rights or the redress of private wrongs..." (emphasis added).

There we find the County or City acting as a "private person" in seeking remedies or recovery. This "status" created by legislation is not and cannot be consistent in any way with the status held by citizens, or more specifically, natural persons under Constitutional protection. Further, the "rights" of these "persons", which are artificial or juristic persons, are not in the same class as fundamental substantial rights held as inviolate by State or Federal government in the Bill of Rights. I submit that these rights are merely equitable interests or claims on property and not the possession of property which is an absolute right, comprehending the complete, undiminished use and dominion of a thing. These are "rights" to action as opposed to rights of ownership and possession. In this sense, they are "property" but must be further defined as personal property and further classified as property or "choses in action." (See Bouvier's Law Dictionary (1914) on property, choses in action, and right (absolute).

These rights, being choses in action, are then recoverable by action in the appropriate court, under the appropriate, enabling statute which confers jurisdiction over that matter and authorizes these special or summary proceedings. Many of the case citings concerning this subject are listed and quoted in I.C. Vol. I; Const. Declaration of Rights; Article I. These citings put forth the law of Idaho as interpreted by its High Court.

Cases in point are: State v. Jutila, 34 Idaho 595; People ex rel. Brown v. Burnham, 35 Idaho 522; Brady v. Place, 41 Idaho 747; Blue Note, Inc. v. Hopper, 85 Idaho 152; Comish v. Smith, 97 Idaho 89 (all on the subject of Common Law right of trial by jury); and on due process of law, or the law of the land: State v. Frederic, 28 Idaho 709; Collins v. Crowley, 94 Idaho 891; Mullen v. Moseley, 13 Idaho 457; Eagleson v. Rubin, 16 Idaho 92; O'Connor v. City of Moscow, 69 Idaho 37; and concerning the 4th Amendment: State v. Petersen, 81 Idaho 233; and concerning fundamental rights: Abrams v. Jones, 35 Idaho 532.

I submit here that the "capacity" mentioned in Black's 5th under personal statutes is a corporate capacity of doing business or operating with limited liability and/or perpetual succession or existence. Any discussion of status must involve the capacities or incapacities, both natural and conventional, belonging to such person deriving, of course, from the nature of the person, whether natural, juristic, or artificial; whether of a substantive origin or merely in contemplation of law.

Of course, persons operating or conducting business under a privilege or commercial contract are a class of persons, just as citizens in full possession of their political and civil rights (see Right in Bouvier's Law Dictionary) are a class of persons. Still they are different classes under the law, some having fundamental or inalienable rights and some having rights arising from legislation. The operation of a statute is upon the class of cases which, from their analogy to the cases that are named (in code books of the state), are within the equity of the statute (see Black's 5th on Equity of a Statute).

To determine jurisdiction then, is to take into account the status of the individuals or persons party to the action, the nature, or cause of the action, the type of relief sought, and finally the power or capacity of the Court itself. A challenge to the jurisdiction of the Court, when based upon the status of Defendant, the service of process, the cause of action or lack of same, and the ability to effect a remedy or the capacity to proceed according to the law of the land, is a matter which will involve much knowledge and understanding of law on the part of the Judge or Magistrate, for it is a question of substantive and procedural law, of Constitution and local usages. The utmost concern and caution of the Court is advisable in such matters, for upon these decisions rest the safety and welfare of the citizenry, Citizen's respect for government, Citizen's continued peaceful and lawful settlement of disputes arising among themselves and between Citizen's and their public servants. An unwarrantable jurisdiction of the civil law or law merchant promulgated by the Legislature and courts cannot help but incite disgust and dissension when the public-at-large becomes aware of a tyranny and despotism in the form of police powers, taxations, summary judgements, and bureaucratic regulation, which is being authorized at every turn by a runaway legislature. The Courts are our basic protection from oppression or excessive rule-making. The Constitution and Bill of Rights are our standards of reason and right. We do not desire to flood the Courts with unseasoned or frivolous banter, but knowledgeable and reasonable arguments of law and clear statements of fact. The weight of the question is great, this issue of status and jurisdiction, and is to be treated solemnly and soberly by all involved. It is regrettable that many public officials have no idea of what is at stake here, but go blindly on, listening to custom and precedent rather than reason or fact. It should be obvious to the learned Court that this Person has no contract and still operates At Law and therefore, not under the jurisdiction of this Court. Wherefore this Accused person moves the Court to dismiss the charges.

NATURAL RIGHT TO COURT TRANSCRIPTS

COMES NOW the Appellant, In Propria Persona, to request relief from the required filing fee, and to be allowed to file an Appeal without cost. The provisions of IC 31-3220 do not apply in this case. Appellant has a natural right to enter the courts without cost, and bases this position on the following law and facts:

PAUPER AND FEES

1. Appellant is a pauper. On record with the court is an Affidavit of Poverty, showing that Appellant has no lawful money of the United States with which to tender a payment of costs, fees, etc. Appellant asks that the Court review that document as a matter of pertinent fact along with the Report to the Gold Commission on Reserve at the Law Library, together with the arguments of law that follow.

Appellant cannot be charged a fee, as no charge can be placed upon a citizen as a condition precedent to his exercise of a constitutional right. A fee is: "A charge fixed by law for services of public officers or for use of a privilege under control of government." Fort Smith Gas Co. v. Wiseman 189 Ark. 675 74 SW. 2d 789, 790, from Black's Law Dictionary 5th Ed.

The accused/appellant sought no service or use of any privilege. It is a rule of law that governments were instituted by the people for the fundamental reason of protection of property rights, as this is the basis of a free society. It is a moot point that the officials of my government should not charge me for the opportunity to exercise this fundamental right of due process. How can mere rules overrun the Law of the Land? They cannot. While members of the bar may be required to tender filing fees for the privilege of entering court, this Defendant in this circumstance cannot.

2. Charging citizens for filing fees appears to be based upon these premises:

A. ALL CASES ARE HANDLED BY LICENSED ATTORNEYS: Usually the defendant is represented by an attorney, who is an officer of the court, practicing law, and requiring a fee for services. As this privilege of being represented by such officer is granted by government to the defendant so choosing, it follows that a fee could be charged for filing appearances in the courts.

It must be remembered that attorneys come into the courts as a matter of business. They enter the courts at the grace of, and as members of the court; not as a matter of fundamental right. It is fundamental that the grantor of any privilege can certainly impose any requirement (filing fees) as a condition on the privilege.

However, in this case, the government has charged this citizen with a crime, and this citizen is simply defending him rights. When the 5th and 14th Amendments guarantee the right to an "opportunity to defend life, liberty, or property" in a court of justice, how can the Clerk of the Court seek to demand, as a condition of this right, a filing fee?

It is an individual's right to be able to defend one's Life, Liberty, and property in the courts. Therefore, it is the duty of the Clerk of the Court to file an answer or response for a Defendant, if he appears In Propria Persona, and not by attorney.

This Appellant is appearing In Propria Persona (in his own person) not Pro Se, which term means "as his own attorney". This Appellant does not choose to be represented by a member of the bar, but chooses to appear in court in person on his own behalf to defend his Life, Liberty, and Property against the claims of the government.

B. HE WHO SEEKS EQUITY MUST PAY: In Equity, the rule is that one comes to equity voluntarily. If two parties of interest wish to enter equity proceedings in order to settle a dispute then, as a minimum, the Plaintiff may be charged a fee to file pleadings. In addition, any attorney may be charged a filing fee whether he represents a party as a Plaintiff or a Defendant and all corporations and regulated enterprises must also pay filing fees. However, this is a criminal case. The Appellant did not bring the action, nor consent to the jurisdiction, as Appellant did not consider the alleged act a proper cause of action.

Where the government seeks to enforce a claim upon rights, and when the Defendant is a citizen and natural person, the due process clauses of our constitutions prevail. This is a substantive rights issue. Due process means at least notification and opportunity to defend. How can the Appellant defend when the rules apply a condition to the right of appeal? Let me remind the Court that: "Where rights secured by the Constitution are involved, there can be no rule making or legislation which would abrogate them." Miranda v. Arizona 384 US 436, 491p " . . . right and justice shall be administered without sale, denial, delay, or prejudice." Idaho Constitution. Article 1, Sec. 18.

STATE BIAS AND RULES

The Appellant is in possession of a document from the Court entitled "ESTIMATED OF CLERK'S RECORD", stating that the clerk of the District Court must have $ for transcript costs for papers needed with the appeal.

The Appellant would like to remind the Court that the Appellant is not in the Court as a Plaintiff, but as a Defendant who has been accused of a crime by his government. The Appellant has been compelled into the judicial system, and does not appear on his own volition. Appellant has been compelled into the judicial system to seek redress of grievance, or his State will deprive him of his Life, Liberty, and/or Property.

The Appellant does not desire to have the transcripts, or even to move forward in this case, but since the State has found it necessary to prosecute this Citizen, this Citizen has no alternative but to defend against the action. In order to properly prepare and adequately defend against the charges of the government, the Appellant must demand and use any and all information available, and all Rights secured by the Constitutions of the United States and the State of Idaho, to include transcripts of past hearings required by the Appellate Court.

In reviewing Rule 5.2, the Appellant notices that both the "Prosecuting Attorney and the Defendant" are entitled to copies of the transcript. Appellant recognizes that Rule 5.2 does not relate to appeals, but must bring it up to show favoritism toward government and bias against the citizen.

From the wording of Rule 5.2, it is only the Defendant who is required to "pay" for justice, as the Prosecuting Attorney is not required to pay for transcripts. Courts cannot adhere to the position that a system of Due Process "without sale" is only for the Prosecuting Attorney at taxpayer expense, and that the State has a right to "sell" justice to the Defendant.

Need the Appellant remind the Court that the Idaho State Constitution states: "Article I, Section 18. justice to be freely and speedily administered. --- Courts of justice shall be open to every person, and a speedy remedy afforded for every injury of person, property, or character, and "right and justice shall be administered without sale" denial, delay, or "prejudice" (emphasis added)

Isn't freely giving transcripts to the Prosecuting Attorney and "selling" transcripts to the Defendant somewhat "prejudicial"? Isn't this administering justice "for sale" rather than "without sale"?

No Accused Person should have to petition his government for justice or, "buy" or "purchase" justice from his government; and no person should be discriminated against or provided "prejudicial" justice "for sale" because a citizen is the Defendant/Appellant rather than a Prosecuting Attorney.

Appellant also notices that Rule 54 (u) states: "These rules shall be construed to provide a just, speedy, and inexpensive determination of all appeals."

The question becomes, less expensive to whom? The Plaintiff or the Appellant? Justice cannot be sold to the Appellant, and it is not appropriate that the Court should order the Appellant to defray any costs to receive Justice, Due Process, and equal protection under the law. The Plaintiff brought the charges forward against the Appellant. Now let the Plaintiff fully accept the burden of defending these wrongful allegations, at public expense, all the way to the United States Supreme Court.

It should also be noted that the estimated cost of the transcript is $. The penal judgement assessed by the Summary Proceedings of the lower Court was only $. As stated above, it appears on the surface, that charges for transcripts are to prohibit and discourage the average Citizen from appealing, as it would be far cheaper and much easier to simply submit to the charges of the "king's agents" and his "chancery" traffic court than appeal to prove one's innocence on appeal.

It is the position of this Appellant that filing an appeal and having it heard in any criminal case is a matter of Right, and there can be no charges to exercise a Right.

Appellant recognizes the excessive cost of preparing transcripts for all appeals, but the Plaintiff is the keeper of the public monies. It is the Plaintiff who brings criminal charges before the Courts. It is the Plaintiff who made the requirement for transcripts and it is the Plaintiff who provides itself transcripts at no cost while charging a sovereign citizen. Therefore, The Plaintiff should be prepared to pay for defence of those charges, at public expense, all the way to the Supreme Court of the United States, and it is the Plaintiff who should be charged the filing fees --- not the sovereign citizen. If the Plaintiff is not so prepared, then the Plaintiff should be a little more selective in whom is charged, arrested, and taken to trial.

The Appellant objects to any "costs for justice" and "Due Process", and shudders to conclude that the only reason the rules require an Appellant to bear the burden of these costs in defense of Life, Liberty, and Property, is to cause an undue expense upon the Appellant in an effort to thwart, hinder, and discourage Appellants from appealing beyond the District Court.

Failure of the Appellant to pay this imposed cost thereby allows the Appellate Court to dismiss the appeal under the provisions of Rule 21 which provides for the dismissal of appeals for failure "...of a party to timely take any other step in the Appellant process..."

NATURAL CITIZENS VS CORPORATIONS

It appears that the filing fee rule was made for subjects of the State, but is being applied to Natural citizens residing within the State. The State is the creator and regulator or most trade, commerce, and industry through the corporate licensing scheme. "...the corporation is a creature of the State. It is presumed to be incorporated for the benefit of the public. It receives certain special privileges and franchises, and holds them subject to the laws of the State and the limitations of its charter. Its rights to act as a corporation are only preserved to it so long as it obeys the laws of its creation. There is a reserved right in the legislature to investigate its contracts and find out whether it has exceeded its powers. It would be a strange anomaly to hold that a State, having chartered a corporation to make certain franchises, could not in the exercise of its sovereignty inquire how those franchises had been employed, and whether they had been abused,..." Hale v. Henkel, 201 U. S. 43; 74, 75.

The State is sovereign over any trade, commerce, and industry it regulates under the police powers of the State. Therefore, the State can pass any statute it desires to control or regulate those entities, to include statutes that would, if applied to a natural Citizen, violate constitutional Rights. The State can control every action of regulated enterprises but cannot apply that class of statutes to a natural Citizen.

The Supreme Court of the United States fully understands the difference between a natural Citizen and a corporation or regulated enterprise and they have stated: "..we are of the opinion that there is a clear distinction...between an individual and a corporation,... The individual may stand upon his constitutional rights as a citizen. He is entitled to carry on his private business in his own way. His power to contract is unlimited. He owes no duty to the State or to his neighbors to divulge his business, or to open his doors to an investigation, so far as it may tend to intimidate him. He owes no such duty to the State, since he receives nothing therefore, beyond the protection of his life and property. His rights are as existed by the law of the land long antecedent to the organization of the State, and can only be taken away from him by due process of law, and in accordance with the constitution... He owes nothing to the public so long as he does not trespass upon their rights." (emphasis added) Hale v. Henkel, supra.

Since a natural citizen "owes no duty to the State", the State cannot require any specific performance from him in the exercise of a right, or that performance abrogates the right.

The legislature can pass any statute, and the courts can make any rule desired, to require corporations, regulated enterprises, and other licensed entities or professions to file fees with the Court or any administrative agency. But where an issue pertaining to a natural citizen who has constitutional rights is concerned, it becomes an issue of substance not mere form, because: "Where rights secured by the constitution are concerned there can be no legislation or rule making that can abrogate them." Miranda v. Arizona, 384 U. S. p. 491

If the legislature or the courts, through legislation and rule making, can impose a tax or a fee upon the right of a natural citizen to petition the courts, then they have abrogated that right, and justice is only for the rich. The principle behind this issue was clearly resolved by the Supreme Court in "The Passenger Cases" where they stated: "...every citizen of the United States from the most remote States or territories, is entitled to free access, not only to the principle departments established at Washington, but also to its judicial tribunals and public offices in every State in the Union..." 2 Black 620; Also see Crandell v. Nevada, 6 Wall 35.

The term here is citizen not corporation or regulated enterprises. If the legislature or the judiciary can charge a citizen $1.00 a page to exercise the right of appeal, it can charge $1,000 per page. Any costs demanded from a natural citizen is a limitation and restriction upon the use of the courts, which amounts to nothing more than a blatant abrogation of rights.

This principle was further expounded upon in an Illinois case in a civil action where a citizen petitioned for a writ of mandate because he couldn't afford the filing fees, and the Court held that a person need not be a pauper to proceed as a poor person. They stated that: "In no event can the court legally require that the application for leave to sue as a poor person should be accompanied by the agreements and the affidavit which are required by the rule and which have been hereinabove in this opinion particularly referred to. We are also of the opinion that it is unnecessary that either the applicant's attorney or the court should be satisfied that the applicant is a pauper. Many persons who are not paupers may rightfully be permitted by the courts to commence and prosecute actions as poor persons. There are other meritorious objections to this rule, but we deem it unnecessary to discuss them." The People v. Chytraus, 228 Ill 194.

Illinois recognizes a difference between poor persons and paupers. It appears that a pauper has no boot nor anything to pour out of it, whereas a poor person may have a boot, but little to pour out of it because of debt servitude to the welfare State. Therefore, in Illinois, citizens have the right to sue in civil cases even when they have limited funds. Can the requirements to appeal in criminal cases be more stringently applied in civil cases?

As pointed out in "The Passenger Cases", citizen have the inalienable right of entry to the Judicial system and cannot be regulated or controlled as can creations of the State.

This Appellant will follow all of the Rules as understood and will not knowingly violate them unless said Rule violates a Constitutional Right, and the Court should not need reminding that Persons acting in their own behalf are held: "...to less stringent standard than formal pleadings by lawyers." Haines v. Kerner, 404 U.S. 519.

The Appellant again reminds the Court that this citizen does not appear in this case of his own volition and the record will clearly show than he has been compelled into an alien and foreign jurisdiction from the Common Law and has been forced to defend or lose Life, Liberty, or Property. Had the Appellant been the moving party in this action, then there may have been some validity in attempting to charge for transcripts. However, in this case the State has criminally prosecuted and the Appellant has the right to all transcripts or any other documentation the State requires for an appeal, and the Appellant hereby demands, as a matter of right, all such documentation.

Wherefore, due to the above mentioned circumstances and facts the Appellant moves the Court to provide the Idaho Supreme Court the transcripts requested as a matter of right and "without sale".

COUNSEL OF CHOICE

The terms "attorney" and "assistance to counsel" are Common Law terms and: "It has been held, and is undoubtedly the law, that, where common law phrases are used in an indictment or information, such phrases must have common law interpretation." Chapman vs People, 39 Mich. 357-359; in re richter (D.C.) l00 Fed. 295-297

The meaning of the Common Law terms is quite clear and the term "Assistance of Counsel" does not necessarily mean that "Counsel" will be a licensed attorney. Certainly a licensed attorney may be a counselor, but all counselors may not be licensed attorneys. "Barristers or counselors-at-law, in England, were never called or appointed by the courts at Westminster, but were called to the bar by the inns of the court." Cooper's Case, 22 N.Y. 67, 90

"They are voluntary societies,..." King v Benchers of Gray's Inn "Of advocates, or (as we generally call them) counsel, there are two species...; barristers and serjeants... serjeants and barristers indiscriminately...may take upon them the protection and defense of any suitors, whether plaintiff or defendant; who are therefore called their clients, like the defendants upon the ancient Roman orators. Those indeed practised gratis, for honor merely, or at most for the sake of gaining influence: and so likewise it is established that a counsel can maintain no action for his fees; which are given, not as 'location vel conduction, but as guiddam honorarium; not as salary or hire, but as a mere gratuity...'" 3 BL. Com. 26-29 "In early times, personal communication between counsel and client 'was necessary'; for there were no attorneys..." It was not until after the statutes of Merton (20 H. III, c. 10), Westminster (3 E. I, c. 33), and Gloucester (6 E. I, c. 1), that suitors were allowed to appear at pleasure by attorney . The counsellor was for many centuries the only person known as a 'lawyer'" Kennedy v Broun, 13 C. B. N. S. 677, 698. "Physicians and counsel usually perform their duties without having a legal title to remuneration. Such has been the general understanding." Veitch v Russell, 3 A., E. N. S. 928, 936 "Attorneys are responsible to their clients for negligence or unskillfulness; but no action lies against the counsel for his acts, if done bona fide for his client. In this respect therefore, the counsel stands in a different position from the attorney." Swinfen v. Swinfel, 1 C. B. N. S. 364, 403 "An advocate at the English bar, accepting a brief in the usual way, undertakes a duty, but does not enter into any contract or promise, express or implied. Cases may indeed occur where on an express promise (if he made one) he would be liable in assumpsit; but we think a barrister is to be considered, not as making a contract with his client, but as taking upon himself an office or duty, in the proper discharge of which not merely the client, but the court in which the duty is to be performed, and the public at large, have an interest....A counsel has complete authority over the suit, the mode of conducting it, and all that is incident to it.   ...No action will lie against counsel for any act honestly done in the conduct or management of the cause." Swinfen v. Chelmsford, 5 H. & N. 890, 920, 922, 923

"English attorneys-at-law (called solicitors since the judicature act of 1873 took effect) were not members of the bar, and were not heard in the superior courts, and the power of admitting them to practice and striking them off the roll had not been given to the inns of the court. That part of the profession which is carried on by attorneys is liberal and reputable, as well as useful to the public,... and they ought to be protected where they act to the best of their skill and knowledge. But every man is liable to error...A counsel may mistake, as well as an attorney. Yet no one will say that a counsel who has been mistaken shall be charged with the debt. The counsel, indeed, is honorary in his advice, and does not demand a fee: The attorney may demand a compensation, but neither of them ought to be charged with the debt for a mistake." Pitt v. Yalden, 4 Burr. 2,060, 2,061 "An attorney-at-law ...is one who is put in the place, stead, or turn of another, to manage his matters of law. Formerly every suitor was obliged to appear in person, to prosecute or defend his suit, ...unless by special license under the king's letters-patent... But... it is now permitted in general, by divers ancient statutes, whereof the first is statute Westm. 3, c. 10, that attorneys may be made to prosecute or defend any action...These attorneys are now formed into a regular corps; they are admitted to the execution of their office by the superior courts of Westminster Hall, and are in all points officers of the respective courts of which they are admitted...No man can practise as an attorney in any of those courts, but such as is admitted and sworn an attorney of that particular court: An attorney of the court of king's bench cannot practise in the court of common pleas; nor vice versa. To practise in the court of chancery, it is also necessary to be admitted a solicitor therein." 3 Bl. Com. 25, 26. "Attorney, in English law, signifies, in its widest sense, any substitute or agent appointed to act in 'the turn, stead, or place of another.' The term is now commonly confined to a class of qualified agents who undertake the conduct of legal proceedings for their clients. By the common law the actual presence of the parties to a suit was considered indispensable, but the privilege of appearing by attorney was conceded in certain cases by special dispensation, until the statute of Merton and subsequent enactments made it competent for both parties in all judicial proceedings to appear by attorney. Solicitors appear to have been at first distinguished from attorneys, as not having the attorney's power to bind their principles, but latterly the distinction has been between attorneys as the agents form ally appointed in actions at law, and solicitors who take care of proceedings in parliament, chancery, privy council, etc. In practice, however, and in ordinary language, the terms are synonymous...The qualifications necessary for admission on the rolls of attorneys and solicitors" are fixed by statute. "They may act as advocates in certain of the inferior courts. Conveyancing, formerly considered the exclusive business of the bar, is now often performed by attorneys. Barristers are understood to require the intervention of an attorney in all cases that come before them professionally, although in criminal cases the prisoner not unfrequently engages a counsel directly by giving him a fee in open court." 3 Enc. Brit. 62; also see Co. Lit. 51 b, 52 a.

The intent of our founding fathers was pretty clear and it is also axiomatic in Law that it is the intent of lawmakers that is law; not the interpretations of others. "The intention of the lawmaker constitutes the law." Stewart v Kahn, 11 Wall, 78 U. S. 493, 504 "As the meaning of the lawmaker is the law, so the meaning of the contracting parties is the agreement." Whitney v Wyman, 11 Otto, 101 U.S.

It has been repeatedly upheld in the courts that: "The framers of the statute are presumed to know and understand the meaning of the words used, and where the language used is clear and free from ambiguity, and not in conflict with other parts of the same act, the courts must assume the legislative intent to be what the plain meaning of the words used import." First National Bank vs United States, 38 F (2nd) 925 at 931 (March 3, 1930). "A legislative act is to be interpreted according to the intention of the legislature, apparent upon its face. Every technical rule, as to the construction or force of particular terms, must yield to the clear expression of the paramount will of the legislature." 2 Pet. 662 "The intention of the legislature, when discovered, must prevail, any rule of construction declared by previous acts to the contrary notwithstanding." 4 Dall 144 "The intention of the law maker constitutes the law." U.S. v Freeman, 3 HOW 565; U.S. v Babbit, 1 Black 61; Slater v Cave, 3 Ohio State 80.

Then, what was the intent of our founding fathers? Our founding fathers wrote the Constitution in plain, simple language and used words that everyone of that day could understand. The Constitution was also written with common words to insure that all of the people could understand its meaning. Otherwise, there was no way the people would submit themselves to it. Hadn't they just rid themselves of a tyrant King? Therefore, each word was chosen very carefully and we need only understand the meaning of the words used in those days. In referring to the American Dictionary of the English Language, First Edition, Noah Webster, 1825, are the following definitions: "COUNSEL, n...which is probably from the Heb... Those who give counsel in law; any counselor or advocate, or any number of counselors, barristers, or serjeants; as the plaintiff's counsel, or the defendant's counsel..."

We need to remember that many of the authors of the Constitution were members of the legal profession, and isn't it interesting that Webster's definition clearly omits any reference to "lawyer" or "attorney" as being counsel? Whatever "COUNSEL" is, counsel can represent both a plaintiff and a defendant.

The word advocate was defined as: "ADVOCATE, n...To call for, to plead for;...In English and American courts, advocates are the same as counsel, or counselors..."

The word Barrister was defined as: "BARRISTER, n. (from bar) A counselor, learned in the laws, qualified and admitted to plead at the bar, and to take upon him the defense of clients;..."

In neither definition are there any references to "lawyers" or "attorneys," nor is anything specifically mentioned about qualifications other than "learned in the laws," and "qualified." Nothing is mentioned about being approved by the Supreme Court nor any other agency or entity.

The word attorney was defined as: "ATTORNEY, n. One who takes the turn or place of another...One who is appointed or admitted in the place of another, to manage his matters in law. The word formerly signified any person who did business for another; ...The word answers to the procurator, (proctor) of the civilians..." "Attorneys are not admitted to practice in courts, until examined, approved, licensed and sworn by direction of some court; after which they are proper officers of the court."

It is important to notice that an attorney could act "FOR" or "IN PLACE OF" an individual. Whereas counselors were restricted to "PLEADING FOR" and "GIVING" of "ADVICE AND COUNSEL" in the presence of the accused or client. Counselors had no authority to "ACT FOR" or "IN PLACE OF" any client.

In those days it was commonplace to handle one's own case, thereby, acting (In Propria Persona) in one's behalf in court. However the court room is an awesome and lonely place when everyone else in the room is a member of the court. Whenever desired, the accused or the plaintiff could have a friend in the court -- A counselor. A friendly person who could and would "SPEAK FOR HIM" or "ADVISE HIM" in court proceedings and matters of law.

Counselors were persons who took pride in their knowledge of the law and used it to the good of the people. They were advisors of the people and, as such, may or may not have been able to collect fee for their services. Under the Common Law, they could charge for their services but could not use the force of law to collect a fee.

Attorneys, on the other hand, were agents of the court, an "officer of the court," who could be "appointed or admitted in place of another to manage his matters in law." Attorneys were schooled in the law, "examined, approved, licensed and sworn, by the direction of some court." As such, they could charge for their services and demand payment under force of law.

Without doubt, our founding fathers knew well the meaning of the word "COUNSEL," and they used that word so the people would be "FREE" to choose counsel of their choice, who may or may not be an attorney. It has only been the rulings of the monopolistic American jurisprudence system that has continuously denied individuals the RIGHT of "ASSISTANCE OF COUNSEL" to the American public.

It has long been recognized under the Common Law that attorneys were different from "counselors." The New York Code recognized the words as having different meanings as it states: "...by an attorney, solicitor, "OR" counselor, or..." NY Code, 4th Ed. Rev., 1885, Article 179, Page 272

In Title 10, Article 303, page 465, I find the same usage as it stated: "...the right of a party to agree with an attorney, solicitor, 'OR' counsel..." (Emp. added)

This usage clearly upholds the Common Law meanings as the words solicitor, attorney, are separated by a comma and attorney, solicitor are separated from counselor by the conjunction "OR".

In the rules of the Supreme Court of New York, it stated: "...shall be alleged, or by his attorney, OR counsel." Rules of Procedure, 1855, Supreme Court of New York, Rule 37, page 666.

And in a footnote (same page): "...by the parties "OR" their attorney "OR" counsel..."

On a trial before Pollock, C.B., it stated: "...The plaintiff, who was in custody, did not appear by either counsel "OR" attorney, "OR" in person;..." Corbett v Hudson (Emp. added)

From the Rules of Procedure in the Supreme Court of Pennsylvania comes the following: "...That counselors shall not practice as attorneys, nor attorneys as counselors in this court." Rules of Procedure, February term, 1790

The Supreme Court of the United States recognizes that there were separate functions and responsibilities for "attorneys" and "counselors" as the two different rolls were maintained by the court. "His name should be taken from the roll of attorneys, and placed on the list of counselors." Ex Parte Hallowell, 3 Dal 411, Feb. 1799

The usage of these words clearly separates functions and responsibilities of attorneys from counselors.

Interestingly enough, when Idaho was founded, the state's founding fathers also recognized the Common Law, and therefore they understood the language and meaning of the Common Law when they wrote: "The Common Law of England, so far as it is not repugnant to, or inconsistent with the Constitution or laws of the United States, in all cases not provided for in these Revised Statutes, is the rule and decision in all the courts of this Territory." Idaho Revised Statutes, 1887, Section 18, Page 63.

The Revised Statutes do provide that: "If any person shall practice law in any court, except a Justice Court, without having received a license as attorney and counsellor, he is guilty of a contempt of court." Idaho Revised Statutes, 1887, Title IV, Section 3996, page 430.

The question now becomes, does this statute apply to criminal or civil cases or both and to whom does it apply? Therefore, in Common Law criminal cases , there is no written Law. The Law is then void, and where the Law is void there can be no arbitrary rule making by any court that can deny an accused the right to "assistance of counsel" of his choice. "Under both our Federal and State Constitutions, a defendant has the right to defend in person or by COUNSEL of his own choosing." People v Price, 262 N.Y. 410, 412, 187 N.E. 298, 299 "This fundamental right is denied to a defendant unless he gets reasonable time and a fair opportunity to secure counsel of his own choice and, with that counsel's assistance, to prepare for trial." People v McLaughlin, 53 N.E. 2d Series 356, 357 "Justice requires that a party should be permitted to con duct his cause in person (subject to reasonable requirements of propriety), or by any agent of good character, and that the test of the agent's character should not be so rigorously applied as to imperil the constitutional right to a fair trial." Concord Mfg. Co. v Robertson, ante, pp. 1, 6, 7; State v Saunders, ante, pp. 39, 72, 73 "It is the responsibility of the court to insure that the court indulge every reasonable presumption against the waiver of fundamental rights." Aetna Ins. Co. v Kennedy, 301 US 389; Ohio Bell Tel. v Public Util. Comm., 301 US 292 "Upon the trial judge rests the duty of seeing that the trial is conducted with solicitude for the essential rights of the accused."

The trial court must protect the right of an accused to have the assistance of counsel. "This protecting duty imposes the serious and weighty responsibility upon the trial judge of determining whether there is an intelligent and competent waiver by the accused. While an accused may waive the right to counsel, whether there is a proper waiver should be clearly determined by the trial court, and it would be fitting and appropriate for that determination to appear upon the record." Johnson v Zerbst, 304 US 458, 465

The constitutional right of Assistance to Counsel is not qualified to only someone who has received a license from some supreme court or other alleged authority. The Constitution says absolutely nothing about a "licensed attorney," but simply says: "In all criminal prosecutions, the accused shall enjoy the right...to have Assistance of Counsel for his defense." United States Constitution, Bill of Rights, Article VI

Since the United States Constitution was ordained and established by the people for their protection, not for the protection of a legal society, and since it may not be superseded or amended by any act of Congress or by any other "law" of this or any other state, this defendant demands the right to exercise such right, and will choose either Counsel or Co-counsel, or both, to help him with his defense.

The language of the Sixth Amendment quoted above is quite clear, unambiguous, and is very precise, and the men who were responsible for its form, very learned and skilled in the Law, and in fact, many were attorneys. Therefore, the conspicuous lack of the words "attorney" or "attorney-at-law" is notable indeed!

While the Bill of Rights was being debated and argued, the same members of Congress were in the process of passing the First Judiciary Act of September 24, 1789. The very same day the President signed this bill, the House and Senate were finally coming to an agreement on the express and explicit language and form of the Bill of Rights. Therefore, their meanings are to be compatible. Williams v Florida, 399 US 78; 90 S. Ct. 1895, 1904. Therefore, it is absolutely clear that the explicit language and form of the First Judiciary Act of 1889 was and is the meaning of the Sixth Amendment. The First Judiciary Act states in part: "Sec. 35. And be it further enacted, That in all the courts in the United States, the parties may plead and manage their own causes personally OR by the assistance of such counsel OR attorneys at law as by the rules of the said courts respectfully shall be permitted to manage and conduct causes therein." First Congress, Session I, Chapter 20, Page 20. Also Section 30, page 89, also refers to counsel as: "...not being of counsel or attorney to either of the parties..." It is the individual who has the absolute Constitutional RIGHT to "ASSISTANCE OF COUNSEL" under the Sixth Amendment and it is the "Will of the Sovereign People" who reign supreme --- not the courts! Numerous court cases support the individual's right to counsel. Some are: "The fundamental right of the accused to representation by counsel must not be denied or unreasonably restricted." Poindexter v. State, 191 S.W. 2d 445. "While the Constitution guarantees to a defendant in a criminal case, the right to be heard by counsel, it also allows him to be heard 'by himself' and where he elects to appear for himself rather than by an attorney, he cannot be compelled to employ counsel, or to accept services assigned by the court." People v. Shapirio, 188 Misc 363. Defendant, in this case, has certainly made a timely and proper demand for "COUNSEL OF CHOICE" --- not necessarily a licensed attorney recognized by the Court. Since one cannot be compelled to accept an assigned attorney, the individual has the basic unalienable right to select "COUNSEL" from among anyone he chooses, because:

"The right of counsel is not formal but substantial." Snell v. U.S., 174 F. 2d 580, US ex rel; Mitchell v. Thompson, (DC-NY), 56 F. Supp 683; Johnson v. U.S., 71 App DC 400, 110 F. 2d

562. This defendant claims and demands the "RIGHT" to "Assistance of Counsel" as imperative, necessary, essential, and the prerequisite to a proper defense of his life, liberty, and property that have been endangered by the fruitful, however unlawful, apprehension and restraint of said defendant. The "RIGHT" to "Assistance of Counsel" may not be limited to any condition, because: "....it is one of the fundamental rights of life and liberty." Robinson v. Johnson, (DC-CAL) 50 F. Supp 774. And finally, "The right to effective "Assistance of Counsel" in a criminal proceeding guaranteed by this amendment is a basic and fundamental right secured to every person by the Due Process Clause of the Fourteenth Amendment." Armine v. Times, (CCA 10), 131 F. 2d 827. This defendant has the "RIGHT" to counsel and because of the above authorities, intends to secure "Assistance of Counsel" of his choice. Inasmuch as such was once well know and understood to be the "RIGHT" of the people as defined in the "Will of the Sovereign People's" Constitution, this defendant here and now asserts his "RIGHT" and takes it back. No governmental entity was ever properly given power or authority, by the "Will of the Sovereign People", to take such a "RIGHT" away. Inasmuch as Defendant believes and knows he cannot receive proper, fair, effective, and conscientious representation from a licensed member of the bar and officer of this court that is trying this Defendant, and because it has become apparent to this Defendant that attorneys neither care to understand nor defend Christian Common Law, nor that which they have sworn a hallowed oath to uphold --- The Constitution of the United States, and therefore; this Defendant must refrain from using, nor can he be forced to use, against his will, a so-called "licensed attorney" because: "If the state should deprive a person the benefit of counsel, it would not be due process of law." Powell v. Alabama, 287 U. S. 45, 70.

And, "If this requirement of the Sixth Amendment is not complied with, the court no longer has jurisdiction to proceed." Johnson v. Zerbst, 304 U.S. 458, 468.

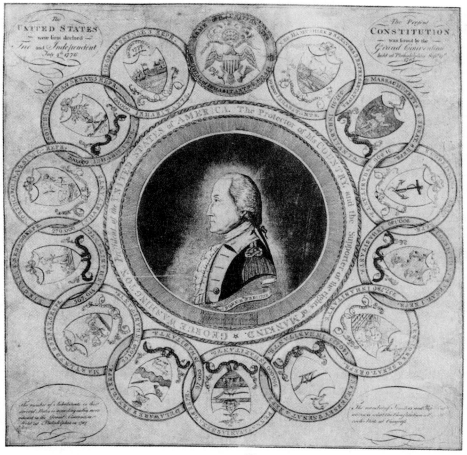

page 82

CORPUS DELICTI

A formal complaint for criminal prosecutions must, on its face, establish a corpus delicti, being 2 conditions: 1. The fact of an injury. 2. The existence of a criminal causation of that injury. Essentially, any act which is defined by a statute as a violation of the law is a crime. The statute must be a public law, and a positive law. "The criminality of the act or omission consists not in the simple perpetration of the act, or the neglect to perform it, but in its being a violation of a quasi-positive law." Schick v. U.S. 195 US 65.

Positive law is distinguished from adjective law:

"The positive law of duties and rights is commonly called Substantive Law; procedure, considered in its relation to substantive law, is called Adjective Law." Bouvier's Law Dictionary 1914.

As substantive law is the law of rights and duties, we might ask the question of Title 49, whether or not these statutes define duties and obligations. From the form of the statutes, this Defendant thinks that statutes are positive laws which define the duties of certain persons in relation to vehicular traffic on the public property. The violation of these statutes, then consists in doing the act prohibited or omitting to do that which is required.

This Defendant has been charged with such omissions, as violations of codes which require certain performance. The nature of the offenses charged being nonfeasance, one would assume that the accused was required by law to do or perform certain conditions or acts. Nonfeasance, in Black's 5th Ed., is: "Nonperformance of some act which ought to be performed, omission to perform a required duty at all, or total neglect of duty." 360 Mass. 591. However, this is the question before the court in this case; is the Defendant subject to the statutes under which he was charged? If the Defendant is not subject to the statutes then the Plaintiff has failed to state a claim upon which relief can be granted, that is, the case stated by the Plaintiff is not sufficient to support a criminal conviction. "There can be no constructive offenses, and before a man can be punished, his case must be plainly and unmistakably within the statute." U.S. v. Lacher 134 US 624. The contention is that if this Defendant had entered into a regulated enterprise or industry, then he would be subject to the duties and obligations, taxes and police powers, etc. which the legislature has defined by statute concerning those businesses. However, such is not the circumstance of this case, as the Affidavit of Defense shows. As this Defendant is not subject to the summary proceedings held in court, all rights at law are demanded as part of the defense.

INTENT

The formal complaint must allege 2 elements of any crime, to be valid and sustain a case. Idaho Code 18-114: Union of Act and Intent -- In every crime or public offense there must exist a union, or joint operation, of act and intent, or criminal negligence. The "tickets" in this case do not allege intent. A fact to be considered by the court is that the Uniform Citations were intended only for charging violations of Title 49, the Traffic Code, by licensed drivers, or those who are required to be licensed. They are not formal complaints, but simply citations for the inferior "offenses" tried in traffic courts. The driver's license is, at least, evidence of intent, for the purposes of the proceedings in this Court. The question asked by the traffic cop is for the license of the driver. This information is then transferred to the "ticket" and becomes part of the evidence before the Court. This is the proof of jurisdiction, being the evidence of the consent of the driver to be regulated by the Code. Therefore, no intent need be proved, and the Defendant cannot raise this to issue. Perhaps licensed drivers have lost a right to have a presumption of good intent. But such is not the case at bar.

DUTY

This Defendant has not performed the duty as required by I. C. 49-307, 49-245, & 49-116, because he could see no lawful requirement therein, as upon his status and circumstance. Plainly stated, the Defendant's position is that only certain persons are, or can be, required to perform or conform to these statutory mandates and prohibitions. An incomplete list is: Corporations conducting business upon the public highways. Franchised persons carrying on occupations not of common right, by vehicular traffic. Natural persons holding themselves out to the public for hire as common carriers, providing services in which the public has an interest. All persons, who for various reasons, are affected with a public interest, and thereby fall under both the police power and the taxing power of the state. The Defendant contends that Title 49, and specifically chapters 1, 2, & 3, are both regulations and taxation of the above "persons", or businesses. The Defendant also contends that the Affidavit of Defense shows that the Defendant is not within the class of subjects of this legislation, and therefore cannot be convicted in this Court.

BURDEN OF PROOF

As corporations, or business, have no conscience or good will, then intent is certainly not at issue in cases brought for violations of the laws prescribing their duties and burdens. This is probably the reason that prosecuting attorneys need not prove intent in traffic cases. But, in the status as a lawful man, no intended evil, nor injury by the Defendant's acts, becomes a presumption of innocence which the state must overcome in its presentation of the case, or else the state fails to establish a prima facie case. "Whether criminal intent is a necessary element of the statutory offense is matter of construction to be determined by the language of the statute in view of its manifest purpose and design." State v. Sterrett 35 Id. 580. The purpose of these statutes is vague, and for the Court to define, in light of the nature of this case. While certain persons may be convicted with no proof of intent, it is a matter of right in this case, which the legislature could not destroy. No attempt is yet made to offer evidence of criminal intent. Therefore, an essential element of the crime has been left out of the "complaint". The "tickets" fail as complaint.

DEMURRER

The Defendant has demurred to this action, and sees no reason why he should be cited to appear in this Court of inferior jurisdiction. The "tickets" which are treated as complaints in this Court, are insufficient upon their faces. The Defendant is pleading the facts by Affidavit, to show not only his status and subsequent right to due process of law, but also the failing of the Plaintiff to show that the Defendant is subject to Title 49, Chapters 1, 2, & 3, specifically the Statutes listed on the ticket(s), by failing to set forth sufficient circumstances surrounding this case.

SUMMARY PROCESS

There should be no question that the proceeding in the traffic court is a summary proceeding established by the legislature. These facts substantiate this premise: The lack of a 12 man jury, as required by the common law.

The lack of a formal complaint to initiate the action. The usual practice of proving only the act or omission, evidence of intent. The equity nature of the case; there being no common law offense alleged. The case actually amounts to nothing more than an infraction of commercial code. A summary proceeding is: "A form of trial in which the ancient established course of legal proceedings is disregarded, especially in the matter of trial by jury." Jones v. Robbins 8 Gray (Mass) 329. However, this Defendant demands the right to due process of law, in all courts to which he may be cited or summoned, and that: ". . . applies conformity with the ancient and customary laws of the English people or laws indicated by Parliament." Davidson v. New Orleans 96 US

97. This means conformity with the common law. "In no case can the party be tried summarily unless when such proceedings are authorized by legislative authority, except perhaps in cases of contempt; for the common law is a stranger to such mode of trial." 4 Bla. Com. 280. (Bouvier's Law Dictionary 1914.)

JURISDICTION

The Defendant further contends that at no time has he set foot outside of the common law jurisdiction of the State. It is not known where or when the State could have gained a claim upon the Defendant's activities or property, and could thereby subject him to a jurisdiction based on regulatory law. In other words, how could this Defendant become affected with a public interest. The equity nature of this case is perhaps fitting and proper for juristic or artificial persons, for requiring them to perform duties prescribed by statute, and inflicting punishments by fines, etc., for violations of these laws. But the entire case fails to support a conviction of this citizen for all the reasons mentioned. The right to due process is demanded. Due process of law is not necessarily satisfied by any process which the legislature may prescribe. See Abrams v. Jones 35 Idaho 532, 207 P. 724. "No change in ancient procedure can be made which disrupts those fundamental principles . . . which . . . protect the citizen in his private right and guard him against the arbitrary action of the government." Ex Parte Young 209 US 123. As shown above, the process in the traffic courts is less than due process, to which the Defendant is entitled. This is a matter of jurisdiction. Asserted as a matter of right, is a demurrer to this action, for the purpose of inquiring of the Court as to the nature of this case, the purpose or constraining need which the state finds as a cause of action in this case. The jurisdiction established by the legislature for this kind of case is in question as concerns this person's rights. If it could be shown that this Defendant is indeed within the statute, then the jurisdiction may be proper to hear and decide the issues and merits. The present Pleading by the Plaintiff are insufficient to grant jurisdiction to the Court. If indeed the nature of this case is equity, then it must be shown that the Defendant has voluntarily entered the jurisdiction, for equity is voluntary, not compulsory. The crime alleged here is not the injury of life, liberty or property, but the infraction of a commercial code, which action is handled in a criminal form of action. Several things stand in the way of conviction. The insufficiencies of the "complaint", the breakdown of service, the vagueness of Title 49, the Rights of the Freeman; all are issues which cry out for judicial determination, before a conviction can be had.

APPLICATION OF LAW

For example, this Defendant did not register as an alien with the U.S. Immigrations this year. Now, supposedly he could be charged with being an illegal alien and would then have to argue the facts of status and circumstances as a defense to the charge. Yet, would the prosecutor contend that he had only to prove the fact that the Defendant had failed to register? Or would the Plaintiff have to prove that the Defendant was required to do this act, by first refuting his testimony and evidence, and showing that the Defendant was "within the statute", before he could be convicted? The same process is demanded here. This issue is hereby clearly laid forth. If the Defendant is not within the statute, as contended, then it is a matter of right that the Defendant challenge the "tickets" and the jurisdiction in this manner, and objects to being rushed to judgment.

SERVICE

The record shows that the Defendant has not voluntarily appeared. The tickets were signed under duress and threat of arrest, which makes the "promise to appear" null and void. Further, the Defendant comes to Court only out of the same fear of force, violence and coercion, for the sole purpose of demanding dismissal.

NOTICE AND DEMAND FOR RIGHTS

COMES NOW the Accused, In Propria Persona appearing specially and not generally or voluntarily herein, to demand all rights under the common law based upon the status of the Accused as a matter of due process of law and to determine what legal rights the Accused has in this court and what rights will be denied, if any, to enable the Accused to determine what jurisdiction the State of Idaho is attempting to apply to this person as: "No change in ancient procedure can be made which disrupts those fundamental principles . . . which . . . protect the citizen in his private right and guard him against the arbitrary action of the government." Ex Parte Young, 209 US 123. When summoned into any court, the first thing a party must do is analyze and identify the nature of the charges, jurisdiction of the court, and the status of the Accused, to determine if the status of the Accused falls within the statute and the jurisdiction of the court. The State and the Court are obviously proceeding based upon Civil Law statutes, and therefore, are using an Admiralty/maritime/equity jurisdiction to proceed rather than the principles and modes of the common law. (See Davison v. New Orleans, 96 U.S. 97; Dartmouth College Case, 4 Wheat 518) Facts supporting this conclusion are:

I JURISDICTION

The Accused recognizes that when jurisdiction is not squarely challenged it is presumed to exist (Burks v. Lasker, 441 US 471). This includes supposed duties, liabilities, and sanctions --- attached by way of statutes --- for violations of said duties (U.S. v. Grimaud, 220 US 506). In this Court there is no meaningful opportunity to challenge jurisdiction, as the Court merely proceeds summarily. However, once jurisdiction has been challenged in the courts, it becomes the responsibility of the Plaintiff to assert and prove said jurisdiction (Hagans v. Lavine, 415 US 533, note 5), as mere good faith assertions of power and authority (jurisdiction) have been abolished. (Owens v. City of Independence, 100 SCt. 1398, 1980).

II THE STATE APPEARS AS THE PLAINTIFF AND AS A PARTY TO THE ACTION:

The state functions in two capacities: 1. In behalf of the "People of the State" in common law actions; and 2. As a person in a corporate capacity to protect and enforce its interests through summary proceedings. But the state in either capacity is still bound by the U. S. Constitution. (Martin v. Hunter's Lesses, 1 Wheat 304)

Since the Plaintiff is the "State of Idaho", it is acting in its own interest and is, therefore, the person who is allegedly complaining. The State is attempting to bring a personal action and is seeking a remedy for an alleged injury of non-existent rights, as rights only exist between moral beings. (Bouvier's Law Dictionary, 1914, p. 2960)

III PUBLIC PROSECUTOR

In order for the Court to be properly set in a common law criminal action, there must be a member of: 1. The judiciary (the judge); 2. The executive (the public prosecutor); and 3. The Accused. In this case the State is proceeding with a city official (city attorney) who is a member of the Judiciary, not an appointed member of the executive branch of state government. The functions of the city attorney are not even outlined or authorized by Code, and he is neither appointed by nor works for the executive branch of government. Therefore, this person is functioning under a statutory Civil Law jurisdiction and not under the provisions of the Common Law. The governor of the state is not discharging his duty to execute the laws of the state, by and through an appointed prosecutor. Instead, the laws of the State are being prosecuted by a municipal city (judicial) officer. Such judicial proceedings are only found in proceedings under the Civil Law.

IV CHARGE NOT BROUGHT BY COMPETENT AUTHORITY

A principle of the Common Law is that the People are the party of the action in a felonious, or public offense. Public offenses are either felonies or misdemeanors (the offense charged in this case). Misdemeanors comprehend all indictable offenses (1 Brish. Cr. L. Section 624; Bouvier's p. 2222) and, therefore, the charges must be brought forth by the People in the form of a grand jury indictment.

V ARTICLE III, SECTION 2, U. S. CONSTITUTION

The original jurisdiction in this case is with the United States Supreme Court because: 1. The State is a Party; 2. The magistrate court is operating in a jurisdiction alien to the Common Law.

VI STATE IS COMPELLING A PERFORMANCE

The State by statute is attempting to compel a performance and the city attorney and the local police are applying said statutes without having to prove whether or not the statute applies to the Accused. Due process of law is not necessarily satisfied by any process which the legislature may prescribe. See Abrams v. Jones 35 Idaho 532, 207 P. 724. "There can be no constructive offenses, and before a man can be punished, his case must be plainly and unmistakably within the statute." U.S. v. Lacher 134 US 624. An action under the common law only exists after there has been a loss or a damage, and it cannot compel a performance. The charges against the Accused are because she did not show a drivers license and display license plates. Punishing a person for not doing a thing is tantamount to compelling a person to do the thing. Therefore, the nature of the action and the kind of relief sought is compelling in nature and not an action under the common law. Under the common law a person cannot be compelled "to purchase, through a license fee or a license tax, the privilege freely granted by the Constitution" Blue Island v. Kozul, 41 N.E. 2d. 515 (As quoted in Murdock v. Pennsylvania (City of Jeanette) 319 U.S. 105, 114. In addition: "A state may not impose a charge for the enjoyment of a right granted by the Federal Constitution. Thus, it may not exact a license tax for the privilege of carrying on interstate commerce." Mc Goldrick v. Bewind-White Co., 309 U.S. 33, 56-58. "Although it may tax the property used in, or the income derived from that commerce, so long as those taxes are not discrimination." Id., p.47 As repeatedly stated, this person is not enfranchised by any state nor engaged in any form of trade, commerce, or industry that makes him subject to any licensing requirement, and therefore, travels on the rights-of-way as a matter of right and: "Where rights secured by the Constitution are involved, there can be no rule making or legislation which would abrogate them." Miranda v. Arizona, 384 U.S. 436, 491. Also see Marbury v. Madison, 1803. The power to tax is the power to destroy and this person claims that the taxing power of the state if it were to pertain to this person in this case would not only control but also suppress and/or abrogate his absolute right to personal liberty (locomotion) as: "The power to tax the exercise of a privilege is the power to control or suppress its enjoyment." Magnano Co. v. Hamilton, 292 U.S. 40, 44-45.

Since the State is attempting to control or suppress the Accused's actions by taxing through the vehicle registration program and operator's license, the state is proceeding in some kind of administrative law not the common law. This type of action is an equitable action brought on by some enfranchisement, license, or contract, which must be shown to establish jurisdiction over this person. As stated by Blackstone: "Let a man therefore be ever so abandoned in his principles, or vicious in his practice, provided he keeps his wickedness to himself, and does not offend against the rules of public decency, he is out of reach of human laws." Blackstone Commentaries, Vol I, p. 113. Since no such conditions exist in this case, no jurisdiction exists in this Court.

VII COUNSEL

The Accused demands unlicensed Counsel of choice. The right to counsel at a criminal trial is deemed so fundamental to the interests of justice that denial thereof automatically vitiates any conviction obtained (the automatic reversal rule). This is true even though there is no showing of any prejudice or unfairness in the proceedings or even any need for counsel. Gideon v. Wainright, 372 US 335. A conviction obtained where the accused was denied counsel is treated as void for all purposes. Lack of counsel of choice can be conceivably even worse than no counsel at all, or having to accept counsel beholden to one's adversary. Burgett v. Texas, 309 US 109.

The right to counsel exists not only at the trial thereof, but also at every stage of a criminal proceeding where substantial rights of an accused may be affected. Mempha v. Rhay, 389 US 128. A state or federal court which arbitrarily refuses to hear a party by counsel, denies the party a hearing and, therefore, denies him due process of law in a constitutional sense. Reynolds v. Cochran, 365 US 525.

VIII NO COMPLAINT

The state is proceeding without any formal complaint. Since no "proper plaintiff" exists who can bring the action for a violation of rights in a common law action, the state is proceeding on the face of a citation which is a proceeding under a Civil Law jurisdiction (probate or admiralty) of licenses and contracts, and which are not applicable to this natural person. The Uniform Citation "tickets" fail as complaints for the following reasons: 1. No corpus delecti is established upon the face of the "tickets". 2. No criminal intent is alleged, nor shown by apparent circumstances surrounding this case. 3. No offer of proof is made that defendant is subject to Title 49, Chapters 1, 2, & 3, and thereby subject to these summary proceedings for lesser offenses. Where no corpus delecti is shown, a conviction cannot be supported.

IX NO INTENT

The formal complaint must allege 2 elements of any crime, to be valid and sustain a case. Idaho Code 18-114: Union of Act and Intent -- "In every crime or public offense there must exist a union, or joint operation, of act and intent, or criminal negligence." The Plaintiff does not have to prove intent in this case as the only issue before the Court is whether Petitioner committed the act or not. Experience has proven that in like cases before this court, there is no presumption of innocence. Since intent will not be a matter of fact before the jury, intent must be a matter of law. Therefore, the state legislature has legislated guilt and the Court is proceeding in a summary process under the Civil Law to regulate corporations and regulated industry. (Almeida-Sanchez, 413 U.S. 266; Colonnade Catering Corp. v. United States, 397 U.S. 72; United States v. Biswell, 406 U.S. 311) Under the Common Law, "intent" is a matter of status and conduct and must be a matter of fact before the jury, and if not so, the proceedings are alien to the common law.

X COMMON LAW JURY

The Accused demands a common law struck jury of twelve of his peers. A trial by jury at the Common law consists of twelve men, neither more or less. Patton et al v. U.S., 281 US 276.

XI JURY TO DETERMINE THE LAW AS WELL AS FACTS

The Accused demands a jury that would be able to determine the law and evidence in this case as well as the facts. This is a common law right. State v. Croteau, 23 Vt 14, 54; State v. Meyer, 58 Vt 457; Appeal of Lowe, 46 Kan 255; Lynch v. State, 9 Ind 541; Hudelson v. State, 94 Ind 426;

People v. Videto, 1 Parker, Gr R. 603; Pleasant v. State, 13 Ark 360; Wohlford v. People, 45 Ill App 188; Commonwealth v. Porter, 51 Mass 263; U.S. v. Watkins, Fed Case No. 16, p. 649 (3 Cranch, C.C. 4411); 4 L.R.A. 675; Beard v. State, 71 Md 275.

XII CAUSE OF ACTION INSUFFICIENT

State has not stated a claim upon which relief can be granted. The complaint naming the State of Idaho as Plaintiff, by the word "Plaintiff" alleges a Cause of Action which is: "Matter for which an action may be brought." "A cause of action implies that there is some person in existence who can bring suit and also a person who can lawfully be sued". "When a wrong has been committed, or a breach of duty has occurred, the cause of action has accrued, although the claimant may be ignorant of it". A cause of action consists of those facts as to two or more persons entitling at least some one of them to a judicial remedy of some sort against the other, or others, for the redress or prevention of a wrong. It is essential to the existence of such facts that there should be a right to be violated and a violation thereof. In this case, no evidence or testimony can be brought before the court to establish any natural person or persons who have suffered a loss of rights and therefore, there can be no cause of action or criminal causation.

XIII MEANINGFUL HEARING

This Court has repeatedly stated on the record that it will not even read or hear any constitutional issues brought before it much less rule on such issues, therefore the Court has denied the Accused due process of law.

XIV THEORY OF THE CASE

Proceedings in the Court during trial will not allow the Accused to address issues of law nor will Petitioner be allowed to express her theory of the law and the case to the jury. The Accused is restricted by the form of the proceedings to restrict her defense solely upon the basis of whether or not she committed the acts, and substantive issues cannot be related to the jury. This clearly shows that the jury proposed by the state is not a common law jury but one operating under statutory and judicial restrictions to satisfy the conscience of the king and his court. This type of jury is prescribed in admiralty/maritime /equity jurisdictions and foreign to the common law.

CONCLUSION

In this case:
1. The Accused is a Free and natural person who has claimed all of her rights at the common law and has denied all other jurisdictions until asserted and proved.
2. The Plaintiff has brought forth charges that, in this case, are not within the jurisdiction of the court.
3. The Court is proceeding in a summary fashion and not according to the rules of procedure of the Common Law.
4. The Plaintiff and the Court are apparently conspiring to defeat the legal/civil rights of the Accused.
5. The Plaintiff and the Court are proceeding in a jurisdiction foreign to the Common law.

REMEDY SOUGHT

Since the action and the proceedings in this case do not conform to the rules and procedures of the common law, the Accused demands that the court to dismiss the charges.

DEMAND FOR PUBLIC PROSECUTOR

In 1748, Baron de la Brede Charles Louis de Second at Montesquieu published his magnum opus L'Esprit des Lois, which contained the original explanation of The Doctrine of the Separation of Powers. Here Montesquieu, a resident of France near Bordeaux, explained his idea of the ideal Constitution, from the point of view of political liberty, as that where the Legislature, the Executive, and the Judiciary are mutually independent of one another. The Fathers of our Constitution adopted the theory of Montesquieu (or what they perceived to be his theory) completely.

Hamilton stated in Number 47 of the Federalist Papers: "The accumulation of all powers, legislative, executive and judiciary, in the same hands, whether of one, a few, or many, and whether hereditary, self-appointed, or elected, may justly be pronounced the very definition of tyranny." Such strong feelings on the part of our Founding Fathers resulted in the following imperatives in our Constitution of the United States:

Article I, Section 1. All legislative powers herein granted shall be vested in a Congress of the United States of America."

Article II, Section 1. The executive Power shall be vested in a President of the United States of America."

Article III, Section 1. The judicial Power of the United States shall be vested in one supreme Court, and such inferior Courts as the Congress may from time to time ordain and establish."

These grants of power clearly and unequivocally ordain that the powers granted are to be divided into three departments and that no one department shall exercise the powers of any of the others. The Founding Fathers of the Idaho Constitution followed the lead of the Federal Constitution when they wrote the Constitution for the State of Idaho. The Idaho Constitution contains the following provisions:

Article II, Section 1. The powers of the government of this state are divided into three distinct departments, the legislative, executive and judicial; and no person or collection of persons charged with the exercise of powers properly belonging to one of these departments shall exercise any powers properly belonging to either of the others, except as in this constitution expressly directed or permitted."

Article III, Section 1. The legislative power of the state shall be vested in a senate and house of representatives."

Article IV, Section 5. The supreme executive power of the state is vested in the governor, who shall see that the laws are faithfully executed."

Article V, Section 2. The judicial power of the state shall be vested in a court for the trial of impeachments, a Supreme Court, district courts, and such other courts inferior to the Supreme Court as established by the legislature." Here again, we have the same separation of powers as is mandated by the Constitution of the United States and as envisioned by Montesquieu. If anything, they are more firmly stated and restated in the Idaho Constitution than in the Federal Constitution.

Each branch of government, then, has its separate functions, of which neither of the other two branches may infringe upon. The functions of the executive branch may be determined by looking at the meaning of the word executive: "Executive, a. Having the quality of executing or performing; as executive power or authority; an executive officer. Hence in government, executive is used in distinction from legislative and judicial. The body that deliberated and enacts laws, is legislative; the body that judges or applies laws to particular cases, is judicial; the body or person who carries the law into effect, or superintends the enforcement of them is executive." Webster's New Twentieth Century Dictionary of the English Language, unabridged. Thus it can be seen that the manner in which our government is intended to operate is for the Legislature to make the laws, the Executive Department, under the supervision of the Governor, to execute the laws, and the Judicial Department to apply the law to particular cases and act as referee and Judge between contending parties.

PUBLIC PROSECUTORS

The execution of the laws include administering the laws and enforcing them by prosecuting those who do not comply with them. In order for the Governor to have the power to prosecute those who fail to comply with the laws passed by the Legislature, the prosecutors must be under his supervision and therefore, prosecutors must be appointed by him. He must have the power to remove them from office if they fail to do his bidding and he cannot do so unless they fill an appointed office.

Article IV, Section 5 of the Idaho Constitution requires the Governor to "see that the laws are faithfully executed," a requirement he cannot fulfill without power over those who prosecute violators of law. Article 1, Section 8 of the Idaho Constitution uses the words "public prosecutor" twice within that section. Therefore, our Founding Fathers understood that a Natural Person was entitled to be prosecuted by a member of the Executive Branch of government --- a "public prosecutor." This is supported by the definition of the word "prosecutor": Prosecutor: "The public prosecutor is an officer appointed by the government to prosecute all offenses: he is the attorney general or his deputy." (emphasis added) Bouvier's Law Dictionary, 1914, page 2753. Interestingly enough, the words "prosecuting attorney" do not even exist in the law dictionaries of those times. The Mandate of Article IV, Section 5, is clear and the Governor is raped of his responsibility and power if he cannot appoint and supervise those who prosecute violators of the laws of the state. The Governor simply cannot perform the duties of his office. He has absolutely no power to discharge his duties as the system is now functioning. He cannot see that the laws are faithfully executed which is the clear mandate of Article IV, Section 5 of the Idaho Constitution. In reality, the Governor is refusing to either accept or carry out his responsibility as he has the power to appoint persons to positions required for him to execute his duties of office. The rule of the Common Law doctrine applies which states that when the Constitution mandates a duty, the Common Law provides the means to carry out that duty. In order for there to be a proper prosecution, At Law, the Governor must appoint public prosecutors who are under his supervision.

PROSECUTING ATTORNEYS

Prosecuting Attorneys exist as a result of Article V, Section 18 of the Idaho Constitution which reads as follows: "Sec. 18. -- A prosecuting attorney shall be elected for each organized county in the state, by the qualified electors of such county, and shall hold office for a term of two years, and shall perform such duties as may be prescribed by law; . . . . " Since the existence of the Prosecuting Attorney is authorized in Article V of the Constitution which is headed "Judicial Department", the Prosecuting Attorney is a member of the Judicial Department and has been held to be so by the Idaho Supreme Court. See State v. Wharfield 41 Id. 14., 236 Pac. 862. According to Article V, Section 18 of the Constitution, the Legislature has the responsibility of assigning the duties of the Prosecuting Attorney. They have done so in Section 31-2604 of the Idaho Code. Among the duties assigned are the prosecution of all cases, criminal and civil, to District or Magistrate Courts in which "The People", the State, or County are a party or have an interest. Therefore, the situation now exists in the court room where a Defendant is not only being prosecuted by a member of the Judicial Department but also being judged and sentenced by a member of that same Judiciary Department. This situation is contrary to The Doctrine of the Separation of Powers and strongly resembles the Star Chamber proceedings in England of old. When Prosecuting Attorneys prosecute a criminal case, they not only violate the State Constitution by usurping duties properly belonging to the Executive Branch, but also violate the Doctrine of the Separation of Powers.

COUNTY OFFICERS

There are other problems with Prosecuting Attorneys representing the County and the State in criminal matters. The Constitution of the State of Idaho provides in Article XVIII, Section 6 for the election of specific County officers. "The legislature by general and uniform laws, shall, commencing with the general election in 1970, provide for the election biennially, in each of the several counties of the state, of county commissioners, and a coroner and for the election of a sheriff, county assessor and a county treasurer, who is ex-officio public administrator, every four years in each of the several counties of the state. All taxes shall be collected by the officer or officers designated by law. The clerk of the district court shall be ex-officio auditor and recorder. No other county offices shall be established, ..." (Emphasis added.) It can be seen that the Constitution clearly states that "no other county offices shall be established" and the office of Prosecuting Attorney is not listed. However, the Idaho Code states: "31-2001. County officers enumerated. -- The officers of a county are:

1. A Sheriff.
2. A Clerk of the District Court, who shall be ex-officio Auditor and Recorder, and ex-officio Clerk of the Board of County Commissioners.
3. An Assessor.
4. A Probate Judge.
5. A Prosecuting Attorney.
6. A County Treasurer, who shall be ex-officio Public Administrator and ex-officio Tax Collector.
7. A Coroner.
8. Three (3) members of the Board of County Commissioners.

The Legislature has clearly decreed by legislative fiat that the Prosecuting Attorney is a county officer. The Legislature has not only violated the Constitution (Article XVIII, Section 6) in designating the Prosecuting Attorney as an officer of the county, but also by designating the Magistrate (Probate Judge) as a county officer.

The salary of the Prosecuting Attorney is determined by the Legislature and is paid by the county, presumably because the Prosecuting Attorneys are by statute county officers. However, even though they are Judicial Officers of the State pursuant to Art. 5, Sec. 18, their salaries are budgeted and paid by the county, not the State. The salary of a Magistrate, in contrast, is budgeted and paid by the State though the Judicial Department not by the county. The inconsistency is striking. It is the sworn duty of judges to uphold the Constitution and whenever a conflict exists between statute and Constitution rights, it is their duty to rule in favor of Constitutional rights. It is also the sworn duty of the Prosecuting Attorney to uphold the Constitution and therefore the Prosecuting Attorney must withdraw from all criminal cases against Natural Persons as he is not a member of the Executive Branch of government.

CITY ATTORNEYS

City attorneys have even less standing as a member of the Executive Branch of government than a Prosecuting Attorney. They are, in fact, simply officials of a municipal corporation acting in behalf of that corporation. Since they are members of a municipal corporation and not members of the Executive Branch of government, they can have no standing in the courts in criminal cases against Natural Persons. Power granted municipal corporations are expressly granted in Idaho Code, Title 50, Chapter 3. Corporate and local self-government powers are: "Cities governed by this act shall be bodies corporate and politic; may sue and be sued;..." IC 50-301. Nowhere in this statute is there a provision giving capacity to the City to act in the behalf of the "State of Idaho" in criminal cases. The wording "sue and be sued" obviously gives the city the capacity to appear in court in civil matters in behalf of the city but that cannot be construed to provide capacity to appear in behalf of the state. The city in enforcing its ordinances and regulations against its subjects (commerce, trade, and industry) should be civil and then the city would have standing in the courts. The city does have a police force which has been granted statutory authority to enforce the laws of the state. City policemen have the authority to arrest but this does not provide any power to the city to prosecute in the name of the state. Criminal prosecutions must be on behalf of the "People of the State" and since the city is merely a municipal corporation within a county it cannot possess Executive Powers of the state. Therefore, the city cannot represent the "People of the State" in court.

REPUBLICAN FORM OF GOVERNMENT

It would appear that Idaho does not provide its citizens a republican form of government as: 1. The Governor has abrogated his Constitutionally mandated duty to "see that the laws are faithfully executed." 2. The legislature has exceeded its Constitutional authority by assigning executive duties to members of the Judicial Department of government. There is also the question of the "party of interest". Is the State of Idaho the party of interest in criminal actions? However, this is not pertinent to this brief, and will be raised at a future time. The State government as it currently exists and functions, appears to be strong evidence of an intention to defraud the citizens of a lawful form of republican government and perhaps there is an ongoing conspiracy causing the Rights of the Accused to be violated.

CONCLUSION

Therefore, neither the prosecuting attorneys nor the City Attorneys have authorization to appear in court to represent the State in the capacity of prosecutors of public offenses in the criminal forms. Such a practice, even if provided for by statute, is a bold violation of the Separation of Powers doctrine, and is a tyrannical abridgment of the provisions of the Idaho Constitution concerning due process of law and separation of powers. The Defendant's rights to constitutional government are not secured in this court due to these fallacious practices. The prosecuting attorney is at best an imposter of the officer who should be in the Plaintiff's chair. The City attorney is therefore an imposter of an imposter.

THEREFORE, the Accused moves the Court to not allow any person to represent the People of Idaho in this case other than a duly appointed member of the Executive Branch of government. The Court should not allow the proceedings to move forward with an agent of the judiciary/city/county who is falsely representing the State in this criminal action against a Natural Person before the bar.

BRIEF ON DRIVER'S LICENSE
AS EVIDENCE OF CONSENT

There can be no jurisdiction in any summary proceeding unless there is consent from the party being moved against. The traffic courts provide nothing more than summary proceedings, there being no due process nor equal protection under the law afforded the Accused except where convenient for the court to do so. The only way any summary process can proceed without due process is when there is some sort of a contract, agreement, or implied consent allowing jurisdiction between two consenting parties.

This was admitted in the Molko case where the opinion of the court states: "...assumed a legal identity other than "freeman" when she availed herself of the privilege of driving on public thoroughfares. Having availed herself of that privilege, she does, indeed, have the duty to specifically perform in accordance with the laws of the state." Cynthia L. Molko v. Milton Birnbaum, L-35855, Decision on Motion for Preliminary Injunction, dated May 27, 1982, in the Third District Court in Canyon County. Driving is a privilege to an artificial person and its employees when conducting trade, commerce, or industry upon the public roadways. However, no privilege exists for a natural person as all natural persons have the inalienable right to personal liberty, which includes the right of locomotion. This is fully explained in the brief entitled "Rights." The issue of "Rights" verses "privilege" is covered in that brief and need not be duplicated herein. It is sufficient to say that no citizen can give up a right for a privilege. "Assuming a legal identity" other than freeman is a voluntary act, or the consent of entering into another capacity of contract requiring a specific performance in some form which is regulatable by the legislature, and evidence of that voluntary act must exist. Any time there is a specific performance there must also be a contract or agreement between the parties involved. Specific performance is defined as: "The actual performance of a contract by the party bound to fulfill it." Bouvier's Law Dictionary, 1914 Any contract requiring specific performance must consist of three things:

1. Perquisite that the contract be founded upon a valuable consideration.
2. Mutual enforcement of the contract must be practicable.
3. Enforcement in specie must be necessary, really important to the plaintiff, and not oppressive to the defendant; and specific performance will not be decreed if it would cause a harsh result, be inequitable, or be contrary to good conscience.

Disregarding 1 and 3, where is the mutual consent for enforcement of any specific performance? Where is the evidence of any contract, express or implied? There can be no consent where there is no proof of contract, and without a contract there can be no mutual consent. Referring again to the Molko case the judge would have us believe that natural citizens: "...have the duty to specifically perform in accordance with the laws of the state."

From this statement it erroneously follows that duties are prescribed by law and that the laws of the state comprise a contract between the state and all persons, natural and artificial. It cannot be disputed that the legislature can pass laws or regulations pertaining to the operation of business and commerce affecting public interest. Any business affected with a public interest can and should be regulated, and the state can lay out the conditions of doing business as following Motor vehicle regulations in the contract of incorporation, which includes obeying all statutes of the state to include the requiring a drivers license for commercial ventures upon the public roadways. However, the natural person cannot be bound by mere statute or the will of the legislature, but is bound by a higher law, that being the "law of the land." A natural person is a sovereign citizen and cannot involuntarily enter upon an "assumed..legal identity" nor can the state compel, by statute, a specific performance from a natural person who has not entered it's authority. A natural person is a Citizen (see brief on "Status"), not bound by contract and, therefore, cannot be required to perform specifically.

The legislature cannot legislate demands upon a citizen forcing, under threat of a criminal action, the carrying or producing of documents nor a specific performance by what is referred to as implied consent legislation as: "....no consent can be given which will deprive the consenter of any inalienable rights." A & E. Encyc; Desty, Cr. L. Section 33.

However, "A central difference between those cases and this one is that businessmen engaged in such federally licensed and regulated enterprises accept the burdens as well as the benefits of their trade, whereas the petitioner here was not engaged in any regulated or licensed business. The businessmen in a regulated industry in effect consents to the restrictions placed upon him." (emphasis added) Almeida-Sanchez v. United States, 413 US 266, 271.

There was no doubt that Sanchez was guilty of hauling marihuana in violation of Federal Code but was stopped and searched without probable cause by law enforcement officers. The U.S., in attempting to support the illegal search, referred to two other cases where the high court had ruled that searches could be made without a warrant. However the court quickly pointed out that in the Sanchez case, he was not in a regulated enterprise nor licensed which would automatically waive his constitutional rights. The Supreme Court, then, has ruled that if Sanchez had been licensed or in a regulated business, the stop and search would have been legal, but since he was not so regulated the stop and search was unconstitutional.

Businesses operating on the public "rights" of way are regulated to protect the public because artificial persons have no conscience and must be controlled through regulation. Therefore, the actions of business operating on the public rights of way are regulated through Motor Vehicle codes and they are required to purchase and carry "evidence of consent" by obtaining licenses. It is well established that the participation in a regulated enterprise, by and through a license, constitutes voluntary consent to regulatory restrictions. The rule is: "There are certain 'relatively unique circumstances'...in which consent to regulatory restrictions is presumptively concurrent with participation in regulated enterprise. See United States v. Biswell, 406 U.S. 311...; Colonnade Catering Corp. v. United States, 397 U.S. 72." (emphasis added) Delaware v. Prouse, 440 U.S. 648, 662. Circumstances are evidences, or more specifically, "evidence of consent" and/or participation in a regulated enterprise.

In the above cases the consent of Biswell and Colonnade was in the license they applied for which allowed them to operate a regulated enterprise. In addition, both were creations of the state and required to abide by the statutes of the states. And one of those statutes is that juristic organizations obtain a driver's/chauffeur's license. The license to drive, then, is a privilege to any juristic person and is prima facia evidence of a regulated enterprise and its state granted privilege to operate motor vehicles on the public rights of way. The drivers/chauffeur's license is the evidence of concurrent consent of a regulated enterprise that it will enter summary proceedings (traffic courts) established by its master (the state) and abide by its regulatory restrictions (Motor vehicle codes). The Supreme Court has ruled that:

"Each licensee is annually furnished with a revised compilation of ordinances that describe his obligation and define the inspector's authority...the dealer is not left to wonder about the purposes of the inspector or the limits of his task." (emphasis added) United States v. Biswell, 406 US 312, 316

The licensee being any person engaged in a regulated enterprise; ordinances being motor vehicle codes; inspector's being the king's agents (city, county, and state police officers); and the dealer being the licensee. A driver's/chauffeur's license then, is nothing more than "evidence of consent" obtained by the licensee establishing that that person is involved in a regulated enterprise.

It could be presumed that a natural person may voluntarily give consent to a privilege through the obtaining of a driver's license, thereby waiving a right to drive on the public rights of way, but that argument is well refuted in the brief entitled "License" and will not be further elaborated upon in this brief. A free and natural citizen drives as a matter of right and cannot be compelled into any foreign or alien jurisdiction or any other summary proceeding.

Even if a natural person were subject to a summary proceeding the complaint fails as there are insufficient facts to form a complaint. There must be the "unique circumstances" of "consent", or the "participation in the regulated enterprise." Therefore, the Plaintiff would have to establish that the accused is either a corporation or a business licensed by the state to conduct business or a regulated enterprise which has consented to regulatory restrictions". The prima facia evidence of these unique circumstances would be the incorporation papers or a driver's/chauffeur's license.

Those natural persons who do not obtain a driver's/ chauffeur's license have not consented to regulatory restrictions nor are they engaged in a regulated enterprise, until proven to the contrary by the Plaintiff.

In every case of a traffic violation the first thing the Plaintiff should establish at the alleged scene of the crime or prior to arraignment is whether or nor the person is natural or artificial, and if natural, whether or nor that person is a person operating on the Public rights of way in a regulated enterprise or licensed, or subject to regulatory restrictions.

The Plaintiff never attempted to establish whether this Accused person was or was not a person required to apply for and obtain a driver's license and otherwise specifically perform under the provisions of motor vehicle codes. Therefore, it was not established that the Accused is a person subject to regulation under motor vehicle codes and, therefore, the complaint fails and the case must be dismissed. This person is a natural person operates a vehicle as a matter of Right and was/is not engaged in any regulatory enterprise or commercial venture on the public roadways and therefore, can only be regulated by his own conscience being fully responsible for any loss, damage, or injury to another person's life, liberty, and property as a result of her actions.

Therefore, the proceedings against this person were without merit, as the Plaintiff did not prove that the Accused was a person subject to the code and since the Plaintiff cannot establish that this person is a person subject to the code the Court has no jurisdiction to proceed against me and the case should be dismissed.

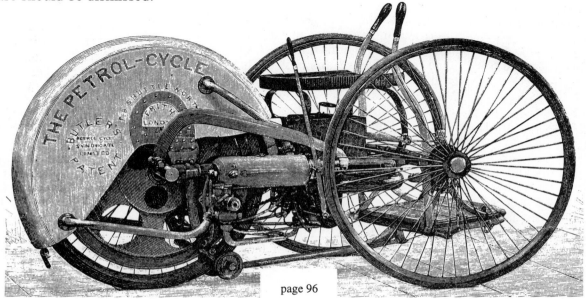

DEMAND FOR JURY OF 12

The details of the origins of the Common Law Jury are lost in the mists of antiquity, Blackstone, 4 Commentaries 365, quotes Cokes who stated: 'Pausanias relates, that at the trial of Mars, for murder, in the court denominated Areopagus from that incident, he was acquitted by a jury composed of twelve pagan deities, and Dr. Hickes, who attributes the introduction of this number to the Normans, tells us that among the inhabitants of Norway, from whom the Normans as well as the Danes were descended, a great veneration was paid to the number twelve: 'nihil sanctius, nihil antiqwuis fuit; ac in ipso hoc numero secreta quaedomm esset religio.' Even before there is a record of the jury system in England, the tribes of Northern Europe had developed traditions which formed the foundations of the Common Law jury system. In Normandy, before the conquest of England by the Normans, the trial by Jury of twelve men was the usual trial among the Normans in most suits, especially in assizes, et juris uturm." 1 Hale's History of the Common Law, 218, 219. Crabbe said: "It cannot be denied that the practice of submitting causes to the decision of twelve men was universal among all the northern tribes (of Europe) from the very remotest antiquity." Crabbe's History of the English Law, p. 32. Also, a Professor Scott wrote: "At the beginning of the thirteenth century twelve was indeed the usual but not the invariable number. But by the middle of the fourteenth century the requirement of twelve had probably become definitely fixed. Indeed this number finally came to be regarded with something like superstitious reverence." A. Scott, Fundamentals of Procedure in Actions at Law, 75-76 (1922) Ranulph De Glanville, writing in the twelfth Century, stated: "By means of such Writs, the Tenant may protect him self, and may put himself upon the Assise, until his Adversary, appearing in Court, pray another Writ, in order that four lawful Knights of the County, and of the Vicinage, who should say, upon their oaths, which of the litigating parties, have the greater right to the land in question. "The Election of the twelve Knights having been made, they should be summoned to appear in Court, prepared upon their oaths to declare, which of them, namely,whether the Tenant, or the Demandant, posses the greater right to the property in question. "When the Assie proceeds to make the Recognition, the right will be well known either to all jurors, or some may know it, and some not, or all may be alike ignorant concerning it. If none of them are acquainted with the truth of the matter, and this be testified upon their oaths in Court, recourse must be had to others, until such can be found who do know of the truth of it.

Should it, however, happen that some of them know the truth of the matter, and some not, the latter are to be rejected and others summoned to Court, until twelve, at least, can be found who are unanimous."

The Magna Carta, signed by King John of England in June, 1215, contains the following sentence: "Nullus liber homo capiatur, vel imprisonetur, aut utlagetur, aut exuletur aut alique modo destrvatur; nec super eum ibimus, nec super eum mittemus, nisi per legale judicium parium suorum, vel per legem terrae." One translation of this passage is by Lysander Spooner in his book entitled, "An Essay on the Trial by Jury," published in Boston by John P. Jewett & Company in 1852, and reads as follows: "No freeman shall be arrested, or imprisoned, or deprived of his freehold, or his liberties, or free customs, or be outlawed, or exiled, or in any manner destroyed, nor will we proceed against him, nor send anyone against him, by force or arms, unless according to the sentence of his peers, and of the Common Law of England. There is some disagreement as to the translation of "vel" in the last phrase of the quotation. However, Justice Black (concurring) in Duncan v. Louisiana, 391 U. S. 169, agrees with the translation by Spooner. Black translated the passage as follows: "No freeman shall be taken, outlawed, banished or in any way destroyed, nor will we proceed against or prosecute him, except by the lawful judgement of his peers and by the law of the land." The phrase, "according to the sentence of his peers," or according to Justice Black's, "except by the lawful judgement of his peers," refers to the Common Law jury of the time who were authorized and impaneled to try and sentence a freeman. Magna Carta does not specify the number of men who were to comprise a jury. This is certainly understandable, because at the time of the Magna Carta, the fact that a jury was composed of twelve men was so firmly embedded in English tradition that it was not necessary to specify the size of a Common Law jury.

Magna Carta was ratified again by Henry III, in 1216, and again several times later. These re-ratifications of the Magna Carta, in essentially an unchanged form, were continued by Henry's successors for at least two hundred years. Coke stated: "....And it seemth to me, that the law in this case delighteth herself in the number of twelve; for there must not only be twelve jurors for the matters of fact, but twelve judges of ancient time for trial of matters of law in the exchequer chamber. Also for matters of state there were in ancient time twelve counsellors of state. He that wageth his law must have eleven others with him, which think he says true. And that number of twelve is much respected in holy writ, as twelve apostles, twelve stones, twelve tribes, etc. "He that is of a jury must be a liber homo, that is, not only a freeman and not bond, but also one that hath such freedom of mind as he stands indifferent as he stands unsworn. Secondly, he must be legalis. And by law, every jurorer that is returned for the trial of any issue or cause, ought to have three properties. "First, he ought to be dwelling most near to the place where the question is moved. "Secondly, he ought to be most sufficient both for understanding, and competency of estate. "Thirdly, he ought to be least suspicious, that is, to be indifferent as he stands unsworn: and then he is accounted in law liber et legalis homo; otherwise he may be challenged, and not suffered to be sworn." 3 Coke's Institutes by Thomas, 459 In regard to civil juries, Blackstone stated: "Then therefore on issue is joined, by these words, 'and this the said A. prays may be inquired of by the country,' or 'and of this he puts himself upon the country,---and the said B. does the like,' the court awards a writ of venire facias upon the role or record, commanding the sheriff 'that the cause to come here on such a day, twelve free and lawful men, libros et legales homines, of the body of his country, by whom the truth of the matter may be better known, and who are neither of kin to the aforesaid A., nor the Aforesaid B., to recognize the truth of the issue between the parties." Blackstone 3 Commentaries 351.

In regard to criminal actions, he stated: "The antiquity and excellence of this trial for the settling of civil property, has before been explained at large. And it will hold much stronger in criminal cases;..." Blackstone, supra.

The first Continental Congress, in the Declaration of Rights adopted October 14, 1774, resolved unanimously: "That the respective colonies are entitled to the Common Law of England, and more specifically to the great and inestimable privilege of being tried by their peers of the vicinage, according to the course of that law." 1 Journals of Congress 28. In the historic case of Thompson v. Utah, the United States Supreme Court stated: "Assuming then that the provisions of the Constitution relating to trials for crimes and to criminal prosecutions apply to the Territories of the United States, the next inquiry is whether the jury referred to in the original Constitution and in the Sixth Amendment is a jury constituted, as it was at common law, of twelve persons, neither more nor less. This question must be answered in the affirmative. When Magna Carta declared that no freeman should be deprived of life, etc., 'but by the judgement of his peers or by the law of the land,' it referred to a trial by twelve jurors." In another case, the Supreme Court stated: "Trial by jury in the primary and usual sense of the term at the common law and in the American constitutions is not merely a trial by a jury of twelve men before an officer vested with authority to cause them to be empaneled, to administer oaths to them and to the constable in charge, and to enter judgement and issue execution on their verdict; but it is a trial by a jury of twelve men, in the presence and under the superintendence of a judge empowered to instruct them on the law and to advise them on the facts." Capital Traction Company v. Hof, 174 US 1. This same number has been reiterated in another case where the high court stated: "That a jury composed, as at common law, of twelve jurors was intended by the Sixth Amendment to the Federal Constitution, there can be no doubt." Maxwell v. Dow, 176 U.S. 581, 586.

Again, it said: "The constitutional requirement that 'the trial of all crimes, except in cases of impeachment, shall be by jury' means, as this court has adjudged, a trial by the historical, common law jury of twelve persons, and applies to all crimes against the United States..." Rassmussen v. United States, 197 U.S. 516, 529. And finally, they stated: "....we must first inquire what is embraced by the phrase 'trial by jury.' That it means trial by jury as understood and applied at common law, and includes all the essential elements as they were recognized in this country and England when the Constitution was adopted, is not open to question. Those elements were --- (1) that the jury should consist of twelve men, neither more or less; (2) that the trial should be in the presence and under the superintendence of a judge having power to instruct them as to the law and advise them in respect of the facts; and (3) that the verdict should be unanimous." Patton et al v. United States, 281 U.S. 276. It can be seen from the foregoing that the concept of the common law jury of twelve men has been our heritage since pre Magna Carta days. The colonists brought the concept of the common law jury to this country and it was firmly embedded in our jurisprudence at the time of our revolution. The Supreme Court of the United States has affirmed and reaffirmed the elements of the common law jury, as specified in Patton supra, so that the elements which constitute a common law jury are beyond all questions or doubt. In spite of the overwhelming evidence supporting the concept of the common law jury as outlined in Patton supra, some people have claimed that the Supreme Court has, in their decision in Williams v. Florida, 399 U.S. 78, put an end to the requirement for a twelve man jury. Nothing could be further from the truth. The Court merely ruled that the Defendant's Fourteenth Amendment rights were not violated by the Florida decision to provide a six man, rather than a twelve man jury. The question of what constitutes a common law jury was neither asked nor answered. It would be difficult to formulate a better discussion of the advantages of the common law jury than that given by Blackstone when he states: "Here therefore a competent number of sensible and upright, chosen by lot from among those of the middle rank, will be found the best investigators of truth, and the surest guardians of public justice. For the most powerful individual in the state will be cautious of committing any flagrant invasion of another's right, when he knows that the fact of his oppression must be examined and decided by twelve indifferent men, not appointed till the hour of trial; and that, when once the fact is ascertained, the law must of course redress it. This therefore preserves in the hands of the people that share which they ought to have in the administration of public justice, and prevents the encroachments of the more powerful and wealthy citizens. Every new tribunal, erected for the decision of facts, without the intervention of a jury (whether composed of justices of the peace, commissioners of the revenue, judges of a court of conscience, or any other standing magistrates), is a step towards establishing aristocracy, the most oppressive of absolute governments. "....It is, therefore, upon the whole, a duty which every man owes to his country, his friends, his posterity, and himself, to maintain to the utmost of his power this valuable constitution in all its rights; to restore it to its ancient dignity, if at all impaired by the different value of property, or otherwise deviated from its first institution; to amend it, wherever it is defective; and, above all, to guard with the most jealous circumspection against the introduction of new and arbitrary methods of trial, which, under a variety of possible pretenses, may in time imperceptibly undermine this best preservation of English liberty. "Upon these accounts, the trial by jury ever has been, and I trust ever will be, looked upon as the glory of the English law. And if it has so great an advantage over others in regulating civil property, how much must that advantage be heightened, when it is applied in criminal cases!...it is the most transcendent privilege which any subject can enjoy, or wish for, that he cannot be affected either in his property, his liberty, or his person, but by the unanimous consent of twelve of his neighbors and equals. A constitution, that I may venture to affirm has, under Providence, secured the just liberties of this nation for a long succession of ages. And therefore a celebrated French writer, who concluded, that because Rome, Sparta, and Carthage have lost their liberties, therefore those of England in time must perish, should have recollected that Rome, Sparta, and Carthage, at the time when their liberties were lost, were strangers to the trial by jury." Blackstone, supra. The Accused reminds the Court that this Free and Natural Person has never entered a plea before the Court, has not granted jurisdiction over this Person, and continually challenges the jurisdiction of the Court over the subject matter and its capability to effect a remedy in this case. In addition, if the Court fails to timely notify this person of "Rights" Sua Sponte or those declared or demanded by this Person, the Court on its own volition denies itself jurisdiction. Although the Accused denies the Court jurisdiction, the Accused readily recognizes certain powers of the Court that the Court can and does exercise whether jurisdiction is valid or not.

The Accused also recognizes that the Court will proceed regardless of proper jurisdiction and, therefore, the Accused has no other alternative but to defend against the loss of Life, Liberty, and Property. The Accused has always demanded his rights under the Constitution of the United States and the Common Law and has never waived them. The Accused, therefore, demands, as a matter of right, a common law jury of twelve men to try all issues of fact, law, evidence, and to impose sentencing in accordance with established procedures of the common law.

JURY TO DETERMINE THE LAW AS WELL AS FACTS

COMES NOW the Defendant, a free and natural person, to demand a trial by Jury which will have all its proper Common Law rights of deciding both law and fact and admissibility of evidence for the following reasons and upon the following grounds:

l. This was formerly the function, right, and duty of a Jury and any diminishment of it is a crime against the Common Law, the inherent and inalienable right of the Defendant, and a denial of justice and the fair trial by an impartial Jury guaranteed by the Sixth Amendment of the Constitution of the United States, and the Constitution of this State. 2. Defendant is entitled to the "trial per pais;" as a plea of "not guilty" was entered for him, he is entitled to, and herein demands, the trial by his country -- or the people -- rather than a trial by the government (the State) or the trial judge. The jury is the accused's instrument of relief.

SUPPORT OF DEFENDANT'S MOTION

"For more than six hundred years -- that is, since Magna Charta , in 1215 -- there has been no clearer principle of English or American constitutional law, than that, in criminal cases, it is not only the right and duty of juries to judge what are the facts, what is the law, and what was the moral intent of the accused; but that it is also their primary and paramount duty to judge of the justice of the law, and to hold all laws invalid that are, in their opinion, unjust or oppressive,and all persons guiltless in violating, or resisting the execution of, such laws. Unless such be the right and duty of jurors, it is plain that, instead of juries being a "palladium of liberty" -- a barrier against the tyranny and oppression of the government -- they are really mere tools in its hands, for carrying into executionary injustice and oppression it may desire to have executed. But for their right to judge of the law, and the justice of the law, juries would be no protection to an accused person, even as to matters of fact; for, if the government can dictate to a jury any law whatever in a criminal case, it can certainly dictate to them the laws of evidence. That is, it can dictate what evidence is admissible, and what inadmisible, and also what force or weight is to be given to the evidence admitted. And, if the government can thus dictate to a jury the laws of evidence, it can not only make it necessary for them to convict on a partial exhibition of the evidence rightfully pertaining to the case, but it can even require them to convict on any evidence whatever that it pleases to offer them. That the rights and duties of jurors must necessarily be such as are here claimed for them, will be evident when it is considered what the trial by jury is, and what is its object. "The trial by jury," then, is a "trial by the country" -- that is, by the people -- as distinguished from a trial by the government. It was anciently called "trial per pais" -- that is, "trial by the country." And now, in every criminal trial (Defendant's note: 1852) the jury are told that the accused "has, for the trial, put himself upon the country; which country you (the jury) are."

The object of this trial "by the country," or by the people, in preference to a trial by the government, is to guard against every species of oppression by the government. In order to effect this end, it is indispensable that the people, or "the country," judge of and determine their own liberties against the government; instead of the government's judging of and determining its own powers over the people. How is it possible that juries can do anything to protect the liberties of the people against the government, if they are not allowed to determine what those liberties are? Any government that is its own judge of, and determines authoritatively for the people, what are its own powers over the people, is an absolute government, of course. It has all the powers that it chooses to exercise. There is no other -- or at least no more accurate -- definition of a despotism than this. On the other hand, any people that judge of, and determine authoritatively for, the government, of course retain all the liberties they wish to enjoy. And this is freedom. At least it is freedom to them because, although it may be theoretically imperfect, it nevertheless corresponds to their highest notions of freedom. (Lysander Spooner, AN ESSAY ON THE TRIAL BY JURY, DaCapo Press, NY, NY) The true trial by Jury, which was the ancient custom of the realm, was established long before Magna Charta, but repeatedly, some Judges, ambitious and jealous of their power, from time to time take from the people, with the aid and abetting of the legislative power -- this inalienable right to be really tried by the country -- or the people! In the famous trial of John Peter Zenger in 1735, Judge Delancy attempted to tell the Jury that truth was not a defense in a criminal libel case. The famous Philadelphia lawyer, Andrew Hamilton, argued that the truth and the good motives of the accused were all important. The judge, in effect, told the Jury, "You decide if Zenger published the material (it had already been admitted) and I'll decide if it was libelous." Hamilton urged the Jury to decide the law and the fact -- which they did in acquitting Zenger -- and the case helped to establish the freedom of the press in America. (See James Alexander, A BRIEF NARRATIVE OF THE CASE AND TRIAL OF JOHN PETER ZENGER, Belknap Press) The ancient right and duty of juries , which was reestablished with Magna Charta, and which has had to be reasserted from time to time by the people with resistance or threatened resistance to the constituted authorities, is well set out in Chapter 39 of Magna Charta: "No free man shall be taken, imprisoned, disseised, outlawed, banished, or in any way destroyed, nor will we proceed against or prosecute him, except by the lawful judgement of his peers and by the law of the land." We should perhaps again then, take note of the inescapable fact, that the "Law of the Land" and "Due Process" have long been held to be synonymous (see Black's Law Dictionary) and: "The term 'due process of law' as used in the Federal Constitution, has been repeatedly declared to be the exact equivalent of the phrase, "law of the land" as used in Magna Charta. (16 Am Jur 2d Sec. 547) Of course, King John was loathe to sign Magna Charta; he was angry and claimed he would not sign that which would take his kingdom away and make him a slave. If the trial by Jury, which the Barons were demanding, meant that the King's government could continue to dictate the rules of evidence and to dictate the law, and all the Jurors could do was to accept the law as the King's court directed, and be a "fact finding group" under the manipulation of the King's court, then King John would have probably been quick to have signed Magna Charta and would have probably felt that he had really given up nothing, for he could still tax and confiscate and convict by enforcing his law and by manipulating the Jurors -- relegated to deciding the fact of, "did the accused, or did not the accused obey the tyrannical law?" So, the Defendant would ask the Court to take judicial notice of this and THINK ABOUT IT because this procedure is rampant in our lower courts today. Although there are many authorities, the Defendant chooses not to even need to cite any -- it is just too axiomatic. ANY "LAW" WHICH IS TYRANNICAL, WHICH IS AGAINST NATURAL JUSTICE, IS NOT LAW -- AND BY THE TRUE LAW OF THE LAND, NEEDN'T BE OBEYED UNLESS A JURY, JUDGING OF THE LAW, BY THEIR OWN CONSCIENCES, NOT BY THE DIRECTION OF A COURT, UNANIMOUSLY AGREE!

This is the message of Magna Charta: It is echoed in the Declaration of Independence and in the 5th, 6th, 7th, 8th, 9th, 10th, 13th, and 14th Amendments of the Federal Constitution -- not to mention the Second Amendment! This is ample evidence to prove that Juries in criminal cases today decide the law as well as the fact. This is obvious when they find a general, rather than a special verdict, but the disturbing part is that many lower court judges, in general, attempt to conceal the power -- and especially the right -- from the Jury! These judges attempt to put the Jury under oath to accept the law as They, the judges, give it to them. This is a degradation of the human personality and spirit. No human being should ever have to swear to follow the instructions and directions of another if this goes against his conscience -- his sense of right and wrong -- his sense of justice and injustice.

Just as incredible is the fact that a member of the Jury has the need to know the Law, because he cannot be held guiltless in a crime himself through ignorance of the Law. Yet, when it comes time to be able to judge the law as well as the fact, he is deemed unable to cope with such matters. In fact, the natural duty and right is simply taken away from him, regardless of what his feelings or abilities would be if all of the facts could be presented."It would be a violation of your sworn duty," says the judge, "to find according to your own sense of right and wrong, or sympathy for the accused," etc. Jurors are sometimes frightened by the judges, to think that they would be perjuring themselves if they rejected the judge's instruction as to the "law." This is an absolute disgrace, especially when the judge may be perjuring himself by neglecting and refusing to uphold his oath to support the Constitution by giving the Jury some statute which he cannot help but know is a flagrant violation of the Constitution.The judge salves his conscience by claiming that he is bound and obligated to uphold judges higher than himself. This is pure unadulterated gobble-de-goup as it is not provided for by the Constitution. Under Article VI of the Constitution, the judge is bound to support the Constitution to the best of his ability -- no matter what some other court has decided! Errors in judgement by lower court judges on matters of Constitutionality should be corrected by a higher court through the appeal process when good cause exists. The practice today, however, is to avoid ruling on the Constitutional issues, thereby denying due process to defendants who are not likely to avail themselves of the appeal process. This tends to aid prosecutors in prosecuting such defendants. Is a lower court judge who will not rule on the constitutionality of statutes any more qualified to sit in judgement of a defendant than the jurors who are constitutionally empowered to veto laws which they feel are detrimental to themselves? A judge should be a referee -- not a prosecutor!

This Defendant points out that NO court has proper jurisdiction over the Defendant's person or the subject matter if the Court thinks it has a higher duty to uphold another court than it does to follow the guidelines of conscience in supporting the Constitution of the United States! The following are some citations and references demonstrating that at the time of the birth of this Republic, corrections of abuses in the Common Law, as practiced in England and in the colonies, had again restricted the power of judges and restored the power of the People, as the supreme sovereign -- as the principle legislature -- to speak through their Juries -- with an absolute veto power over the courts, the legislature, and the President! In other words, the Jury could not pass legislation, but they could veto it in that case by the simple expedient of refusing to find against the accused and refusing to apply an unjust or harsh law -- and they knew it and were advised of it. AND THEY ARE ENTITLED TO KNOW IT -- AND BE ADVISED OF IT TODAY!!! Thus the Defendant does so demand of this Court today.

"Nevertheless the historical tradition is that in the course of this controversy William Cushing (Defendant's note: The same Cushing who was Associate Justice of the Supreme Court, and who was united with Jay, Blair, Wilson, and Patterson in the Jury charge in Georgia v. Brailsford, infra), decided that the clause in the 1770 Massachusetts Constitution that declared that "all men free and equal" was, in effect, the equivalent of abolishing slavery in Massachusetts. As Cushing points out, the law in Massachusetts at this time was stated by the jury and not in opinions of the court." (Article on William Cushing by Herbert Alan Johnson, in Friedman & Israel's Vol. I, THE JUSTICES OF THE UNITED STATES SUPREME COURT, 1789-1969, Chelsea House Publishers, N.Y.) (emphasis added) The following provision is Section 5 of the Constitution of Maryland, of 1776. Similar phrases are found in other states' constitutions. The phrase is implicit that not even legislators who pass statutes which are upheld by courts can make them binding upon the people without the consent of the "country," or of the "people" speaking through their Juries:"The doctrine of non-resistance, against arbitrary power and oppression, is absurd, slavish, and destructive of the good and happiness of mankind." (Maryland Constitution, Section 5, 1776) Since the Supreme Court has held that "Due Process means the 'Law of the Land' of Magna Charta -- and since that meant that a Jury could veto any "law" -- a meaning becomes quite apparent 63 years later in the Constitution of Kentucky of 1850 wherein it states: "That the ancient mode of trial by jury shall be held sacred, and the right thereof remain inviolate, subject to such modifications as may be authorized by this Constitution." (Section 8) The "ancient mode of trial by jury" was the mode where the unanimous consent of 12 peers was needed before the government could punish, exile, banish, fine, forfeit, seize, or in any way proceed against an accused.

It is stated clearly in Chapter 39, Magna Charta. Anything less than this would not have been, and was not, acceptable at Runnymede. Does anyone think the Barons would have risked their lives to have a King continue to control his own courts enforcing his own laws with his own judges' controlling instruction to Juries and the admissibility of evidence? Does anyone think that our revolutionary Forefathers risked their "lives, fortunes, and sacred honor," fighting with frozen bleeding feet in the snow for the right to trials by government wherein government could control instructions to Juries; control interpretation of statutes; control the evidence; and control the selecting of Jurors, and then make the jury swear to uphold as "Law" that which was dictated to them by a judge?My patriotic champions and heroes did not risk their everything for such a "thank you for nothing" privilege. The colonists fought, bled, and died for independent Juries who could think and act for themselves -- bound only to their consciences to do justice -- and if that meant refusing to impose an unjust government law -- that was exactly what the colonists wanted! And that's exactly what the Defendant is demanding.The colonists knew that representative government would not solve their problems -- they knew that government is always the enemy of liberty, and that it must be watched with suspicion and diligence, and must be "bound down by the chains of the Constitution." If not, then pray tell, why did the State of Massachusetts have Juries, rather than the courts deciding the law? (Cushing, supra) Why did the Constitution of Maryland call for Juries to decide the law as well as the fact in all criminal cases? Why did the State of Idaho, in 1889, declare without any significant amendment even until today: "Right to trial by jury. --- The right to trial by jury shall remain inviolate;..." Article I, Section 7

Article II, Sec. 10, of the Colorado State Constitution in 1876 stated: "Freedom of speech and press. -- No law shall be passed impairing the freedom of speech; every person shall be free to speak, write, or publish whatever he will on any subject, being responsible for all abuse of that liberty; and in all suits and prosecutions for libel the truth thereof may be given in evidence, and the jury, under the direction of the court, SHALL DETERMINE THE LAW AND THE FACT." (Emphasis added)

Why does the Constitution of Maryland still provide that the Jury shall decide the law as well as the fact in criminal cases? Why does Wyoming? And why do nearly all of the states' constitutions (or by statement) provide that all cases of criminal libel shall be decided by the Juries -- both as to LAW and FACT? And why do some of these add, "under the direction of the court," as in other cases? Does someone mean that we have one type of Jury for libels and another type of Jury for other cases? Doesn't "direction of the court" refer to its oral charge to a Jury that they are to be told that they have the duty and right to try both law and fact? Is this the ancient mode of trial by Jury we are supposed to hold sacred and inviolate? The Constitution of Delaware of 1792 states:" And in all indictments for libels the jury may determine the facts and the law, as in other cases."

Doesn't this seem odd? In nearly every state the judiciary attempts to make the citizens think that in libel cases there is an exception to the Jury finding only the facts -- that in libel cases the judges concede that the Jury can actually find the law.

Then, pray tell, why does the citation just above say, "AS IN OTHER CASES?" Doesn't that mean this was already established procedure and it became also applicable to the libel cases? From the Mississippi Constitution's Declaration of Rights, Section 13: "....and in all prosecutions for libel the truth may be given in evidence, and the jury shall determine the law and the facts under the direction of the court; AND IF IT SHALL APPEAR TO THE JURY THAT THE MATTER CHARGED AS LIBELOUS IS TRUE, AND WAS PUBLISHED WITH GOOD MOTIVES AND FOR JUSTIFIABLE ENDS, THE PARTY SHALL BE

ACQUITTED." Here we have, again, a principle emerging which the judiciary of many jurisdictions have attempted to smother and hide that the truth is justification, that good motives, and for justifiable ends, must be seriously considered in "criminal intent." Some Judges are attempting to make Juries swear to follow the judges' lead in declaring patriotic resistance to certain tyrannical and unconstitutional statutes a violation of the law. Judges have no right to do this! They may permit the parties to argue the law and they may give their own opinion of it to the Jury, but they have no right to make a Jury think they would be violating their oath if they did not take the same view of a statute as that held by the judge -- and they do not have the right to prevent the Jury from seeing and hearing how the statute is in conflict with the Constitution. Again, Judges are referees -- not prosecutors.

In the Constitution of Delaware, of 1792, Article I, Sec. 5, we have: "...and in all indictments for libels the jury may determine the facts and the law, AS IN OTHER CASES." (Emphasis added) Juries DID decide the law as well as the fact in other than libel cases. Since the Constitution provided this, is not the Jury entitled to be told by the court that they have not only the power, but the constitutional right to decide the law in the case? I contend that the Jury must be told of the Common Law and of their right and duty to decide the law as well as the facts. I wonder who started this nonsense about a Jury being instructed that "it would be a violation of your sworn duty not to take the 'law' as it is given to you by the court in this case"? What kind of a "railroad and greased-skid" Jury trial did our forefathers risk their lives for? Surely not for the types we see before us today. "As where rights secured by the Constitution are involved, there can be no legislation or rule making which would abrogate them." Miranda vs. Arizona 384-US 491 Who, anywhere, has the right to force a man to swear to follow another's thinking as to what is proper law? Let him first honor his own oath to support the Constitution. Does it make a judge feel better who thinks he has to follow superior judges into error to force a Jury to also follow him and them into error? When the blind lead the blind they both fall into the ditch.

This Defendant will shortly show beyond all refutation that defendants had the right for juries to decide law and fact, and will also show that Juries were entitled to know and understand the same. Finally it should be highly suggestive of impropriety when courts appear to be so insulated that a defendant wants a Jury to decide the law as well as fact.

Most attorneys and judges are aghast at the very thought of juries being able to determine the law and the facts of a case; they act as if theirs, the most learned profession in the world, has been slandered by the very mention of the possibility that a jury has any right to determine the law.Before listing the citations, a sober look at a situation that has been repeating itself is in order: "The history of the present king of Great Britain is a history of repeated injuries and usurpations, all having in direct object the establishment of an absolute Tyranny over these States. To prove this, let Facts be submitted to a candid world."He has combined with others to subject us to a jurisdiction foreign to our constitution, and unacknowledged by our law; giving his Assent to their acts of pretended Legislation."For depriving us in many cases, of the benefits of Trial by Jury. "For taking away our Charters, abolishing our most valuable Laws, and altering fundamentally the Forms of our Governments. "In every stage of these Oppression We have Petitioned for Redress in the most humble terms:Our repeated Petitions have been answered only by repeated injury. A Prince, whose character is thus marked by every act which may define a Tyrant, is unfit to be the ruler of a free people..."We, therefore...." Declaration of Independence I contend that a Court that would subvert my Common Law Jury is, in fact, a prince who is unfit to be the ruler of a free people.

We can readily see from the above that the situation that faced our forefathers is not much different than that which we face today and is all the more reason that the true function of Juries to decide the law as well as the facts in criminal cases must be restored. "The common law right of the jury to determine the law as well as the facts remains unimpaired." State v. Croteau, 23 Vt

14, 54 "There is no qualification of the right of the jury, in a criminal cause, to disregard the instructions of the court as to the law, and they may adopt their own theory of the law, even if more prejudicial to the accused than the instructions of the court." State v.Meyer, 58 Vt 457, 3 A 195 "Comp. laws 1885, p. 360, S 275, which provides that, in prosecutions for criminal libel, the jury, after having received the direction of the court, shall have the right to determine,at their discretion, the law and the facts is constitutional." Appeal of Lowe, 46 Kan 255, 26 P 749"It seems that the court instructs juries in criminal cases not to bind their consciences, but to inform their judgements, but they are not in duty bound to adopt its opinion as their own."Lynch v. State, 9 Ind 541 "An instruction that the jury have no right to determine whether the facts stated in the indictment constitute a public offense is in error." Hudelson v. State, 94 Ind 426 "The jury have a right to disregard the opinion of the court, in a criminal case, even on a question of law, if they are fully satisfied that such opinion is wrong." People v. Videto, 1 Parker, Gr R. 603 "The court below having charges the jury, in a trial for a capital offense, that "they were the judges of the law and the evidence," in unqualified terms, the supreme court remarked that if the court had charged the jury, that they were bound to receive the law when given from the court, but that, in cases where the issue involves a mixed question of the law and testimony, in order to determine the criminal intent with which the act was done, it would have saved to the defendant the full benefit of his right to have an impartial trial; by jury, and the court would , at the same time, have maintained its own dignity and constitutional authority. Pleasant v State, 13 Ark 360 "Where the jury are made the judges of the law,as well as the facts, it is within the discretion of the trial court to permit counsel to read judicial opinions and legal textbooks to the jury." Wohlford v. People, 45 III App 188 "In a criminal case, counsel may, in summing up, argue the law of the case to the jury." (Ind 1857) Lynch v State, 9 Ind 541 (Mass 1854) Commonwealth v Porter, 51 Mass (10 Metc) 263; (Tenn 1883) Hannah v State, 79 Tenn (11 Leal 201) "Counsel will not be permitted to argue, before the jury, questions of law not involved in the instruction asked and submitted to the court." (Ask for them) (US v Watkins, Fed Ca No 16, 649) (3 Cranch, C.C. 4411) "Counsel should be allowed, on the trial of a criminal case, to read to the jury suitable statements of the law from works of approved authority." (Winkler v State, 32 Ark 539) "On a trial for murder, the court charged the jury that 'the jury are not only judges in the facts of the case, but they are judges of the law. The court is a witness to them as to what the law is. After the court has stated the law to them, then, if they believer it to be different, they can disregard the opinion of the court. If the jury err in favor of the defendant, their judgement is final, and cannot be reversed by the Supreme Court.' Held, there was no error in so charging a jury in a criminal case." Nelson v State, 32 Tenn 482 "Though the Constitution gives to the jury in criminal cases the right to determine the law, it is not error the court to instruct them not to disregard the law." Blacker v State, 130 Ind 203, 29 NE 1077 "Defendant cannot complain of an instruction that it is the court to instruct it as to the law of the case, but the instructions are advisory merely, and it has the right to disregard them, and determine the law for itself." Walker v State, 136 Ind 663, 36 NE 356 "In criminal cases, the jury are judges of the law as well as of the facts; and it is error in the court to restrict them to 'the law as given in charge of the court'" McGuthrie v State, 17 Ga 497.

"On trial for larceny, the presiding judge, after charging the jury that they were judges of the law and the evidence, added that, if they thought they knew more of the law than the judge, it was their privilege to so believe. Held, not to be error." State v Johnson 30 La Ann 904 "In a prosecution under a law against liquor selling, the accused claimed that the act was unconstitutional, and asked the court to charge the jury that they were judges of the law as well as of the facts. The judge instructed the jury that in a criminal case they were judges of the law as well as of the facts, but that they were under the same obligation in the matter with the judge on the bench, and were not authorized to say that is not law which is so; that the Supreme Court had decided the act to be constitutional, and that in his opinion it was constitutional, that if they decided that to be unconstitutional which the Supreme Court had decided to be constitutional they would disturb the foundations of law; but that, after all, they were judges of the law and if on their consciences they could say that the act was unconstitutional they ought to acquit the accused. Held , on motion of the accused for a new trial, that the charge was correct." State v Buckley, 40 Conn 246 "Const. Art. l5, S. 5, declaring that the jury shall be judges as well of law as of fact in criminal cases, does not prohibit the court from instructing the jury on the law, when they unanimously request it." Beard v State,   71 Md 275, 17 Atl 1044, 17 Am St Re 536, 4 L.R.A. 675 "...and in all indictments for libels, the jury shall have a right to determine the law and the fact, under the direction of the court, as in other cases." Constitution of Kentucky, 1850; Art. XIII, Sec. 10 "In all criminal cases whatever the jury shall have the right to determine the law and the facts." Constitution of Indiana, 1851; Sec. 19 "...and in all prosecutions for libel the truth may be given in evidence, and the jury shall determine the law and the facts under the direction of the court; and if it shall appear to the jury that the matter charged as libelous is true, and was published with good motives and for justifiable ends, the party shall be acquitted." Constitution of Mississippi; Sec. 13 (apparently from their Declaration of Rights) "...and in all indictments for libels the jury may determine the facts and the law, as in other cases." Constitution of Delaware, 1792, Sec. 5

"Upon all general issues, the jury find not the fact of every case by itself, leaving the law to the court; but find for the plaintiff or defendant upon the issue tried, wherein they resolve both law and fact by itself." Remarks by Lord Chief Justice Vaughan (Vaughan, 136) wherein the English government tried to punish a jury which had defied the court's instructions as to the law in a trial of William Penn in England, and; "To what end must they have, in many cases, the view, for their exacter information chiefly? To what end must they undergo a verdict by the dictates and authority of another man, under pain of fines and imprisonment, when sworn to do it according to the best of their own knowledge? A man cannot see by another's eye, nor hear by another's ear; no more can a man conclude or infer the thing to be resolved, understanding or reasoning." (The judge's interpretation of the law -- defendant's note)

In Indiana, the Supreme Court, under the Constitution of 1816, having alternately denied and affirmed the right of the jury in criminal cases to decide the law, the people, by the constitution which took effect in November, 1851, declaring that, "in all criminal cases whatever the jury shall have the right to determine the law and the fact," and this right has since been maintained by that court, even when the constitutionality of a statute was involved. Townsend v State (1828) 2 Blackford, 151; Warren v State (1836) 4 Blackford, 150; Carter v State (May 1851) 2 Indiana, 517; 1 Charters and Constitutions, 513, 526; Lynch v State (1857) 9 Indiana, 541; McCarthy v State (1877) 56 Ind 203; Hudelson v State (1883) 94 Ind 426; Blake v State (1891) 130 Ind 203. From the dissenting opinion of Gray, Sharas, J.J. of Sparf and Hansen v U.S., 156 US 51 (1895) at page 153.The provision of Section 3 of the Act of Congress of July 14, 1798, c 74, for punishing seditious libels, that "the jury who shall try the cause shall have a right to determine the law and the fact, under the direction of the court, as in other cases," (1 Stat 597) is a clear and express recognition of the right of the jury in all criminal cases to determine the law and the fact in all cases -- not just liable cases -- as is manifest by the words, "as in other cases." The words "direction of the court," as used here, like the words "opinion and directions" in the English libel act, do not oblige the jury to adopt the opinion of the court, but are merely equivalent to instruction, guide or aid, and not to order, command, or control. The provision is in affirmance of the general rule, and not by way of creating an exception; and the reason for inserting it was that the right of the jury had been more often denied by the English courts in prosecution for seditious libels than in any other class of cases (ibid).Until nearly forty years after the adoption of the Constitution of the United States, not a single decision of the highest court of any state, or of any judge of a court of the United States, has been found, denying the right of a jury upon the general issue in a criminal case to decide, according to their own judgement and consciences, the law involved in that issue -- except the two or three cases, above mentioned, concerning the constitutionality of a statute. And it cannot have escaped attention that many of the utterances, above quoted, maintaining the right and duty of the jury to decide both the Law and facts, were by some of the most eminent and steadfast supporters of the Constitution of the United States, and of the authority of the national judiciary. (Gray, Shiras, J.J., dissenting opinion, Sparf and Hansen v U.S.)

The jury are perjured if the verdict be against their own judgement although by direction of the court, for their oath binds them to their own judgement. T. Jones, 13, 17 (Bushell case -- England)Quoting again from Justice Gray and Shira, in Sparf and Hansen v U.S: "Within six years after the Constitution was established, the right of the jury, upon the general issue, to determine the law as well as the fact in controversy, was unhesitatingly and unqualifiedly affirmed by this court, in the first of the very few trials by jury ever had at its bar, under the original jurisdiction conferred upon it by the Constitution."

That trial took place at February term, 1794, in Georgia v Brailsford, et al, 3 Dall 1, which was an action at law by the State of Georgia against Brailsford and others, British subjects... After the case had been argued for four days to the court and jury, Chief Justice Jay, on February 7, 1794, as the report states, "delivered the following charge:

"This cause has been regarded as of great importance, and doubtless it is so. It has accordingly been treated by the counsel with great learning, diligence and ability; and on your part it has been heard with particular attention. It is, therefore, unnecessary for me to follow the investigation over the extensive field into which it has been carried; you are now, if ever you can be, completely possessed of the merits of the cause. "The facts comprehended in the case are agreed; the only point that remains is to settle what is the law of the land arising from those facts; on that point, it is proper that the opinion of the court should be given. It is fortunate on the present, as it must be on every occasion, to find the opinion of the court unanimous; we entertain no diversity of sentiment; and we have experienced no difficulty in uniting in the charge which it is my province to deliver."

The Chief Justice, after stating the opinion of the court in favor of the defendants upon the questions of law, proceeded as follows: "It may not be amiss, here gentlemen, to remind you of the good old rule, that on questions of fact it is the province of the jury, on questions of law it is the province of the court to decide. But it must be observed that by the same law, which recognizes this reasonable distribution of jurisdiction, you have nevertheless a right to take upon yourselves to judge of both, and to determine the law as well as the fact in controversy. On this, and on every other occasion, however, we have no doubt you will pay that respect which is due to the opinion of the court; for, as on the one hand, it is presumed that juries are the best judges of facts; it is, on the other hand, presumable that the courts are the best judges of law. But still both objects are lawfully within your power of decision." (emphasis added)

Here we have Chief Justice of the Supreme Court, Jay, who was one of the three authors of the Federalist Papers, urging adoption of the United States Constitution -- former president of the Continental Congress -- and who became the first Chief Justice of the Supreme Court, unanimously, along with Justices Cushing, Wilson, Blair, and Paterson. (Defendant's note, Iredell was not present) after four days of trial -- where there were no facts in dispute -- and where the jury was listening to arguments by counsel about the law -- gave an instruction to the jury, giving them the court's opinion of the applicable law -- but clearly informing the jury that they were to decide the law in the case.

It is clearly seen here that in the early days of this Republic there was no doubt among the highest judicial authorities, of the jury's RIGHT AND DUTY in all criminal cases to determine the law as well as the fact! The Constitution cannot be altered, save by amendment; the Supreme Court set the example here in the Brailsford case. Any Court that does not follow this Supreme Court lead does attempt to amend the Constitution by rule -- not by amendment. I contend, therefore, that the lower courts must refrain from this unlawful usurpation of law in favor of our common heritage -- the Common Law -- as exemplified by the Supreme Court of the United States. Defendant only wants his right as clearly exists from ancient times to this day.

Continuing with the opinion in Sparf and Hansen v U.S., supra, Supreme Court Justices Gray and Shira state: "That Georgia v Brailsford was not a criminal case, nor a suit to recover penalty; had it been, it could hardly have been brought within the original jurisdiction of this court." Wisconsin v Pelican Ins. Co., 127 US 265,294. "But it was a suit by a State to assert a title acquired by an act of its legislature in the exercise of its sovereign powers in time of war against private individuals. As the charge of the court dealt only with the case before it, without any general discussion, it does not appear whether the opinion expressed as to the right of the jury to determine the law was based upon a supposed analogy between such a suit and a prosecution for crime, or upon the theory, countenanced by many American authorities of the period, that at the foundation of the Republic, as in early times in England, the right of the jury extended to all cases, CIVIL OR CRIMINAL, tried upon the general issue. "However that may have been, it cannot be doubted that this court, at that early date, was of opinion that the jury had the right to decide for themselves all matters of law involved in the general issue in criminal cases; and it is certain that in the century that has since elapsed there has been no judgement or opinion of the court, deciding or intimating, in any form, that the right does not appertain to the jury in such cases. And the opinions expressed by individual justices of the court upon the subject, near the time of the decision in Georgia v Brailsford, or within forty years afterwards, of which reports are known to exist, tend, more or less directly, to affirm this right of the jury. That there is not a greater accumulation of evidence to this effect is easily accounted for when it is remembered that comparatively few reports of trials were printed, and that the right of the jury was considered to be so well settled, that it was seldom controverted in practice, or specially noticed in reporting trials." 156 US 51

The conclusion is obvious, since the Jury once had the right to decide the law in all criminal cases, the jury still has the right to decide the law as well as the fact and the defendant also has the right to argue the Law to the Jury and he must be allowed to in order for him to receive a fair and just trial. The Jury must have a copy of the Constitution with them and need to swear to support IT like all judicial officers. -- otherwise they are simply agents of the State and like the prosecutor are clearly prejudiced against the Defendant! The law and precedent is clear. There is no new law espoused by this Defendant. I advocate, therefore, a return to the Law as it was, and as it is established by the highest judicial office of our land; and that we not deviate from that mode of trial by Jury so long established by our heritage, nor pollute it by foreign and alien modes of trial held by our forefathers to be tyranny.

ANSWER TO OBJECTIONS

In 1852, Lysander Spooner, wrote of why it is imperative that Juries rather than judges decide the issues of a case: "The following objections will be made to the doctrines and the evidence presented in the preceding chapters. "

l. That it is a maxim of the law, that the judges respond to the question of the law, and juries only to the question of fact. "The answer to this objection is, that, since Magna Charta, judges have had more than six centuries in which to invent and promulgate pretended maxims to suit themselves; and this is one of them. Instead of expressing the law, it expresses nothing but the ambitious and lawless will of the judges themselves, and of those whose instruments they are." It is not my intention here to impugn all judges, as the Supreme Court and higher court judges generally understand the Constitution and the Common Law and rule wisely. However, many lower court judges do not rule in a way consistent with Constitutional principles, and do violence to our heritage.

Many judges do not even live up to that part of their own maxim, which requires jurors to try the matter of fact. By dictating to them the laws of evidence, that is, by dictating what evidence they may hear and what they may not hear, and also by dictating to them rules for weighing such evidence as they permit them to hear, they of necessity dictate the conclusion to which they shall arrive; and thus the court really tries the question of fact, in every cause. It is clearly impossible, in the nature of things, for a jury to try a question of fact, without trying every question of law on which the fact depends."

2. It will be asked, 'Of what use are the justices if the jurors judge both of law and fact?' "The answer is, that they are of use, (1) To assist and enlighten the jurors, if they can, by their advice and information; such advice and information to be received only for what they may chance to be worth in the estimation of the jurors; (2) To do anything that may be necessary in regard to granting appeals and new trials; to conduct the proceedings as a referee with total impartiality."

3. It is said that it would be absurd that twelve ignorant men should have power to judge, while justices learned in the law would be compelled to sit by and see the law decided erroneously. "The answer to this objection is, that the powers often are not granted to them on the supposition that they know the law better than the justices; but on the grounds that the justices are untrustworthy, that they posed to bribes, are themselves fond of power and authority, and are also the dependent and subservient creatures of the legislature; and that to allow them to the law, would not only expose the rights of parties to be sold for money, but would be equivalent to surrendering all the property, liberty, and rights of theirs unreservedly into the hands of arbitrary power (the legislature) to be disposed of at its pleasure. The powers of juries, therefore, not only place a curb over legislators and judges, but imply also an imputation upon their integrity and trustworthiness; and these are the reasons why legislators and judges only entertained the intensest hatred of juries, and so fast as they could do it without alarming the people for their liberties, have, by indirection, denied, and practically destroyed their power. And it is only since all the real power of juries has been destroyed, and they have become mere tools in the hands of legislators and judges, that they have become favorites with them. "Legislators and judges are necessarily exposed to all the temptations of money, fame, and powered them to disregard justice between parties, and sell the rights, and violate the liberties of the people. Jurors, on the other hand, are exposed to none of these temptations. They are not liable to bribery, for they are not known to the parties until they come into the jury box. They can rarely gain either fame, power, or money by giving erroneous decisions. Their offices are [temd] they know that when they shall have executed them, they must return to the people, to hold all their own rights in life subject to the liability of such jury their successors, as they themselves have given an example for. "The laws of human nature do not permit the supposition that twelve men, taken by lot from f people, and acting under such circumstances, will all prove dishonest. It is a supposable case that they may not be sufficiently enlightened to know and do their who duty, in all cases whatever; but that they should all prove dishonest, is not within the range of probability. A jury, therefore, insures to us -- what no other court does -- that first and indispensable requisite in a judicial tribunal, integrity. "

4. It is alleged that if juries are allowed to judge of the law, they decide absolutely; that their decision must necessarily stand, be it right or wrong; and that this power of absolute decision would be dangerous in their hands, by their ignorance of the law. "One answer is, that this power, which juries have of judging of the law, is not a power of absolute decision in all cases, it is a power to declare imperatively that a man's property, liberty, or life, shall not be taken from him; but it is not a power to declare imperatively that they shall be taken from him."

Magna Charta does not provide that the judgments of the peers shall be executed, so far as to take a party's goods, rights or person, thereon. "A judgment of the peers may be reviewed, and invalidated, and a new trial granted. So that practically a jury has no absolute power to take a party's goods, rights, or person. They have only an absolute veto upon their being taken by government. The government is not bound to do everything that a jury may adjudge. It is only prohibited from doing anything -- (that is, from taking a party's goods, rights or person) -- unless a jury have first adjudged it to be done." An Essay on the Trial by Jury, by Lysander Spooner, (Who's Who), Da Capo Press N. Y., N. Y.

SUMMARY

1. Under the Common Law the Jury has the right to decide the law and the facts of every criminal case.
2. Under the Common Law the Jury has the duty to judge of the justness of the law, and of the intent and motives of the accused, and to hold guiltless those accused of violating what in their opinion were unjust or oppressive laws.
3. "Trial per pais" means "trial by the country," or "by the people"; it does not mean "trial by the judge or government".
4. The Common Law Jury has not only 'veto' power over all legislation of the king, but over all legislation of "representative government" AND THEY KNEW IT ! AND WERE TOLD IT !
5. Juries could not be bound or sworn to follow the Court's instructions as to the "law"; they were only sworn to follow their own consciences -- to convict the guilty and acquit the innocent, but they would decide whether the law was proper!
6. Freedom can only be properly maintained where the People through their Juries, maintain a veto over the legislature and judges.
7. The victory for freedom at Runnymede was not that the Barons convinced King John to continue dictating the law and evidence in the courts with or without Juries -- it was that, henceforth, the ancient custom of the realm would be enforced -- and that no life, liberty, or property could, henceforth, be taken without the unanimous consent of a Jury of peers -- undictated to by government as to either law or fact. Magna Charta was not new law but, like Miranda, a reaffirmation of the Law as it had always existed.
8. "Law of the Land" and "Due Process" have been held to be the equivalent of the Law of the Land of Magna Charta.
9. Under the Common Law or Law of the Land, no "law" which was oppressive and unjust could be Law, and the Jury had the right and duty not to impose it against an accused if this was against their conscience.

This undertone of justice, under the Common Law and Magna Charta, is echoed in the Declaration of Independence, which many states have affirmed by their Enabling Acts; it is also echoed in the first ten, the 13th and 14th Amendments of the United States Constitution.
10. No human being can morally be subjected to the present degradation (being practiced in some of the courts) of being sworn to uphold the Judge's interpretation of the "law". This is an insult to all self respect and one's own religion!
11. The only proper addition to the Common Law Oath of Jurors would be their sworn support of the Constitutions of the United States and of this State.
12. A jury is sworn to uphold the Constitution -- not some other Judge, which would be a violation of one's own conscience, and the supremacy clause of the U.S. Constitution.
13. The Court lacks jurisdiction over the person of the accused and over all the subject matter if it refuses to permit a properly sworn Jury to decide both law and fact in this case!
14. Representative government is no bar to tyranny and oppression without the added safeguard of Juries judging the law which the representatives pass and the judges attempt to uphold as is apparent in often flagrant violation of the Constitution they are sworn to uphold. (But, when will a traitor impeach a traitor?)
15. Apparently a majority decision in the Sparf and Hansen case (156 US 51) in 1895 has led to a steady and widespread repudiation of the true function of the Common Law Jury; and it is no longer permitted to decide the law without being made to feel as perjurers if they dare challenge the Judge's interpretation of the "law".
16. Assuming Congress and the Supreme Court and the legislatures and the State Courts go

along with this changing of the function of a Jury -- IT IS INVALID -- IT AMOUNTS TO CHANGING OR AMENDING THE CONSTITUTION BY REDEFINING A WORD INSTEAD OF THROUGH THE PROPER AMENDMENT PROCESS !

17. This Defendant cannot have the trial by an impartial Jury which he is guaranteed by the Sixth Amendment, if the Judge instructs them that a statute is not in conflict with the Constitution when the Defendant KNOWS that it is, and if the Defendant cannot argue the law to the Jury, THEN THE JURY IS "SENSITIZED" or made PARTIAL by the Judge.

18. The principle reason for Juries deciding the law is not that they are more learned or wise than Judges, but that they are less susceptible to worldly temptations and political pressures, assuring the likelihood of more integrity in their decisions.

CONCLUSION

Alas, the time has come when the People may again have to leave for Runnymede to face and challenge a tyrannical Caesar. Must they again remove the blinds which were so craftily placed on their eyes while they slept and are beginning to exercise the "horse sense" to which any thinking person must give them credit of having. Their past monumental work stand as living testaments to their mental, physical, and spiritual abilities, and maybe they are again beginning to exercise the great muscle of our Republic by demanding that Juries be given back their ancient rights and duties to the last, -- but most important, -- bar to justice for all!

Under the Common Law and under the Constitution of the United States, this Defendant DEMANDS that his Jury be appraised of their right and duty to decide the law, and the fact and the admissibility of evidence.

In the alternative, he respectfully asks the Court for an Order to Dismiss with Prejudice.

"Scene at the Signing of the Constitution of the United States"

JURY INSTRUCTION

EXAMPLE 1: Ladies and Gentlemen of the Jury, you are instructed that any person under the age of nineteen (19) years who shall by any means represent to any person licensed to sell beer at retail, or to any agent or employee of such retail license, that he is nineteen (19) or more years of age for the purpose of inducing such retail licensee, his agent or employee, to sell, serve or dispense beer to him or her shall be guilty of a misdemeanor. Boise City Code 5-5-13-C

EXAMPLE 2: Ladies and Gentlemen of the Jury, you are instructed that where a state statute talks about a subject and an ordinance of a city talks about a subject, the state statute has precedence. Article 12, Section 2, Idaho State Constitution Idaho Code 50-302 In re Ridenbaugh, 5 ID 371,375 State v. Musser, 67 ID 214, 219

EXAMPLE 3: Ladies and Gentlemen of the Jury, you are instructed that all persons are capable of committing crimes, except those belonging to the following classes:
1. Persons who committed the act or made the omission charged, under an ignorance or mistake of fact which disproves any criminal intent.
2. Persons who committed the act charged without being conscious thereof.
3. Persons who committed the act or made the omission charged, through misfortune or by accident, when it appears that there was not evil design, intention or culpable negligence.
4. Persons (unless the crime be punishable with death) who committed the act or made the omission charged, under threats or menaces sufficient to show that they had reasonable cause to and did believe their lives would be endangered if they refused. Idaho Code 18-201

EXAMPLE 4: Ladies and Gentlemen of the Jury, you are instructed that whenever any person licensed to sell beer, his agent or employee, shall have reasonable cause to doubt that any person who attempts to purchase or otherwise procure beer from or through such retail licensee, his agent or employee, is nineteen (19) or more years of age, such retail licensee, his agent or employee, shall require such person to execute a certificate that he or she is nineteen (19) or more years of age, and to exhibit acceptable proof of age and identity. The form of such certificate, the manner in which it shall be executed, the record to be kept thereof, the responsibility of the retail licensee, his agent or employee, with respect to the execution of said certificate, and a determination of what shall constitute acceptable proof of age and identity, shall be in accordance with such regulations as the director shall prescribe relating thereto. Idaho Code 23-1025

EXAMPLE 5: Ladies and Gentlemen of the Jury, you are instructed that the law implies conformity with the natural and inherent principles of justice and forbids the taking of one's property without compensation, and requires that no one shall be condemned in person or property without opportunity to be heard. Holden v. Hardy, 169 U. S. 366

EXAMPLE 6: Ladies and gentlemen of the jury, you are instructed that the claim and exercise of a constitutional right cannot be converted into a crime. Miller v. U. S., 230 F. 486 at 489

EXAMPLE 7: Ladies and gentlemen of the jury, you are instructed that there can be no sanction or penalty imposed upon one because of his exercise of constitutional rights. Sherar v. Cullen, 481 F. 2d 946

EXAMPLE 8: Ladies and gentlemen of the jury, your are instructed that it can never be admitted as a just attribute of sovereignty in a government, to take the property of one citizen and bestow it upon another. The exercise of such power is incompatible with the nature and object of all government and is destructive of the great end and aim for which government is instituted and is subservice of the fundamental principles upon which all free governments are organized. White

v. White, 5 Barb 474, 484-5

EXAMPLE 9: Ladies and Gentlemen of the Jury, you are instructed that malice is defined as "that state of mind which is reckless of law and of the legal rights of the citizen". Alabama News Employees' Benevolent Soc v. Agricola, 200 So. 748,755 240 Ala.668 ---Evens-Jordan Furniture Co. v. Hartzog, 187 So. 491, 493, 237 Ala. 407 ---Bowles v. Lowery, 59 So. 695, 697, 5 Ala. app. 555

EXAMPLE 10: Ladies and Gentlemen of the Jury, you are instructed that malice is defined as "a state of mind that is reckless in its nature, implying a determination to do a thing regardless of legal rights or for the purpose of inflicting an injury". Lusk v. Onstatt, Tex Civ. app. 178 S.W. 2d 549, 553, 554

EXAMPLE 11: Ladies and Gentlemen of the Jury, you are instructed that malice is defined as "an intention to vex, injure, or annoy another person". Oregon Cawrse v. Signal Oil Co., 103 P.2d 729, 731, 164. Or. 666, 129 A.L.R. 174

EXAMPLE 12: Ladies and Gentlemen of the Jury, you are instructed that malice is "an intent to do an unlawful act without legal justification or excuse. Calif. People v. Faylor, 36 Cal. 38 C.J. P 347 note 22

EXAMPLE 13: Ladies and Gentlemen of the Jury, you are instructed that malice "involves a mere disregard of duty which is apparent from the intentional doing of a willful act to the injury of another" New Mexico-Rea v. Motors Ins. Corporation, 144 P2d 676, 680, 48 N.M. 9

EXAMPLE 14: Ladies and Gentlemen of the Jury, you are instructed that malice "It has been said that a wanton or conscious or intentional disregard of the rights of another is equivalent to legal malice. Georgia-Investment Securities Corporation v. Cole, 194 S.E. 411, 414, 57 Ga. app. 97. Mc Gill v. Vaxin, 106 So. 44, 48, 213 Ala 649

EXAMPLE 15: Ladies and Gentlemen of the Jury, you are instructed that malice has been held to mean the same as improper motives and any unjustifiable motive constitutes legal malice. Michigan-Oyler v. Fenner, 248 N.W. 567, 569 263 Mich. 119. North Dakota-Redahl v. Stevens, 250 N.W. 534, 536, 64 N.D. 154

EXAMPLE 16: Ladies and Gentlemen of the Jury, you are instructed that malice in its legal sense means a motive from which flows the act injurious to another person, done intentionally and without lawful excuse. Arkansas-Gaylor v. State 70 S.W. 2d 844, 845, 188 Ark 1167

EXAMPLE 17: Ladies and Gentlemen of the Jury, you are instructed that "malice is a performed purpose to do a wrongful act without sufficient legal provocation or just excuse". South Carolina-State v. Judge, 38 S.E. 2d715, 719,208 S.C. 497-State v. Hayward, 15 S.E. 2d 669, 671, 197 S.C. 371

EXAMPLE 18: Ladies and Gentlemen of the Jury, you are instructed that "malice has been judicially described as the spirit of evil which sometimes grips individuals and nations; it is the venomous spirit that motivates those who delight in doing harm to others". Pennsylvania-Caskie v. Philadelphia Rapid Transit Co. 5 A 2d 368, 372, 334 Pa. 33

EXAMPLE 19: Ladies and Gentlemen of the Jury, you are instructed that "Actual malice devotes the desire to do harm for the satisfaction of doing it or conduct which in effect amounts to the same thing". California Gudger v. Manton, 134 P 2d 217, 221, 21 Cal. 2d 537

EXAMPLE 20: Ladies and Gentlemen of the Jury, you are instructed that when the right of privacy must be reasonable yielded to the right of a search, is as a rule, to be decided by a judicial officer, not by a policeman or government enforcement agent. Johnson v. U.S. 333 U.S. 10, 14

EXAMPLE 21: Ladies and Gentlemen of the Jury, you are instructed that a complaint may not be dismissed on motion if it states some sort of claim, baseless though it may prove to be and artistically as the complaint may be drown.This is particularly true where the plaintiff is not represented by counsel. Brooks v. Pennsylvania R. Co. 91 F. sup 101 (D.CS.D

EXAMPLE 22: Ladies and Gentlemen of the Jury, you are instructed that by the great weight of authority it is acknowledged that generally 'Public Officials are not immune from suit when they allegedly violate the rights of citizens' and that "A Public Officials defence of immunity is to be sparingly applied in these kinds of eases. James v. Ogilvie (1970, D.C. Ill.) 310 F. sup 661, 663

EXAMPLE 23: Ladies and Gentlemen of the Jury, you are instructed that; "A public official does not have immunity simply because he operates in a discretionary situation.Public servants are to be held liable when they abuse their discretion or act in a way that is arbitrary, fanciful or clearly unreasonable. Littleton v. Berbling, (1972 Ca. 7 Ill.) 467 F 2d 389. The seventh Circuit Court of Appeals

EXAMPLE 24: Ladies and Gentlemen of the Jury, you are instructed that the decisions have, indeed, always imposed a limitation upon the immunity that the officials act must have been within the scope of his powers, since they exist only for the public good, never cover occasions where the public good is not their aim, and hence that to exercise a power dishonestly is necessarily to overstep its bounds. Gregoire v. Biddle 177 F 2d 579, 581, (Ca 2 1949)

EXAMPLE 25: Ladies and Gentlemen of the Jury, you are instructed that "Where rights secured by the Constitutional are involved there can be no rule making or legislation which would abrogate them." Miranda vs. Arizona 384 U.S. 432, 491.

EXAMPLE 26: Ladies and Gentlemen of the Jury, you are instructed that malice is "the purposely doing of a wrongful act, without justifiable excuse, which may or may not profit him who does it and injures the rights of him against whom it is directed". Ohio-Ricketts v. Halm, 53 N.E. 2d 202, 205, 72 Ohio app. 478.

EXAMPLE 27: Ladies and Gentlemen of the Jury, you are instructed that malice is "the willful doing of an act which one knows is liable to injure another regardless of the consequences". U.S. - U.S. v. Reed,C.C. N.Y., 86 F. 308, 312.

EXAMPLE 28: Ladies and Gentlemen of the Jury, you are instructed that "Malice," in a legal sense, has been defined as the willful violation of a known right;a conscious violation of the lawful rights of another to his prejudice. Arizona-Meason v. Ralston Purina Co., 107 P. 2d 224, 228, 56 Ariz. 291. Florida John B. Stetson University v. Hunt, 102 So. 637, 639, 88 Fla. 510. Illinois-Kemp v. Division No 241 A.A. S. & E. R.E., 153 Ill. app 344, 365.

EXAMPLE 29: Ladies and Gentlemen of the Jury, you are instructed that malice is "an act wantonly done against another which a person of reasonable intelligence must know to be contrary to his duty and purposely prejudicial to another;" U.S.-KVOS, Inc. v. Associated Press, D.C. Wash., 13 F. sup. 910, 911, 912.

EXAMPLE 30: Ladies and Gentlemen of the Jury, you are instructed that "Malice is also defined as unjustifiable action causing injury". North Carolina-Rose v. Dean 135 S.E. 348, 349, 192 N.C. 556.

EXAMPLE 31: Ladies and Gentlemen of the Jury, you are instructed that malice is "an action flowing from any wicked and corrupt motive, a thing done malo animo, where the fact has been attended with such circumstances as carry in them the plain indications of a heart regardless of social duty, and fatally bent on mischief". Illinois-People v. Wilson, 174 N.E. 398, 401, 342 Ill. 358. Mass.-Commonwealth v. Webster, 5 Cush 295, 304, 52 AM. D. 711. Wisconsin-State v. Scherr, 9 N.W. 2d 117, 11, 243 Wis. 65.

EXAMPLE 32: Ladies and Gentlemen of the Jury, you are instructed that malice is "a wrongful act, done intentionally, without just cause or excuse even though it is from good motives and without express malice". Massachusetts-Whitcomb v. Reed-Preutice Co. 159 N.E. 922, 925, 262 Mass. 348.

EXAMPLE 33: Ladies and Gentlemen of the Jury, you are instructed that it is not necessary to show that the particular act was willfully or wantonly done, but it is necessary that the actor know that the act was wrongful, since it is not merely doing an act intentionally that is wrongful. Missouri-Beckler v. Yates 89 S.W. 2d 650, 653 338 Mo. 208-Greaves v. Kansas City Junior Orpheum Co., 80 S.W. 2d 228, 235, 229 Mo. app 663.

EXAMPLE 34: Ladies and Gentlemen of the Jury, you are instructed that "Malice has been defined as a wish to injure another person or to do a wrongful act; a desire to injure; a wish to vex, annoy, or injure another person, or an intent to do a wrongful act; a wish or desire to vex, harass, or annoy another; a specific desire to vex or injure another from malevolence or motives of ill will; a desire to be avenged on a particular person. California-People v. George, 109 p. 2d 404, 406, 42 Cal. app. 2d 568. Michigan-Glieberman v. Fine, 226 N.W. 669, 670, 248 Mich 8.38 C.J.p 351 note 31. North Dakota-Briggs v. Coykendall, 224 N.W. 202, 205, 57 N.D. 785 38 C.J. p 348 note 49. Arizona- Statutory definition- Fears v. State, 265 p. 600, 601 33 Ariz. 432. Montana-Wray v. Great Falls Paper Co., 234 p. 486, 487, 72 Mont. 461. North Dakota-Lux v. Bendewald, 227 N.W. 550, 553, 58 N.D. 761. South Dakota-Kerley v. Germscheid, 106 N.W. 136, 137, 20 S.D. 363. U.S.-Johnson v. Ebberts, C.C. Or. 11 F. 129 131, 6 Lawy. 538. Florida-Corpus Juris quoted in Parker v. State, 169 So. 411, 414, 124 Fla. 780. North Carolina-Swain v. Oakley, 129 S.E. 151, 152, 190 N.C. 113.

EXAMPLE 35: Ladies and Gentlemen of the Jury, you are instructed that the purpose of a due process hearing is to safeguard from deprivation the liberty or property rights of protected persons, and this can only be done where the requisite hearing is held before the decision maker so that the decision maker can sift through the facts, weigh the evidence and reach the appropriate conclusion. (U.S.C.A. Const. Amend 5 Ponce vs. housing authority of Tulore Co. 389, F. sup. 635 D.C. Cal. 1975)

EXAMPLE 36: Ladies and Gentlemen of the Jury, you are instructed that failure to secure a valid court order must be punishable for those conducting a search or seizure without it if the rights of the fourth amendment of the Constitution are to be maintained." If no penalty will be ever attached to a failure to seek a warrant, as distinguished from the officers making their own, correct, determination of probable cause, warrants will never be sought". (Quotation of Niro v. U.S., 338 F. 2d 535 at 539 (1st Cir. Ct.) Cited in U.S. v. Mason 290 F. sup 843 (1968).

EXAMPLE 37: Ladies and Gentlemen of the Jury, you are instructed that all persons born or naturalized in the United States, and subject to the jurisdiction thereof, are Citizens of the United States and of the State wherein they reside.No State shall make or enforce any law which shall abridge the privileges or immunities of citizens of the United States; nor shall any State deprive any person of life, liberty, or property, without due process of law; nor deny to any person within its Jurisdiction the equal protection of the laws.Amendment XIV United States Constitution.

EXAMPLE 38: Ladies and Gentlemen of the Jury, you are instructed that even where probable cause exists, a warrantless search is forbidden unless made incident to a lawful arrest. Agnello vs. United States. 269 U.S. 20 46 S. Ct. 4 70 LED 145, (1925).

EXAMPLE 39: Ladies and Gentlemen of the Jury, you are instructed that private property may be taken for public use, but not until a just compensation, to be ascertained in the manner prescribed by law, shall be paid therefor.Idaho Constitution Article 1 Sec. 14.

EXAMPLE 40: Ladies and Gentlemen of the Jury, you are instructed that he has erected a multitude of new offices, and sent hither swarms of officers to harass our people, and eat out their substance.Declaration of Independence.

EXAMPLE 41: Ladies and Gentlemen of the Jury, you are instructed that No person shall be deprived of life, liberty, or property, without due process of law; nor shall private property be taken for public use, without just compensation.Amendment V of the Constitution of the United States.

EXAMPLE 42: Ladies and Gentlemen of the Jury, you are instructed that all men are by nature free and equal, and have certain inalienable rights, among which are enjoying and defending life and liberty; acquiring, possessing and protecting property; pursuing happiness and securing safety.Idaho Constitution Article 1 Sec. 1.

EXAMPLE 43: Ladies and Gentlemen of the Jury, you are instructed that the state of Idaho is an inseparable part of the American Union, and the Constitution of the United States is the supreme law of the land. Idaho Constitution Article 1 Sec. 3.

EXAMPLE 44: Ladies and Gentlemen of the Jury, you are instructed that No person shall be deprived of life, liberty or property without due process of law. Idaho Constitution Article 1 Sec. 13.

EXAMPLE 45: Ladies and Gentlemen of the Jury, you are instructed that "Malice includes not only anger, hatred and revenge, but every other unlawful and unjustifiable motive." 30 Idaho 259 at 266

EXAMPLE 46: Ladies and Gentlemen of the Jury, you are instructed that "Malice, although in its popular sense it means hatred, ill will or hostility to another, yet, in its legal sense, has a very different meaning and characterizes all acts done with an evil disposition, a wrong and unlawful motive or purpose; the willful doing of an injurious act without lawful excuse." 30 Idaho 259 at 266

EXAMPLE 47: Ladies and Gentlemen of the Jury, you are instructed that "Malice, in common acceptation, means ill will against a person; but in its legal sense it means, a wrongful act, done intentionally, without just cause or excuse......" 30 Idaho 259 at 266.

EXAMPLE 48: Ladies and Gentlemen of the Jury, you are instructed that the rule is, malice is implied for any deliberate and cruel act against another, however sudden, which shows an abandoned and malignant heart.24 Idaho 252 at 265.

EXAMPLE 49: Ladies and Gentlemen of the Jury, you are instructed that "Malice not only includes anger, hatred and revenge, but every other unlawful and unjustifiable verb."30 Idaho 261.

EXAMPLE 50: Ladies and Gentlemen of the Jury, you are instructed that intentionally to do that which is calculated in the ordinary course of events to damage, and which does, in fact, damage another's property or trade, is actionable if done without just cause and excuse; and such intentional infliction of damage without justification or excuse is malicious in law. Hitchman Coal & Coke Co. v Mitchell, 245 US 229, LRA1918C497, 38 S Ct. 65.

EXAMPLE 51: Ladies and Gentlemen of the Jury, you are instructed that malice, in common acceptation, means ill will against a person; but in its legal sense it means a wrongful act, done intentionally, without just cause or excuse. Tinker v Colwell, 193 US 473, 24 S Ct. 505. State v Rogers, 30 Idaho 259 at 26

EXAMPLE 52: Ladies and gentlemen of the Jury, you are instructed that a municipality has no sovereign immunity.Owens v City of Independence 445 US 622 with Justice Brennan delivering the opinion of the court:"We hold, therefore, that the municipality may not assert the good faith of its officers or agents as a defence to liability under 1983". (page 638)"Yet in the hundreds of cases from that era awarding damages against municipal governments from wrongs committed by them, one searches in vain for much mention of qualified immunity based on the good faith of municipal officers. Indeed, where the issue was discussed at all, the courts had rejected the proposition that a municipality should be privileged where it reasonably believed its actions to be lawful." Owen v. City of Independence 445 US 622 with Justice Brennan delivering the opinion of the court:"The central aim of the Civil Rights Act was to provide protection to those persons wronged by the misuse of power, possessed by virtue of state law and made possible only because the wrongdoer is clothed withthe authority of state law." Monroe v. Pape, 365 US, at184 (quoting United States v. Classic, 313 US 299, 326 (1941) Owens v. City of Independence 445 US 622 with Justice Brennan delivering the opinion of the court:"By creating an express federal remedy, Congress sought to "enforce provisions of the Fourteenth Amendment against those who carry a badge of authority of a State and represent it in some capacity, whether they act inaccordance with their authority or misuse of it." Monroe v. Pape, supra, at 172. Owen v. City of Independence 445 US 622 with Justice Brennan delivering the opinion of the court:"By its terms, (Title 42) 1983 'Creates a species of tort liability that on its face admits of no immunities 'Imbler v Pachtman 424 US 409, 417 (1976). Its language is absolute and unqualified; no mention of any privileges, immunities, or defenses that may be asserted. Rather the act imposes liability upon "every person" who, under color of state law or custom, subjects, or caused to be subjected, any citizen of the United States...to the deprivation of any rights, privileges, or immunities secured by the Constitution and laws 11/6 and Monell held that these words were intended to encompass municipal corporations as well as natural "persons. (page 635)

EXAMPLE 53: Ladies and Gentlemen of the Jury, you are instructed that a municipality is not entitled to defeat liability by claiming it has acted in good faith. Owen v. City of Independence 445 US 622 with Justice Brennan delivering the opinion of the court:"We hold, therefore, that the municipality may not assert the good faith of its officers or agents as a defence to liability under 1983". (page 638)" Yet in the hundreds of cases from that era awarding damages against municipal governments from wrongs committed by them, one searches in vain for much mention of qualified immunity based on the good faith of municipal officers. Indeed, where the issue was discussed at all, the courts had rejected the proposition that a municipality should be privileged where it reasonably believed its actions to be lawful." Owen v. City of Independence 445 US 622 with Justice Brennan delivering the opinion of the court: "The central aim of the Civil Rights Act was to provide protection to those persons wronged by the" '(M) issue of power, possessed by virtue of state law and made possible only because the wrongdoer is clothed with the authority of state law'." Monroe v. Pape, 365US., at 184 (quoting United States v. Classic, 313 US 299, 326 (1941). Owens v. City of Independence 445 US 622 with Justice Brennan delivering the opinion of the court: "By creating an express federal remedy, Congress sought to "enforce provisions of the Fourteenth Amendment against those who carry a badge of authority of a State and represent it in some capacity, whether they act in accordance with their authority or misuse of it." Monroe v. Pape, supra, at 172. Owen v. City of Independence 445 US 622 with Justice Brennan delivering the opinion of the court: "By its terms, (Title 42) 1983 'Creates a species of tort liability that on its face admits of no immunities 'Imbler v Pachtman 424 US 409, 417 (1976). Its language is absolute and unqualified; no mention of any privileges, immunities, or defenses that may be asserted. Rather the act imposes liability upon "every person" who, under color of state law or custom, subjects, or caused to be subjected, any citizen of the United States...to the deprivation of any rights, privileges, or immunities secured by the Constitution and laws 11/6 and Monell held that these words were intended to encompass municipal corporations as well as natural "persons. (page 635)

EXAMPLE 54: Ladies and Gentlemen of the Jury, you are instructed that even if a municipality did have sovereign immunity, agents of the municipality acting beyond their authority may not claim the city's sovereign immunity. Owen v. City of Independence 445 US 622 with Justice Brennan delivering the opinion of the court: "We hold, therefore, that the municipality may not assert the good faith of its officers or agents as a defence to liability under 1983". (page 638)"Yet in the hundreds of cases from that era awarding damages against municipal governments from wrongs committed by them, one searches in vain for much mention of qualified immunity based on the good faith of municipal officers.Indeed, where the issue was discussed at all, the courts had rejected the proposition that a municipality should be privileged where it reasonably believed its actions to be lawful." Owen v. City of Independence 445 US 622 with Justice Brennan delivering the opinion of the court: "The central aim of the Civil Rights Act was to provide protection to those persons wronged by the" '(M) issue of power, possessed by virtue of state law and made possible only because the wrongdoer is clothed with the authority of state law'."Monroe v. Pape, 365US., at 184 (quoting United States v. Classic, 313 US 299, 326 (1941). Owens v. City of Independence 445 US 622 with Justice Brennan delivering the opinion of the court:"By creating an express federal remedy, Congress sought to "enforce provisions of the Fourteenth Amendment against those who carry a badge of authority of a State and represent it in some capacity, whether they act in accordance with their authority or misuse of it." Monroe v. Pape, supra, at 172. Owen v. City of Independence 445 US 622 with Justice Brennan delivering the opinion of the court:"By its terms, (Title 42) 1983 'Creates a species of tort liability that on its face admits of no immunities 'Imbler v Pachtman 424 US 409, 417 (1976). Its language is absolute and unqualified; no mention of any privileges, immunities, or defenses that may be asserted. Rather the act imposes liability upon "every person" who, under color of state law or custom,subjects, or caused to be subjected, any citizen of the United States...to the deprivation of any rights,privileges, or immunities secured by the Constitution and laws 11/6 and Monell held that these words were intended to encompass municipal corporations as well as natural "persons. (page 635)

EXAMPLE 55: Ladies and Gentlemen of the Jury, you are instructed that a damages remedy against the offending party is a vital component of any scheme for vindicating cherished constitutional guarantees. Owens v. City of independence 445 US 622 with Justice Brennan delivering the opinion of the court:"How uniquely amiss" it would be, therefore, if the government itself - "the social organ to which all in our society look for the promotion of liberty, justice, fair and equal treatment, and the setting of worthy norms and goals for social conduct"--were permitted to disavow liability for the injury it has begotten. See Adickesv. Kress & Co., 398 U.S. 144, 190 (1970) (opinion of BRENNAN, J.). A damages remedy against the offending party is a vital component of any scheme for vindicating cherished constitutional guarantees, and the importance of assuring its efficacy is only accentuated when the wrongdoer is the institution that has been established to protect the very rights it has transgressed. Yet owing to the qualified immunity enjoyed by most government officials, see Scheuer v. Rhodes, 416 U.S. 232(1974), many victims of municipal malfeasance would be left remediless if the city were also allowed to assert a good faith defense. Unless countervailing considerations counsel otherwise, the injustice of such a result should not be tolerated." "Moreover, Sec. 1983 was intended not only to provide compensation to the victims of past abuses, but to serve as a deterrent against future constitutional deprivations, as well." See Robertson v. Wegmann, 436U.S. 584, 590-591 (1978); Carey v. Piphus, 435 U.S. 247,256-257 (1978).

EXAMPLE 56: Ladies and Gentlemen of the Jury, you are instructed that the parties have stipulated that the following facts are true.1.That <owners name> is the owner of the property in question at all pertinent times.

EXAMPLE 57: Ladies and Gentlemen of the Jury, you are instructed that Rights are:"neither accorded to the passive resistant, nor the person who is ignorant of his rights, not to one indifferent thereto. It is a fighting clause. Its benefits can be retained only by sustained combat. It cannot be claimed by an attorney or solicitor. It is valid only when insisted upon by a belligerent claimant in person." (United States vs. Johnson, 76F Sup 538)

EXAMPLE 58: Ladies and Gentlemen of the Jury, you are instructed that Seizure is the act of taking possession of property, e.g., for a violation of law or by virtue of an execution.The term implies a taking or removal of something from the possession, actual or constructive, of another person or persons. Molina v. State 53 Wis. 2d 662, 193 N.W. 2d 874, 877.

EXAMPLE 59: Ladies and Gentlemen of the Jury, you are instructed that a civil suit is a proper remedy against officers or agents of a city who use color of law and authority to unconstitutionally deprive U.S. citizens of their property.Owens v. City of Independence 445 US 622 with Justice Brennan delivering the opinion of the court:"When there is a substantial showing that the exertion of state power has overridden private rights secured by that Constitution, the subject is necessarily one for judicial inquiry in an appropriate proceeding directed against the individuals charged with the transgression."(page 649).

EXAMPLE 60: Ladies and Gentlemen of the Jury, you are instructed that Idaho Code 18-2403 says:THEFT. - (1) A person steals property and commits theft when, with intent to deprive another of property or to appropriate the same to himself or to a third person, he wrongfully takes, obtains or withholds such property from an owner thereof. (2) Theft includes a wrongful taking, obtaining or withholding of another's property, with the intent prescribed in subsection (1) of this section, committed in any of the following ways: (a) By deception obtains or exerts control over property of the owner; (b) By conduct heretofore defined or known as larceny; common law larceny by trick; embezzlement; extortion; obtaining property, money or labor under false pretenses; or receiving stolen goods.

EXAMPLE 61: Ladies and Gentlemen of the Jury, you are instructed that Idaho Code 18-2403 says: (2)(c) By acquiring lost property. A person acquires lost property when he exercises control over property of another which he knows to have been lost or mislaid, or to have been delivered under a mistake as to the identity of the recipient or the nature or amount of the property, without taking reasonable measures to return such property to the owner; or a person commits theft of lost or mislaid property when he: 1. Knows or learns the identity of the owner or knows, or is aware of, or learns of a reasonable method of identifying the owner; and 2. Fails to take reasonable measures to restore the property to the owner; and 3. Intends to deprive the owner permanently of the use or benefit of the property.

EXAMPLE 62: Ladies and Gentlemen of the Jury, you are instructed that Idaho Code 18-2407. Grading of theft.- says: (1) Grand theft. (b) A person is guilty of grand theft when he commits a theft as defined in this chapter and when: 1. The value of the property exceeds one hundred fifty ($150); or 4. The property, regardless of its nature or value, is taken from the person of another;.

EXAMPLE 63: Ladies and Gentlemen of the Jury, you are instructed that: Idaho Code, 49-1109, states that; (a) The authority to make an arrest is the same as upon an arrest for a felony when any person is charged with any of the following offenses: 1. Negligent homicide. 2. Driving, or being in actual physical control, of a vehicle while under the influence of intoxicating liquor. 3. Driving a vehicle while under the influence of any narcotic drug, or driving a vehicle while under the influence of any other drug to a degree which renders the person incapable of safely driving a vehicle. 4. Failure to stop, or failure to give information, or failure to render reasonable assistance in the event of an accident resulting in death or personal injuries. 5. Failure to stop, or failure to give information, in the event of an accident resulting in damage to a vehicle or to fixtures or other property legally upon or adjacent to a highway. 6. Reckless driving. (b) Whenever any person is arrested as authorized in this section, he shall be taken without unnecessary delay before the proper magistrate as specified in section 49-1115, except that in the case of either of the offenses designated in paragraphs 5]&]6, a police officer shall have the same discretion as is provided in other cases in section 49-1111.

EXAMPLE 64: Ladies and Gentlemen of the Jury, you are instructed that:Idaho Code, 49-1111, states: Whenever any person is halted by a police officer for any violation of this act and is not required to be taken before a magistrate as herein before provided, the person shall, in the discretion of the officer, either be given a traffic citation as hereinafter provided, or be taken without unnecessary delay before the proper magistrate as specified in section 49-1115 in any of the following cases: 1. When the person does not furnish satisfactory evidence of identity or when the officer has reasonable and probable grounds to believe the person will disregard a written promise to appear in court. 2. When the person is charged with a violation of section 49-843, relating to vehicles transporting explosives. 3. When the person is charged with a violation of sections relating to the refusal of a driver of a vehicle to submit such vehicle to an inspection and test. 4. When the person is charged with a violation of sections relating to the failure or refusal of a driver of a vehicle to submit the vehicle and load to a weighing or to remove excess weight therefrom.

EXAMPLE 65: Ladies and Gentlemen of the Jury, you are instructed that:Idaho Code, 49-1112 states; (a) All of the provisions of this article apply both to residents and nonresidents of this state, except the special provisions in this section which shall govern in respect to nonresidents under the circumstances herein stated. (b) A police officer at the scene of a traffic accident may arrest without a warrant any driver of a vehicle who is a non-resident of this state and who is involved in the accident when, based upon personal investigation, the officer has reasonable and probable grounds to believe that the person has committed any offense under the provisions of this act in connection with the accident, and if the officer has reasonable and probable grounds to believe the person will disregard a written promise to appear in court. (c)Whenever any person is arrested under the provisions of this section, he shall be taken without unnecessary delay before the proper magistrate as specified in section 49-1115.

EXAMPLE 66: Ladies and Gentlemen of the Jury, you are instructed that Idaho Code 49-1113 states; (a) Whenever a person is halted by a police officer for any violation of this act punishable as a misdemeanor and is not taken before a magistrate as herein before required or permitted, the officer shall prepare in quadruplicate a written traffic citation containing a notice to appear in court, the name and address of the person, the state registration number of his vehicle, if any, the offense charged, the time and place when and where the person shall appear in court, and such other pertinent information as may be necessary. (b) The time specified in the notice to appear must be at least 5 days after the alleged violation unless the person charged with violation shall demand an earlier hearing. (c) The place specified in the notice to appear must be before a magistrate as designated in section 49-1113. (d) The person charged with violation may give his written promise to appear in court by signing at least one (1) copy of the written traffic citation prepared by the officer, in which event the officer shall deliver a copy of the citation to the person and thereupon, the officer shall not take the person into physical custody for the violation. (e) Any officer violating any of the provisions of this section is guilty of misconduct in office and shall be subject to removal from office.

EXAMPLE 67: Ladies and Gentlemen of the Jury, you are instructed that Idaho Code 49-1116 states;Whenever any person is taken into custody by an officer for the purpose of taking him before a magistrate or court as authorized or required in this article upon any charge other than a felony of the offenses enumerated in paragraphs 1, 2, 3, and 4 of subsection (a) of section 49-1109, and no magistrate is available at the time of arrest, and there is no bail schedule established by any such magistrate or court and no lawfully designated court clerk or other public officer who is available and authorized to accept bail upon behalf of the magistrate or court, such person shall be released from custody upon the issuance to him of a written traffic citation and his signing a promise to appear as provided in section 49-1113.

EXAMPLE 68: Ladies and Gentlemen of the Jury, you are instructed that:Idaho Code 49-1114 states; Except for felonies and those offenses enumerated in paragraphs 1, 2, 3, and 4 of subsection (a) of section 49-1109, a police officer at the scene of a traffic accident may issue a written traffic citation, as provided in section 49-1113, to any driver of a vehicle involved in the accident when, based upon personal investigation, the officer has reasonable and probable grounds to believe that the person has committed any offense under the provisions of this act in connection with the accident.

EXAMPLE 69: Ladies and Gentlemen of the Jury, you are instructed that Idaho Code 49-1110 states; 122   122122`   `   122 Whenever any person is halted by a police officer for any violation of this act not amounting to a felony, he shall be taken without unnecessary delay before the proper magistrate as specified in section 49-1115 in any of the following cases:1.When the person demands an immediate appearance before a magistrate.2.In any other event when the person is issued a traffic citation by an authorized person and refuses to give his written promise to appear in court as hereinafter provided.

EXAMPLE 70: Ladies and Gentlemen of the Jury, you are instructed that Idaho Code 49-1119 states; No evidence of the conviction of any person for any violation of this act shall be admissible an any court in any civil action.

EXAMPLE 71: Ladies and Gentlemen of the Jury, you are instructed that Idaho Code 49-1118 states; The foregoing provisions of this article shall govern all police officers in making arrests without a warrant for violations of this act, but the procedure prescribed herein shall not otherwise be exclusive of any other method prescribed by law for the arrest and prosecution of a person for an offense of like grade.

EXAMPLE 72: Ladies and Gentlemen of the Jury, you are instructed that Idaho Code 49-1115 states; Whenever any person is taken before a magistrate or is given a written traffic citation containing a notice to appear as herein before provided, the magistrate shall be a magistrate within the county where the offense charged is alleged to have been committed and who has jurisdiction of the offense, or any magistrate in any other county with jurisdiction over the alleged offense which is agreed to be more convenient by both the officer and the defendant. Whenever a person is taken immediately before a magistrate as herein before provided, it shall be any magistrate within the state who has jurisdiction of the alleged offense. For the purposes of posting bail bonds or cash bail, waivers of trial or entering pleas of guilty, the officer shall take the defendant before any magistrate or other designated person within the state who has sufficient jurisdiction to accept the bond, waiver or plea. For the purpose of this chapter, the terms "magistrate" and "court" include magistrates and courts having jurisdiction of offenses under this chapter as committing magistrates and courts and those having jurisdiction of the trials of such offenses.

EXAMPLE 73: Ladies and Gentlemen of the Jury, you are instructed that the question has been raised whether at the time of the occurrence Mike Candor and Kith Schultz was the agent of Richard Noble or was an independent contractor.One is the agent of another person at a given time if he is authorized to act for, or in place of, such other person. The term "agent" includes servants and employees.If you find that one person has the right to control the actions of another at a given time, you may find that the relation of principal and agent exists, even though the right to control may not have been exercised.An independent contractor is one who undertakes a specific job where the person who engages him does not have the right to direct and control the method and manner of doing the work. ADJ 255

EXAMPLE 74: Ladies and Gentlemen of the Jury, you are instructed that willful and wanton misconduct is present if the defendant intentionally does or fails to do an act, knowing or having a reason to know facts which would lead a reasonable man to realize that his conduct not only creates unreasonable risk of harm to another, but involves a high degree of probability that such harm would result. ADJ 225

EXAMPLE 75: Ladies and Gentlemen of the Jury, you are instructed that the plaintiff has the burden of proving each of the following propositions:1.That the defendant took plaintiff's property 1-1965 Chevrolet Automobile and 1-1972 Motorcycle without a right to do so;2.That the plaintiff was consequently deprived of possession of that property 1-1965 Chevrolet Automobile and 1-1972 Motorcycle;3.The nature and extent of the damages to plaintiff and the amount thereof.If you find from your consideration of all the evidence that each of these propositions has been proved, then you verdict should be for the plaintiff; but, if you find from you consideration of all the evidence that any of these propositions has not been proved, then you verdict should be for the defendant.

EXAMPLE 76: Ladies and Gentlemen of the Jury, you are instructed that in the exercise of ordinary discretion, the defendants should have known the dangers that existed and realized the possibility of injury from them. ADJ 260-2

EXAMPLE 77: Ladies and Gentlemen of the Jury, you are instructed that if you decide for the plaintiff on the question of liability with respect to his claim, you must then fix the amount of money which will reasonably and fairly compensate him for any of the following elements of damage proved by the evidence to have been approximately caused by the wrongful conduct of the defendants:1.Loss of the car.2.Loss of the Motorcycle.3.Loss of use of the car.4.Loss of use of the motorcycle.Whether any of these elements of damage has been proved by the evidence is for you to determine. ADJ 901

EXAMPLE 78: Ladies and Gentlemen of the Jury, you are instructed that you must fix a reasonable amount which will compensate plaintiff for all actual detriment proximately caused by the defendant's wrongful conduct. ADJ 920-1

EXAMPLE 79: Ladies and Gentlemen of the Jury, you are instructed that for damages, if any, to plaintiff's property you may award the reasonable rental value of 1-1965 Chevrolet Automobile and 1-1972 Motorcycle. ADJ 912

EXAMPLE 80: Ladies and Gentlemen of the Jury, you are instructed that the market value of the property 1-1965 Chevrolet Automobile and 1-1972 Motorcycle at the time it was taken by the defendant; The reasonable value of the use of the property 1-1965 Chevrolet Automobile and 1-1972 Motorcycle while the defendant continued to detain it from plaintiff; Plaintiff's expenses and damages reasonably incurred incident to defendant's taking of the property. ADJ 915

EXAMPLE 81: Ladies and Gentle of the Jury, you are instructed that the Idaho Code 49-1109 states the "The authority to make an arrest is the same as upon an arrest for a felony when any person is charged with any of the following offenses: 1. Negligent homicide. 2. Driving, or being in actual physical control, of a vehicle while under the influence of intoxicatingliquor. 3. Driving a vehicle while under the influence of anynarcotic drug, or driving a vehicle while under theinfluence of any other drug to a degree which renders the person incapable of safely driving a vehicle. 4. Failure to stop, or failure to give information, orfailure to render reasonable assistance, in the event of an accident resulting in death or personal injuries. 5. Failure to stop, or failure to give information, in the event of an accident resulting in damage to a vehicle or to fixtures or other property legally upon or adjacent to a highway. 6. Reckless driving.

EXAMPLE 82: Ladies and Gentlemen of the Jury, you are instructed that the Idaho Code 49-1110 states that "Whenever any person is halted by a police officer for any violation of this act not amounting to a felony, he shall be taken without unnecessary delay before the proper magistrate as specified in section 49-1115 in any of the following cases: 1. When the person demands an immediate appearance before a magistrate. 2. In any other event when the person is issued a traffic citation by an authorized person and refuses to give his written promise to appear in court as hereinafter provided.

EXAMPLE 83: Ladies and Gentlemen of the Jury, you are instructed that the Idaho Code 49-1111 states that "Whenever any person is halted by a police officer for any violation of this act and is not required to be taken before a magistrate as hereinbefore provided, the person shall, in the discretion of the officer, wither be given a traffic citation as hereinafter provided, or be taken without unnecessary delay before the proper magistrate as specified in section 49-1115 in any of the following cases: 1. When the person does not furnish satisfactory evidence of identity or when the officer has reasonable and probable grounds to believe the person will disregard a written promise to appear in court. 2. When the person is charged with a violation of section 49-843, relating to vehicles transporting explosives. 3. When the person is charged with a violation of sections relating to the refusal of a driver of a vehicle to an inspection and test. 4. When the person is charged with a violation of sections relating to the failure or refusal of a driver of a vehicle to submit the vehicle and load to a weighing or to remove excess weight therefrom.

EXAMPLE 84: Ladies and Gentlemen of the Jury, you are instructed that the Idaho Code 49-1112 states that (a) All of the provisions of this article apply nothing to residents and nonresidents of this state, except the special provisions in this section which shall govern in respect to nonresidents under the circumstances herein stated. (b) A police officer at the scene of a traffic accident may arrest without a warrant any driver of a vehicle who is a nonresident of this state and who is involved in the accident when, based upon personal investigation, the officer has reasonable and probable grounds to believe that the person has committed any offense under the provisions of this act in connection with the accident, and if the officer has reasonable and probable grounds to believe the person will disregard a written promise to appear in court. (c) Whenever any person is arrested under the provisions of this section, he shall be taken without unnecessary delay before the proper magistrate as specified in section 49-1115.

EXAMPLE 85: Ladies and Gentlemen of the Jury, you are instructed that Property in a thing consists no merely in its ownership and possession, but in the unrestricted right of use, enjoyment and disposal. Anything which destroys any of these elements of property, to that extent destroys the property itself. The substantial value of property lies in its use. If the right of use be denied, the value of the property is annihilated and ownership is rendered a barren right. Therefore, a law which forbids the use of a certain kind of property, strips it of an essential attribute and in actual result proscribes its ownership. O'Conner v. City of Moscow, 69 Idaho 37.

EXAMPLE 86: Ladies and Gentlemen of the Jury, you are instructed the Idaho Code Title 49-301 (13) states "Street or highway" means the entire width between property lines of every way or place of whatever nature when any part thereof is open to the use of the public, as a matter of right, for purposes of vehicular traffic."

EXAMPLE 87: Ladies and Gentlemen of the Jury, you are instructed that "Highways are public roads which every citizen has a right to use. 3 Angel Highways 3.

EXAMPLE 88: Ladies and Gentlemen of the Jury, you are instructed that the ownership of property implies its use in the prosecution of any legitimate business which is not a nuisance in itself. In re Wong Wah, 82 F. 623

EXAMPLE 89: Ladies and Gentlemen of the Jury, you are instructed that "It must be conceded that there are such rights in every free government beyond the control of the State. A government which recognizes no such rights, which held the lives, the liberty, and the property of its citizens subject at all times to the absolute disposition and unlimited control of even the most democratic depository of power, is after all but a despotism.It is true it is a despotism of the many, of the majority, if your choose to call it so, but it is nevertheless a despotism. Loan Association v. Topeka, 20 Wall 655, 662

EXAMPLE 90: Ladies and Gentlemen of the Jury, you are instructed that "Where rights secured by the Constitution are involved there can be no rule making or legislation which would abrogate them." Miranda v. Arizona, 384 U.S. 432,491

EXAMPLE 91: Ladies and Gentlemen of the Jury, your are instructed that "The individual may stand upon his constitutional rights as a citizen. He is entitled to carry on his private business in his own way.His power to contract is unlimited. He owes no duty to the State or to his neighbors to divulge his business, or to open his doors to an investigation so far as it may tend to incriminate him. He owes no such duty to the State, since he receives nothing therefrom, beyond the protection of his life and property. His rights are such as existed by the law of the land long antecedent to the organization of the State, and can only be taken from him by due process of law, and in accordance with the Constitution.Among his rights are a refusal to incriminate himself, and the immunity of himself and his property from arrest or seizure except under a warrant of the law.He owes nothing to the public so long as he does not trespass upon their rights. Hale v. Henkel, 201 U.S.43

EXAMPLE 92: Ladies and Gentlemen of the Jury, you are instructed that "Arbitrary power, enforcing its edicts to the injury of the persons and property of its subjects, is not law, whether manifested as the decree of a personal monarch or of an impersonal multitude.And the limitations imposed by our constitutional law upon the action of the governments, both State and national, are essential to the preservation of public and private rights, notwithstanding the representative character of our political institutions.The enforcement of these limitations by judicial process is the device of self-governing communities to protect the rights of individuals and minorities, as well against the power of numbers, as against the violence of public agents transcending the limits of lawful authority, even when acting in the name and wielding the force of the government. Hurtado v. California, 110 U.S. 516,536.

EXAMPLE 93: Ladies and Gentlemen of the Jury, you are instructed that the Idaho Code 18-114 states that "In every crime or public offense there must exist a union, or joint operation, of act and intent, or criminal negligence.

EXAMPLE 94: Ladies and Gentlemen of the Jury, you are instructed that all men are by nature free and equal, and have certain inalienable rights, among which are enjoying and defending life and liberty; acquiring, possessing and protecting property; pursuing happiness and securing safety. Idaho Constitution, Article I, Section 1.

EXAMPLE 95: Ladies and Gentlemen of the Jury, you are instructed that the state of Idaho is an inseparable part of the American Union, and the Constitution of the United States is the supreme law of the land. Idaho Constitution, Article I, Section 3.

EXAMPLE 96: Ladies and Gentlemen of the Jury, you are instructed that the Idaho Code 18-201 states that "All persons are capable of committing crimes, except those belonging to the following classes: 1. Persons who committed the act or made the omission charged, under an ignorance or mistake of fact which disproves any criminal intent. 2. Persons who committed the act charged without being being conscious thereof. 3. Persons who committed the act or made the omission charged, through misfortune or by accident, when it appears that there was not evil design, intention or culpable negligence. 4. Persons (unless the crime be punishable with death) who committed the act or made the omission charged, under threats or menaces sufficient to show that they had reasonable cause to and did believe their lives would be endangered if they refused.

EXAMPLE 97: Ladies and Gentlemen of the Jury, you are instructed that the following essential elements are required to be proved beyond a reasonable doubt by the prosecution in order to establish the guilt of the defendant, John S. Curtis, as charged in the Summons and Complaint:
1.That John S. Curtis was driving a vehicle.
2.That John S. Curtis and the vehicle he was driving was approaching a stop sign.
3.That he was not directed to proceed by a police officer.
4.That he was not directed to proceed by a traffic control signal.
5.That he did not stop at a clearly marked stop line or before entering the crosswalk on the near side of the intersection, at the point nearest the intersecting roadway where the driver has a view of approaching traffic on the intersecting roadway roadway before entering it.That there existed either a clearly marked stop line or an intersecting roadway with a crosswalk on the near side of the intersection. Idaho Code49-643

EXAMPLE 98: Ladies and Gentlemen of the Jury, you are instructed that the words 'life, liberty and property' and constitutional terms and are to be taken in their broadest sense.They indicate the three great subdivisions of all civil rights.The term 'property' in this clause embraces all valuable interests which a man may possess outside himself.That is to say, outside of his life and liberty. It is not confined to mere technical property, but literally to every species of vested right. Camp v. Holt, 115 U.S. 620

EXAMPLE 99: Ladies and Gentlemen of the Jury, you are instructed that "Undoubtedly the right of locomotion, the right to remove from one place to another according to inclination, is an attribute of personal liberty, and the right, ordinarily, of free transit from or through the territory of any State is a right secured by the Fourteenth Amendment and by other provisions of the Constitution."Williams v. Fears, 179 U.S. 270, 274

EXAMPLE 100: Ladies and Gentlemen of the Jury, you are instructed that "A highway is a passage, road, or street, which every citizen has a right to use." Bouvier's Law Dictionary 1870 p. 667

EXAMPLE 101: "I must tell the jury the laws are constitutional and they are bound by them. Then what they do is up to them.That is why we developed the jury system, you know, so the king could not put bad laws over on the people.While the jury is told to obey the law, if they don't, they is nothing anybody can do about it.That is our system of justice and it has worked out pretty well."Pre-trial hearing, June 8, 1979 Boise, Idaho CR 10027,U.S. District Court

CODE HAS NO FORCE OF LAW

COMES NOW the Accused, appearing specially and not generally or voluntarily herein, to move the court to dismiss the charges against this Free and Natural Person as the Boise City Code has no force of law over this Accused person.

1. IC 1-701. District courts established.--- The District courts were established in each county for "the purpose of hearing and determining all matters and causes arising under the laws of the state."
2. IC 1-2208 allows the District Court to assign any and all cases within its jurisdiction to the magistrates division for misdemeanor and quasi-criminal actions and proceedings to prevent the commission of crimes.
3. The City of Boise is a municipality, an administrative body, an incorporated town with certain privileges and has no Sovereign powers. The City's privileges are quite limited by its master, the State, and like any artificial being, it must petition its master for any privileges it desires.
4. Since a municipality, city, or town has no sovereignty it cannot create laws pertaining to the citizens of the state. It can only enforce the laws of its master (LAWS OF THE STATE) however, the city can regulate those artificial beings it creates or natural persons it employs.
5. In this case, Boise City Code has no authority of law as the Accused is not an employee of the City nor a created being of the City; nor has he a license, permit, or any other agreement or contract with the City. Therefore, this proposed action is in direct violation of the laws of the state and cannot be enforced against this free and natural person. It is axiomatic that no municipality can create any code that is in conflict with its creator's law. The Idaho State Constitution states: "Any county or incorporated city or town may make and enforce, within its limits, all such local police, sanitary and other regulations as are not in conflict with its charter or with the general laws." Article 12, Section 2, Idaho State Const.

This has been upheld numerous times by the Idaho Supreme Court and a few of the cases are as follows: "This provision of the Constitution authorizes the council of Boise City to make and enforce ordinances that are not in conflict with the general laws, and forbids the making and enforcing of any ordinance in conflict with the general laws." (emphasis added) In re Ridenbaugh, 5 Idaho 371, 375.

"This power, vested by direct grant, is as broad as that vested in the legislature itself, subject to two exceptions: It must be local to the county or municipality and must not conflict with general laws." (emphasis added) State v. Musser, 67 Idaho 214, 219.

The Boise City Code is administrative in nature, and only applies to those it regulates or employs. If this city code were construed to apply to persons other than those mentioned, it would violate the rights of other classes of persons and exceed its authority under Article 12, Section 2, of the Idaho State Constitution and IC 50-302 which states in part: "Cities shall make all such ordinances, by laws, rules, regulation (regulations) and resolutions not inconsistent with the laws of the state of Idaho.... to maintain the peace, good government and welfare of the corporation and its trade, commerce and industry."

In this regard, it is only fitting and proper that the Boise City code regulate those whom it controls. IC 50-302 talks about the "welfare of the corporation and its trade, commerce, and industry." There can be no doubt that the Boise City code applies to those artificial entities as well as natural persons hired by the city. However, the City Code cannot be stretched to apply to other persons not within its control (State v. Musser) or there exists a conflict between the Idaho Code and the Boise City Code. Or perhaps the City of Boise believes their code supersedes the Idaho Code, and that the Idaho Code does not pertain within its geographical boundaries. Therefore, the City code abrogates the Idaho Code. If so, the City's logic is ad absurdism. In any event, this Court has jurisdiction over the subject matter only so long as the charges being brought before it are authorized by the District Court. The District Court has delegated certain classes of cases to the magistrate court, and any complaint filed under any provisions of the Boise City Code is not within the jurisdiction of the Court. In this case, the Court has no authority to proceed as a complaint based upon a Boise City Code cannot be heard in the District Court, as the District Court only has the power to hear cases pertaining to the laws of the state and the laws of the state are those passed by the legislature not the Boise City Council.

"The legislative power of the state shall be vested in a senate and house of representatives." Article III, Section 1, Idaho State Constitution.

The legislature of this state is the only body that can pass laws of the state. This is further explained under the enabling clause for corporations, municipal. "The legislature shall provide by general laws for the incorporation, organization and classification....which laws may be altered.... by the general laws." (emphasis added) Article XII, Section 1, Idaho State Constitution.

Only the legislature can pass general laws or laws of the state as no where in the Idaho State Constitution did the Sovereign People give any entity, other than the state legislature, the ability to pass laws of the state. Local municipalities.(counties, cities, and towns) were only authorized to make regulations. "Any county or incorporated city or town may make and enforce, within its limits, all such local police, sanitary and other regulations as are not in conflict with its charter or with the general laws." (emphasis added) Article XII, Section 2, Idaho State Constitution. The state legislature is authorized to enact general laws/laws of the state and any other governmental entity or municipality are only authorized to make regulations ---- not enact laws of the state.

Regulations do not have the force and effect of law on all citizens. Regulations only pertain to certain classes of persons. Regulations are defined as: "Such are issued by various governmental departments to carry out the intent of the law." Black's law Dictionary, 5th edition, p. 1156 "Regulations are implementary to existing law." Gibson Wine Co. v. Snyder, 194 F. 2d 329, 331 Regulations then, are things issued to carry out the intent of law but of and by themselves are not law. In short, they can only be considered administrative procedures and edicts.

"Agencies issue regulations to guide the activity of those regulated by the agency and of their own employees and to ensure uniform application of the law." (emphasis added) Black's supra Regulations, within constitutional provisions that municipalities may enforce such local police, sanitary and other regulations as are not in conflict with general laws, refers to rules relating for instance, to operation of a police department,..." (emphasis added) State ex rel. Lynch v. City of Cleveland, 132 N.E. 2d 118, 121 Regulations then, are written to guide a specific agency in its operation, to guide those being regulated by the agency, and to guide the employees of the agency. In the case of the municipality of Boise, their code is to guide in the operation of the corporation, to guide those controlled by the corporation, and to guide the employees of the corporation ---- not the citizenry at large. "Regulations are not the work of the legislature and do not have the effect of law..." Black's supra.

"The terms by-laws, ordinances, and municipal regulations have substantially the same meaning, and are the laws of the corporate district made by the authorized body, in distinction from the general laws of the state. They are local regulations for the government of the inhabitants of the particular place. They are not laws in the legal sense, though binding on the community affected. They are not prescribed by the supreme power of the state, from which alone a law can emanate, and therefore cannot be statutes, which are the written will of the Legislature, expressed in the form necessary to constitute parts of the law." (emphasis added) Rutherford v. Swink, 35 S.W. 554, 555.

"An ordinance of a municipal corporation is a local law, and binds persons within the jurisdiction of the corporation." (emphasis added) Pittsburgh, C., C. & St L. Ry. Co. v. Lightheiser, 71 N.E. 218, 221; Pennsylvania Co. v. Stegemeier, 20 N.E. 843.

"An ordinance is a local law, a rule of conduct prospective in its operation, applying to persons and things subject to local jurisdiction." (emphasis added) C.I.R. v. Schnackenberg, C.C.A., 90 F. 2d 175, 176.

"Ordinances...are laws passed by the governing body of a municipal corporation for the regulation of the corporation." (emphasis added) Bills v. City of Goshen, 20 N.E. 115, 117.

"The terms ordinance, by-law, and municipal regulation...are local regulations for the government of the inhabitants of a particular place, and though given the force of law by the charter for the purposes of the municipal government, yet relate to that solely, and prosecutions for their violation have no reference, as a general rule to the administration of criminal justice of the state." (emphasis added) State v. Lee, 13 N.W. 913.

"Ordinances are laws of municipality made by authorized municipal body in distinction from general laws of the state and constitute local regulations for government of inhabitants of particular place." (emphasis added) State v. Thomas, 156 N.W. 2d 745.

"...defining the term criminal offense as any offense for which any punishment by imprisonment or fine, or both, may by law be inflicted, a violation of a city ordinance is not a criminal offense...an ordinance being a regulation adopted by a municipal corporation and not a law in the legal sense." (emphasis added) Meredith v. Whillock, 158 S.W. 1061, 1062.

"A city ordinance is not a law of the same character as a statute. It is merely a regulation; a rule of conduct passed by the common council for the direction and supervision of its citizens." (emphasis added) People v. Gardner, 106 N.W. 541, 545.

"An ordinance prescribes a permanent rule for conduct of government." (emphasis added) 76 N.W. 2d 1, 5; 61 A.L.R. 2d 583.

"An ordinance is not, in the constitutional sense, a public law. It is a mere local rule or by-law, a police or domestic regulation, devoid in many respects of the characteristics of the public or general laws." (emphasis added) State v. Fourcade, 13 So. 187, 191; McInerney v. City of Denver, 29 P. 516.

Since regulations are the work of a corporation, they can only apply to members of that corporation. From IC 50-302 we know that the City of Boise can only make regulations: "to maintain the peace, good government and welfare of the corporation and its trade, commerce and industry." IC 50-302 does not even mention persons either natural or artificial but it does specifically mention the corporation and its trade, commerce, and industry. Trade commerce and industry are all artificial entities and either licensed by the state and city or are corporations both of with have an agreement with the state or city and through that agreement, those businesses must adhere to the Boise City Code. However, Natural citizens who are not engaged in trade, commerce, or industry and do not have any agreements with their state or city, cannot be bound by the Boise City Code. The Boise city code is not the law of the State and, this Court has no jurisdiction to proceed. Therefore, if the Plaintiff wishes to proceed in this case with charges brought about based upon the Boise City Code, this case will have to be dismissed and a new action brought before a court of proper jurisdiction. Since this natural person is not a member of the municipal corporation; nor licensed by, nor has any other legal connection with the city; and since the City has no courts, there is no proper court of jurisdiction to hear an action against this Accused natural citizen under the provisions of the Boise City Code.

Free and natural citizens are only subject to the Idaho Code, as stated in IC 19-301, and said Code states, in part: "Every person is liable to punishment by the laws of this state..." The Accused may be subject to the laws of the State under the provisions of this Code, but nowhere does this Code charge the Accused, or any other person, to be liable to punishment by the code of the City of Boise. Laws of this state are those brought into being by the legislature of the state of Idaho, not by an administrative municipality, town, or city. The courts have often said that the state of the law in Idaho is the Idaho Code. The Idaho Code is very specific in what laws a person is liable to, that being laws of the state, not laws of the municipality. This Court may have jurisdiction over those persons who voluntarily submit to the Boise City Code. However, this Court can have no jurisdiction over a free and natural person who challenges the jurisdiction of this Court over a complaint based upon the Boise City Code, and once jurisdiction has been challenged by the Accused, the Court can not proceed until the Plaintiff has not only asserted, but proven jurisdiction. The Plaintiff must overcome every single argument of the Accused and have additional matter, before the Court can have jurisdiction and proceed. In addition, the Court can not assume jurisdiction by mere act or estoppel. It only follows that if a municipality has the authority to create a code, that code can only apply to its subjects or members. As the code pertains to those persons, it may grant them privileges and regulate their actions. However, this free and natural person is not a member, subject, or slave of the municipality and in no way depends upon the City for his welfare, nor is he a corporation, or involved with trade, commerce, or industry (see IC 50-302) with or within the City of Boise, and this person absolutely refuses to enter into any foreign jurisdiction asserted by Boise City for its subjects, employees, and members. I would like to remind the learned court that: "A municipal corporation possesses only such powers as the state confers upon it,.. "Any ambiguity of doubt arising out of the terms used by the legislature must be resolved in favor of the granting power. Regard must also be had to constitutional provisions intended to secure the liberty and to protect the rights of citizens..." (emphasis added) State v. Frederick, 28 Idaho 709, 715.

In this regard, the state legislature must preserve and protect the rights of citizens at all times. The State must maintain legislative power over all citizens throughout the state and therefore the laws of the state are the only laws applicable to natural citizens. "It is settled law, that the legislature in granting it, does not divest itself of any power over the inhabitants of the district which it possessed before the charter was granted. Laramie County v. Albany County et al, 92 U.S. 307, 308.

The City is forbidden from making any regulations or from enforcing any ordinance in conflict with the general laws (re Ridenbaugh, Supra) and the general law (IC 50-302) of Idaho has not granted the city of Boise the power to make laws pertaining to free and natural citizens. It can only make regulations to affect its employees and the trade, commerce and industry it regulates. Therefore, for the above causes, the Accused moves the Court to dismiss the charges.

ACT ALLEGING CRIME IS A BILL OF ATTAINDER

The Parking ticket or complaint is issued out of the mind and hand of the Executive Branch of City Government and imposes a predetermined punishment on persons in the form of a fine or penalty without any Judicial process or trial. A Bill of Attainder is defined as: "Legislative acts, no matter what their form, that apply to persons in such a way as to inflict punishment on them without a judicial trial is nothing more than a Bill of Attainder" (pains and penalties). U. S. vs Brown, 381 U.S. 437, 448-49. U.S. vs Lovett, 328 U. S. 303, 315.

"A special act of the legislature which inflicts a punishment less than death upon persons supposed to be guilty...without any conviction in the ordinary course of judicial proceedings." 2 Wood. Lect. 625. "The clause in the constitution prohibiting bills of attainder includes bills of pains and penalties." Story, Const. Sec 1338; Hare Am. Const. L. 549; Cummings v. Missouri, 4 Wall. 323; Fletcher v. Peck, 6 Cran. 138.

The issue of what is a bill of attainder and of pains and penalties was well settled in the case of Cummings v. Missouri where the United States Supreme Court stated: "The theory upon which our political institutions rest is, that all men have certain inalienable rights -- that among those are life, liberty, and the pursuit of happiness: and that in the pursuit of happiness all avocations, all honors, all positions, are alike open to every one, and that in the protection of these rights all men are equal before the law. Any deprivation or suspension of any of these rights for past conduct is punishment, and can be in no otherwise defined." Cummings v. Missouri, supra, p. 321-2. "A bill of attainder is a legislative act which inflicts punishment without judicial trial." "If the punishment be less than death, the act is termed a bill of pains and penalties. Within the meaning of the Constitution, bills of attainder include bills of pains and penalties. In these cases, the legislative body, in addition to its legitimate functions, exercises the powers and and office of judge; it assumes, in the language of the textbooks, judicial magistracy; it pronounces upon the guilt of the party, without any of the forms or safeguards of trial; it determines the sufficiency of the proofs produced, whether conformable to the rules of evidence or otherwise, and it fixes the degree of punishment in accordance with its own notions of the enormity of the offence." Cummings, supra, p. 323.

Obviously parking ticket meet all of the criteria elaborated upon by the Supreme Court. The parking ticket regulation allows the city to exercise the powers and office of judge (individual has been convicted by city and fined), pronounce guilt without trial (guilt announced by demand for payment of fine which can only transpire after conviction of guilty), determine proof (proof of guilt has been predetermined to be the person to whom the vehicle is registered), and fix punishment (as indicated on the parking citation).

The high Court went on to say: "Bills of this sort,...have been most usually passed .... in .... periods, in which all nations are most liable (as well the free as the enslaved) to forget their duties, and to trample upon the rights and liberties of others." Cummings, supra. The Supreme Court reiterated the validity of the Cummings case in U.S. vs Lovett. In the Lovett case they also referred to Ex Parte Garland, 4 Wall 333, in which they stated that these type of bills. "...stand for the proposition that legislative acts no matter what their form, that apply either to named individuals or to easily ascertainable members of a group in such a way as to inflict punishment on them without a judicial trial are bills of attainder prohibited by the Constitution." United States v. Lovett, 328 U.S. 303, 315. Continuing in the same case they said: "The Constitution outlaws this entire category of punitive measures. The amount of punishment is immaterial to the classification of a challenged statute. But punishment is a prerequisite. "Punishment presupposes an offense, not necessarily an act previously declared criminal, but an act for which retribution is exacted." U. S. V. Lovett, supra, p. 324; Also see Garner v. Los Angeles Board, 341 U.S. 716; and

Christie v. Lueth, 61 N.W. 2d 338, 341. These type of acts clearly fall within the scope of Constitutional prohibition. United States Constitution, Article 1, Section 9, Clause 3; and Article 1, Section 10 states: "No Bill of Attainder or ex post facto law shall be passed." (emphasis added)

And: "No State shall...pass any Bill of Attainder,..." On the face of each parking complaint it plainly states: "The fine for this violation is $ if paid within 24 hours. You may pay this by placing $ in this envelope and mailing it to Ticket Section, City Hall... Delinquencies are subject to additional penalties." (emphasis added) The City is issuing complaints, determining guilt of individuals, and imposing punishments in the form of a fine all without due process and judicial trial. Prima facia proof of this fact is in the wording of the alleged citation. On the face of the citation it states "the fine for this violation is..." This statement amounts to a blatant confession that the city has charged the individual, found him guilty, and is requiring the individual to pay a specific dollar amount, all without the benefit of due process and Judicial trial. From the wording "Delinquencies are subject to additional penalties," it is obvious that guilt has been further predetermined. Since guilt has been predetermined, and when some individual does not pay the fine (punishment) entered on the face of the parking complaint, that person will be further subjected to additional punishment for his predetermined guilt through delinquency charges. This demand of and imposition of a delinquency charge for an unproven offense is further prima facie evidence of predetermined guilt without judicial trial. Offering some sort of delayed due process to those who forget, refuse or otherwise do not pay the appropriate amount for their predetermined guilt after filing the charge, predetermining guilt, and imposing of a fine does not negate the invalid status of the enactment creating the offense. As applied to Free and Natural Persons it is plainly a Bill of Attainder (Bill of Pains and Penalties) and violates the law of the land.

The full significance of the clause "law of the land" is said to be that statutes which would deprive a citizen of the rights of person or property without a regular trial according to the course and usage of the common law would not be the law of the land. Hoke v. Henderson, 15 N.C. 15, 25. "By law of the land is more clearly intended the general law, a law which hears before it condemns; which proceeds upon inquiry, and renders judgement only after trial. The meaning is that every citizen shall hold his life, liberty, property and immunities, under the protection of the general rules which govern our society. Everything which may pass under the form of an enactment is not, therefore, to be considered the law of the land." (emphasis added) Dartmouth College Case, 4 Wheat 518.

The enactment authorizing such summary proceedings by the city is clearly applied to Natural persons in such a way as to inflict punishment on them without judicial trial and is therefore unconstitutional bill of pains and penalties as applied to Natural persons. There can be no doubt that this act can and does pertain to those artificial subjects and members who are wards or creations of the State and City, therefore, in those cases it is not unconstitutional. Government has the right to control, limit, restrict, and regulate the actions of those artificial persons they create, and therefore, those artificial persons are the legal subjects of parking citations. The Accused hereby declares to his accusers that he is a Free and Natural Person who is not engaged in any business, commerce, trade, or industry within the city, nor does he represent, nor is he a voluntary member or subject of any artificial being (person) or entity.

Therefore, the Accused moves the court to dismiss the charges against this Free and Natural Person because any enactment attempting to impose punishment without due process and judicial trial upon a Free and Natural Person is a bill of pains and penalties.

STATUTE EXCEEDS
THE POLICE POWERS OF THE STATE

Each law relating to the police power of a state involves the questions:

First, is there a threatened danger? Second, does the regulation involve a constitutional right? Third, is the regulation reasonable? 1. First, is there a threatened danger? Here the question needs to be asked, just what is a threatened danger? Can there be a danger in simply carrying a firearm? Is it a threat to carry a flask of nitro? Is it a threat to have blasting caps in one's possession? Is it a threat to drive an automobile? Is it a threat to be a karate expert? Is it dangerous to carry a long pointed and sharpened pencil? What kills more people per year --- guns or automobiles? How about war or automobiles? Isn't it a fact that more people were killed in one single year from automobile accidents than there were Americans killed in ten years of fighting in Vietnam? What then is a threatened danger to society? Is it the mad husband or wife? 2. Second, does the regulation involve a constitutional right? The State possesses the police power to protect the public health, morals, and safety by any legislation appropriate to that end which does not encroach upon the rights guaranteed by the national constitution. (emphasis added) Missouri K & T Ry. Co. v. Haber, 169 U.S. 628. Rights founded in law or statute are mere legal rights. However, inalienable rights are not granted by government through codes or statutes and can only inhere in and exist between moral beings. The People of a country organize the government and give government its powers, and in the case of the United States of America, the People reserved for themselves all inalienable Rights and so declared them through the Declaration of Independence, the Constitution, and the Bill of Rights. Rights then, proceed government or the establishment of states.Rights are acknowledged above government and their states, which is better expressed by the maxim "Ne ex regula jus sumatur, sed ex jurequod est, regula fiat." Both legal rights and inalienable rights are protected by the Constitution of the United States and statutory laws enacted by Congress or legislative bodies. However, government does not create the idea of rights or original rights, it simply acknowledges them.

Inalienable Rights then, are claims of the People that in here in the very nature of man himself. Rights can only inhere in and exist between moral beings, not between government and man, nor government and government. Government can give Civil rights, or what are more commonly referred to as privileges, to any entity it regulates or creates as in the case of corporations, but since government is not a moral being it cannot give that which it does not itself possess, and government possesses no inalienable rights.

To secure the Rights of the People, the Declaration of Independence, the Constitution of the United States, and the Bill of Rights were penned and is the Supreme Law of the land. "The constitution is either a superior paramount law, unchangeable by ordinary means, or it is on a level with ordinary legislative acts, and like other acts, is alterable when the legislature shall please to alter it. "If then, the courts are to regard the constitution,and the constitution is superior to any ordinary act of legislation, the constitution, and not such ordinary act must govern the case to which they both apply." Thus, the particular phraseology of the constitution of the United States confirms and strengthens the principle, supposed to be essential to all written constitutions, that a law repugnant to the constitution is void; and that courts as well as other departments, are bound by the instrument." Marbury v. Madison, 1 C 137, 176-179It is also clear that no State Constitution can espouse anything that would be in contravention with the Federal Constitution. If any State Constitution violates the principles stated in the Federal Constitution, that provision or statement is null and void from its inception as though it had never existed as:" An unconstitutional act is not law; it confers no rights; it imposes no duties; it affords no protection; it creates no office; it is in legal contemplation, as inoperative as though it had never been passed;..."Norton v. Shelby County,p. 442.

And, "An unconstitutional law is void, and is as no law. An offense created by it is not a crime. A conviction under it is not merely erroneous, but is illegal or void, and cannot be a legal cause of imprisonment." Ex Parte Siebold, U. S. page 376.

For example, in the Constitution for the State of Idaho, Article VI, Section 3, it states that "No person is permitted to vote, serve as a juror, or hold any civil office who ... is living in what is known as a patriarchal plural or celestial marriage..."

It should go without saying that this provision in our own State constitution abrogates a right granted by the Federal Constitution and is, therefore, null and void.

The general police power is reserved to the states, subject to the limitation that it may not trespass on the Rights and powers vested in the national government. (emphasis added)re Huff, 197 U.S. 488.

In addition, in exercising the police powers of a state, there are no limits except the restrictions outlined in the written constitution. (emphasis added) McLeon v. Arkansas, 211 U.S. 539; Jacobson v. Massachusetts, 197 U.S. 11; 1 Thayer Constitutional Law, 720. In this case the right which is being abridged or infringed is the right of personal liberty.

This person hereby lays claim to the absolute inalienable rights of contract, freedom, and liberty -- that is, the claim of unrestricted action except so far as the claim of others necessitates restriction, and the right to free locomotion. .. Personal liberty is defined as: "Freedom from physical and personal restraint;...freedom to go where one chooses...." "....right to travel...." "....freedom to move about as one pleases...." Munn v. Illinois, 94 U.S. 142; Slaughter House Cases, 16 Wall, 106; Butcher's Union Co. v. Slaughter House Co., 111 U.S. 757

It is ludicrous on one hand to say a person has the freedom of movement and on the other to say government has the authority to restrict or regulate that freedom of movement by foot, horse, automobile or whatever. However, it also goes without saying that government may exercise its authority to insure each person is capable of exercising said right. Personal liberty has also been defined as:"....the power of locomotion, of changing situation, of removing one's person to whatever place one's inclination may direct...."1 Bla. Com.134; Hare, Cons. Law 777.

And: "Liberty means.... the facility of willing, and the power of doing what has been willed without influence from without." Am. Republic; Ord. Cons. Leg. "Liberties are nothing until they have become rights -- positive rights formally recognized and consecrated. Rights, even when recognized, are nothing so long as they are not entrenched within guarantees. And guarantees are nothing so long as they are not maintained by forces independent of them in the limit of their right. Convert liberties into rights -- surround rights by guarantees --- entrust the keeping these guarantees to forces capable of maintaining them. Such are the successive steps in the process of free government." 1 Guizot, Rep. Gov. Lect. 6. However, it goes without saying that no person can do whatever he pleases when that act infringes, abridges, or abrogates the rights of another free and natural person." As soon as any part of a person's conduct affects prejudicially the interests of others, society has jurisdiction over it."Mill, Liberty.c. 4.

There is a monstrous difference in restricting or regulating the ability of a person to exercise a right than in prohibiting and commanding actions, or the lack of, and punishing by penalty, fines, and imprisonment persons who fail to comply when the action committed by the person has not, in fact, caused any loss or damage of another's life, liberty, or property as opposed to those classes of crimes where another's life, liberty, or property has been damaged or lost. Restriction and regulation of various functions and privileges on certain classes of commercial travelers and other juristic persons may be necessary; and in those cases government can certainly exercise its authority in prohibiting or commanding an action and may punish by penal action when a violation has occurred.

A penal action is nothing more than an action or information brought on by an "agent of the king" and in which the penalty goes to the "king" (government). (Bouvier Law Dictionary, P. 2551)

Any FREEMAN who claims his rights cannot be forced to comply with penal offenses. Under the Common Law there can be no constructive offenses. United States V. Lacher, 134 US624; Todd V. United States, 158 US 282. It should be understood that a constructive offense is nothing more than an act which may or may not be performed; the doing that which a penal law forbids to be done, or omitting to do what it commands.

Penal statutes are essentially those actions which impose a penalty or punishment arbitrarily extracted for some act or commission thereof on the part of some person.(Black's Law Dictionary, 5th Ed., P. 1019) Such statutes operate to compel a performance (Black, P. 1020) and inflict a punishment by statute for its violation. (The Strathairly, 124 US 571)

In any appearance of the this Free and Natural Citizen, it must be noted that I recognize no jurisdiction other than the Common Law and expressly exclude executive chancery. This denial includes Idaho codes that are in violation of the rights of free and natural persons, and in this case a code demanding a specific performance commanding that a certain thing can or cannot be done, making said statute an unconstitutional statute if an attempt is made to apply that statute to this person. 3. Third, is the regulation reasonable? The definition of a criminal is one who takes what you have without your permission. When my government takes my gun in contravention of the Idaho Constitution, are they acting in a criminal capacity? When my government wants to limit my right to keep and bear arms, thereby abridging my rights, is my government acting as a criminal? When my government prosecutes me for exercising an alienable right, are they acting as a criminal? Who, then, is the criminal? The free and natural citizen exercising his inalienable right, or an oppressive government abridging the free person's ability and inalienable rights?

Therefore in view of the above cause, the Accused moves the court to dismiss the charges as the code, in this case, exceeds the police powers of the State.

INDEX

Index

| | 3 1405 02761 5495 | M |

Phone, fax or write if you would like a copy of our catalog listing all
books, videos, etc. that we produce and distribute.

Telephone Orders: Call 505-474-0998 and charge to your VISA or MasterCard.
Fax Orders: 505-471-2584
Mail Orders: The Message Company
RR2 Box 307MM
Santa Fe, NM 87505

CODE	TITLE	QUANTITY	PRICE	TOTAL
D20101	**History of the American Constitional or Common Law** with Commentary concerning Equity and Merchant Law. Paperback	x	$11.95 =	_____
D20039	**Universal Law** **Keely's Secret** Using the Sci Vibration. 28		$19.95 =	_____
D20047	**Grazing Thr** **Herb Man:** I wild edible pl		$19.95 =	_____

TRUSSVILLE PUBLIC LIBRARY
201 PARKWAY DRIVE
TRUSSVILLE, AL 35173-1125
(205) 655-2022

GAYLORD

SUBTOTAL _____

SHIPPING $2.00 _____

NM RESIDENTS ADD SALES TAX 5.75% _____

TOTAL $_____

❏ Enclosed is a check or money order for total.
❏ Please charge to my [   ] VISA [   ] MC [   ] AE

NAME _____

CARD # _____ EXP. DATE _____

ADDRESS _____

CITY / STATE / ZIP _____

SIGNATURE

PHONE _____